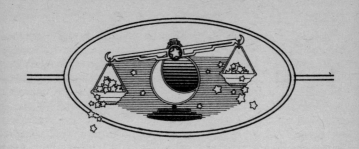

Libra

SEPTEMBER 24—OCTOBER 23

QUANTITY SALES

INDIVIDUAL SALES

Dell Horoscope

PRESENTS

1991

DAY-BY-DAY

Libra

SEPTEMBER 24—OCTOBER 23

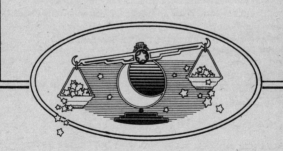

A DELL BOOK

Published by
Dell Publishing
a division of
Bantam Doubleday Dell Publishing Group, Inc.
666 Fifth Avenue
New York, New York 10103

ISBN: 0-440-20696-0

Printed in the United States of America

Published simultaneously in Canada

August 1990

10 9 8 7 6 5 4 3 2 1

EDITOR'S NOTE

For the second year in a row, the editors of *Dell Horoscope Magazine* present a series of twelve astrological books—one for each sign in the zodiac. With the resources of the world's most popular astrology magazine at our disposal, we bring you a capsule of the history of astrology, your personal and professional astrological indicators; sign descriptions; financial, health, and career advice; hobbies and pastimes inherent in your personal sign; advice for parents; relationship guidance; unique stellar combinations; how to determine where each planet was at the time of your birth and its astrological meaning; and fifteen months of daily predictions from two of *Horoscope*'s most experienced and skilled forecasters—all of which can help you to achieve personal fulfillment and greater self-understanding, assist you in decision-making for your important life choices, and aid you in your quest to find greater peace of mind in your place on this planet and within the boundaries you share with your closest associations.

I'd like to extend a special thanks to Edward Kajkowski for his efforts in research and his astrological and editorial wisdom; to Jack Pettey for his wonderful introduction and his keen editorial and astrological advice; to Julia Lupton Skalka, Heidi Rain, and Evy Tishelman for the many valuable and insightful articles they wrote exclusively for this series; and to Lloyd Cope and Doris Kaye for their top-notch daily forecasts.

RONNIE GRISHMAN
Editor

CONTENTS

INTRODUCTION

Today, while the tenth and final decade of the twentieth century is still young, curious minds and seekers within the astrological field have vast resources at their fingertips. If we want to check a point to back up a statement we have made or a belief that we hold, if we want to gain a better understanding of the meaning of a particular aspect in a friend's birth-chart, or if we want to grasp a more psychological approach to the underlying mythological background of the natal chart, we have but to go, in some cases, to our own home libraries. In most large cities we can travel to a top-notch New Age bookstore and ask to be directed to the subject of our inquiry. Or we can take a class and start with the basics of astrology, building up a storehouse of knowledge that we can trust, add to, and draw on as time-tested theories wedge their way into the accepted lexicon of astrology.

Many centuries ago, when time, as we know it, was nascent and humankind consisted of primitive beings who had no means of committing thoughts, environmental conditions, or progress to words, the only reference book in existence was the great expanse of sky overhead—a seemingly stable and stationary rooftop of bright, some not so bright, shining lights that appeared each night in a sea of dark. Early humankind's experience of the heavens was virtually the same from day to day, year to year. But against the starry backdrop of this upper world came the nocturnal visitations of one object in particular—noticeable to those below by its much more rapid movement across the sky. This was the Moon. And during the day a bright shining ball coursed across the sky from one side of the known world's existence to its opposite point 180 degrees away. This was the Sun, and living in a totally physical world, humans soon noticed five other relatively rapid moving lights across the sky. These were the five visible planets—Mercury, Venus, Mars, Jupiter, and Saturn—and the ancient world came to know them as wanderers because they did not stay in the same place like the other stars.

Speculation has it that as early as 8000 B.C. humans became fascinated with the movements occurring overhead and soon thereafter began to note physical earthly connections to the shifting patterns above. The earliest inhabitants soon learned what time was best to grow and harvest crops. The ancient Egyptians noticed that the rising of the Dog Star, Sirius, the brightest star in the Northern Hemisphere, coincided with the flooding of the Nile Valley. Some noticed that the ocean rose and fell with the tides and connected this to the pull of the Moon's rays. Was there a natural order to the universe, some accountability for the birth and death, the growth and decay that were such a noticeable part of the environment? Could it be possible that individual destinies were part of the plan, if indeed it was a plan at all? Life was filled with mysteries for those first observers of the sky to unravel.

Astrology was born of observation and mathematical calculation. An overview of the evolution of astrology is contained in the first chapter of this book. The Chaldeans of ancient Babylonia are credited as the first astrologers. They combined astronomy and astrology in a marriage of science and divination or spirituality until it came under attack by the outbreak of rationalism during the Age of Reason of the eighteenth century. They were first to use the twelve principal constellations as forerunners of the zodiac as we know it today. Every two hours the constellations shifted one-twelfth of a complete circle or thirty degrees. The constellations consist of seven bestial figures, four human, and one that is neither (Libra, the sign of justice or the scales). The system of houses is separate from that of the constellations, although there were delegated twelve houses, equal to the number of zodiac signs. Numbering from the east down below the horizon and around to complete the circle, the Chaldeans designated these twelve sections to encompass twelve areas or planes of the life experience.

THE DEVELOPMENT OF THE CALENDAR

It is reasonable to assume that early inhabitants of the planet Earth, having noted the difference between day (the Sun) and night (the Moon), next perceived the changes in climate and the recurring pattern of these changes. The lunar month became the guidepost of the first calendars. Time after time people saw the Moon increasing in light (the waxing Moon), followed by a period when it became smaller or decreased in light (the waning Moon). This cycle became the lunar month, and its repetition in the skies was easily discernible. The need for a reliable timetable grew out of the requisites for the success of agriculture. The planting of crops could not operate by human whim, for the ripening of vegetables and grains had to occur before winter. Humankind's intelligence soon learned that there was a regular pattern to climate, and it was by observation of celestial patterns and the two main bodies or wanderers of the solar system (the Sun and Moon, called the Lights) that mastery of agricultural practices might take place. Julius Caesar, with the help of Egyptian astronomers, established the Julian calendar in 46 B.C. Using the solar rotation as a guide, he fixed the length of the year at 365¼ days. Since the Egyptians had discovered that every four years Sirius, by which they set the start of their year, rose one day late, Caesar decreed that every fourth year should have 366 days to make up for the accumulation of quarter days.

The modern calendar, as we know it, is the Gregorian calendar, which corrects the length of the solar day. This revision, initiated under Pope Gregory XIII in 1582, allowed the spring equinox to remain at March 21 because the Julian calendar was eleven minutes and fourteen seconds out of step with the Sun each year. All this is just a very brief and sketchy synopsis of the progress of the calendar, presented here to stress the importance of the Sun and Moon in guiding humankind to an understanding of time to the present day and as important celestial markers of our day-to-day lives. If we live our every waking moment to the rhythm of the Sun and the Moon, as evidenced by the invention of the modern-day calendar, then might we not also be influenced by the other heavenly bodies?

THE BIRTH CHART AND THE TWELVE ZODIACAL SIGNS

Like the calendar and its constant need for revision to keep up with the unflagging pace and tempo of the Earth's Lights, the twelve signs of the zodiac, as we know them by the passage of our Sun through each constellation, are not fixed in precise time from year to year. For instance, the Sun enters Leo this year on July 22 (9:23 P.M. EST), but next year it will enter Leo on July 23 (3:12 A.M. EST). The Sun enters Aquarius in 1991 on January 20. Thus, the dates differ from year to year for each of the signs, and an ephemeris (a daily account of each planet's place in the heavens) is required to know one's correct sun placement.

The birth chart is a circular depiction of the ten known planets (Sun and Moon included here as planets) in relationship to the planet Earth. Some are above the horizon; some are below. Others may be east or west of the meridian (the imaginary line separating the north and south points of the horizon—the top and bottom of the visual chart). Therefore, when you view the pictograph of the individual birth chart which represents your entrance into this life, you must visualize yourself as at the exact center of the chart, with its twelve pielike slices constituting the circle. At the center is the planet Earth, and on it you are being born. The exact time of birth (the first intake of human breath) is required because what you are actually getting in the picture of your birth chart is a depiction of the exact placements of the Sun, the Moon, and the eight planets as they relate to the time and location of your birth. The birth chart, then, is a picture of the self within you, the individual essence that you are, the center of your being. It does not tell us your sex or your racial and collective background. What it does portray is the conscious level you are living on, the stage of development you have reached to be lived out in this lifetime. It has often been said that the construction of the chart is a science (astronomy) and the interpretation of the chart is an art (astrology).

The sign where a planet is placed is like the adjective that modifies a noun. The planets are energies, but the signs tell us how these energies are predisposed to action; they are the background that colors the affairs of the individual planet. We all know that there are twelve astrological signs and that these signs correspond to the twelve constellations that constitute the outer circle of our universe. Brief overviews of each sign appear later in this book (see "Sun Signs Around The Zodiac"), but here we present a different way of regarding the signs—a mythological overlay that can serve as a kind of archetypal guidepost.

ARIES is the point of all beginnings. It is the first sign in the natural zodiac and thus begins the system of the twelve houses. It begins with the spring equinox, when day and night are of equal length and winter's thaw gives rise to new birth. Symbolically life renews itself and begins again. This is why many astrologers refer to Aries as the new-start sign, for it encourages pioneerism and the conquering of new vistas. Early Christians chose to celebrate Easter at a time close to the spring equinox because it marked a time of rebirth and renewal. "I am," cries Aries, for here is born the concept of individuality. The myth behind Aries (whose bestial symbol is the battering ram) is that of the conquering hero (the self) who slays the dragon (the overthrowing of the old order) and asserts his independent and individual spirit. The old order is dead (the ruling structure into which the hero is born—i.e., the father), and a free spirit is born. This is the embodiment of Aries, and inherent in this concept is a sense of the rugged, outdoorsy physical self. Aries, Mars (its ruler), and the first house rule the physical body. Aries men and women often outwardly display a physical sensibility that is common to their sign. You see them in physical jobs, at the gym, at home in the military, and working with tools in their backyards. In summation, then, Aries is the solar hero, who has courage and confidence and faces challenges easily; he sets his own rules, wants to see results immediately, and then seeks out a new challenge in the ever-present spirit of moving onward. You may detect shades and gradations of this solar hero in friends who have a number of planets in Aries, many first-house planets, Aries rising, or just a strongly placed Aries Sun. Aries is the search for a separate identity.

TAURUS represents the earth of springtime, ripe with fertility and ready to receive the seed which will ultimately result in prosperity. This mental image conjures up visions of creativity and wealth. The earth gives rise to produce, and Taurus says, "I have; I own; I possess." Symbolized by the bull, the zodiac's second bestial figure, Taurus cannot be pushed into activity unwillfully. The attachment to comfort, security, and beauty which Taurus feels is the inherited structural foundation of this sign. Venus, its ruler, is renowned for her feeling nature, creative impulses, love of beauty, and sociable tendencies. The myth behind this sign is that of King Minos, who claimed the throne of Crete by divine right. Covetousness motivated him to keep for himself a bull sent by the god Poseidon and offer in sacrifice a substitute. Of this subterfuge was born the Minotaur, whose ogreish reputation was enhanced by the literal feeding of youths and maidens to appease him in his labyrinthine prison. As tyrant-monster the Minotaur represents the challenge for Taurus, that of single-minded covetousness and overwhelming senses, as opposed to the earthly power to accrue wealth as a natural unadulterated gift of true merit. Those who have many planets in Taurus, the second house, Taurus rising, or even just a very strong Taurus Sun placement are being asked to examine their resources, both inner and outer (material possessions), and find their own true value system. Taurus is involved in a lifelong search for meaning, an evolution leading to the inner realms through earthly dealings with the world of matter.

GEMINI, the sign of duality, says to the world, "I think." As opposed to the feeling type of person, Gemini lives his life in the head; he sifts experience through the analytical sieve of the mind, filtering out emotional baggage. This youthful sign represents the eternal adolescent, for unlike Taurus/earth (the seed which must ripen and mature) and Aries/fire (the young and virile hero), the mind grows in wisdom but has no intrinsic properties that connect with physical aging. Mercury, the Messenger, is the planetary ruler of this sign, whose symbol is that of the twins. This is the first human symbol found in the natural zodiac, implying that the process of thought is what distinguishes human from beast. Gemini's underlying myth, some say, is that of the twins Castor and Pollux, one mortal, the other divine. The theme implied here is that of two forces in opposition—one a force of dark, the other of light. Gemini must learn to face his own oppositeness, which he will ultimately experience through another. Here there is the need to focus, to reason out conflicts with rivals (often a sibling). Gemini stands at a crossroads and must learn to unite the two selves within. You'll notice the playfulness, anxiety, and duality in those who have many Gemini planets, planets in the third house, Gemini rising, or a strong Gemini Sun.

CANCER, the fourth sign and first of the water element, has as its nonhuman symbol that crustacean of the sea, the slow-moving crab. Insecure, the crab is never far from home because it carries its home on its back; the shell is its fortress against life's frequent invasions. "I feel," says Cancer, for like the tides of the ocean, Cancer swells with highs and lows of emotional pulse. Cancer's lifelong search is for security, emotional and otherwise. Just as the crab might clamp its pincers to your toe and not let go, the person of this sign clings to people in his or her life. Emotional, nondirect, protective, mother-loving (the home), Cancerian imagery evokes creative, earth mother symbolism. The Moon, symbol of women and the mother in particular, rules Cancer, and mythology offers us examples of mother-goddess figures that would opt for destruction of their offspring rather than lose their dominant and emotional hold on them to the forces of free will and individual selfhood. Confronting life via the search for emotional security is a predominant theme in those with fourth-house planets, several planets in Cancer, a strongly placed Cancer Sun, and Cancer rising.

LEO rules the Sun in the natural zodiac and is symbolized by the lion, the hot-blooded fiery beast of the jungle. In myth the story always involves the taming of the beast; the lion is not permitted to remain in its aggressive impassioned state but must come to its individuality through the creative process of self-discovery. As king of the jungle, the lion embodies the animal form (showmanship, self-involvement) before the sign evolves to compassion and maturity through life's experiences. Leo's quest to shine (like the sun) in the limelight grows out of a strength of will and the passion of the heart for self-recognition; Leo's search for the self must surpass erotic leanings and hedonism and strive for more spiritual and compassionate involvement in life to be successful. Individualism, Leo must learn, grows out of the journey away from insensitive self-involvement toward a sense of spiritual inner meaning. You will find that people with many fifth-house planets or planets in Leo, like Leo rising and the Leo Sun, have honesty, nobility, creativity, a sense of joy about them, and a spirit of generosity when they have evolved beyond the base ego of their bestial form.

VIRGO, the sign of humble service, looks at life and its workings with the motor blades of the mind turning, analyzing, and assimilating experience. A materialistic earth sign, Virgo leads a search for perfection—oftentimes through service to others. This sign has a fondness for order and precision. Virgo's symbol is that of the Virgin or Maiden holding a sheaf of barley or wheat, this itself a symbol of the earth's harvest. Virgo is the second human symbol in the zodiac, and its mission or search for a meaningful way to employ human energy and to be productive in this lifetime is integral to the experience of humanity, as opposed to beasthood, just as Gemini accents the human gift of intelligent selection. Virgo shares its ruler, Mercury, with Gemini. Mercury (or Hermes), in mythology is the clever and cunning messenger who has access to all worlds—that above, the mortal realm, and that below, or Hades. Mercury's flexibility via access to heavenly, earthly, and subterranean realms has important implications in its rulership of Virgo. Virgo must come to its sense of purity and perfection by traveling to the inner world of the subconscious and making choices according to inner laws rather than live life according to what is expected by the outer world. People with a strong Virgo Sun, Virgo rising, many planets in the sixth house, or a preponderance of Virgo planets are guided by a strong inner moral ethic when evolved. They can be overly critical, anxious, high-strung, and shy, at times, but through the lessons of humble service and patience, Virgos can reach the highest perfection.

LIBRA marks the beginning of the fall season and is the seventh sign in the natural zodiac. Thus, it is a turning point because one half of the circle of twelve signs has been completed. The journey now veers from that of the personal (or personality) to the universal (or soul). Strategic in this midway point, Libra says to the world, "I balance." The symbol for Libra, that of the scales of justice, is the only one in the zodiac that is neither human nor beast. It is an inanimate and tactile object. As opposite to the first house of the self (Aries), this turning point embodies the self in alliance with another or others; it is the house of you and me, the area of our partnerships and how we relate to others in this life. Venus is the planetary ruler of this sign of fairness and impartiality, and congenial Venus has a great desire to receive affection and appreciation from others. The mythological background of this friendly sign is constructed around the need to make fair and objective assessments, to judge according to personal and ethical codes, thereby upholding a moral balance of the universal principles of right and wrong. Libra's search for the perfect balance extends beyond the temporal quest for a complementary partner or soul mate for this life. The indecision associated with this sign stems from the thrusting of decision-making situations into Libra's life and a strong desire not to violate the principles of idealism inherent in this individual's deep inner value system. You will note that people with several seventh-house planets, a number of planets in Libra, strong Libra Sun Signs, and perhaps Libra rising can be very diplomatic, thoughtful, civilized, and sometimes quite vacillating as they deal with the relationships that enter their daily lives.

SCORPIO is often cited as the most complex of the twelve signs; it is called the mystery sign of the zodiac and is the one many astrologers find hardest to read for. The dark imagery of this sign's background is reflected in Scorpio's association with murky water—those waters with superficial oil spillings or clouded debris that do not allow one to see beneath the surface to what may lie below. In the natural zodiac Scorpio rules the eighth house of sex and death, indisputably two of life's most mystifying experiences. Mythic images pit the individual against the dark and destructive dragon, suggesting that Scorpio's battle lies in coping with evil and rage and emotional darkness in order to give birth to change and light. Scorpio is called upon to meet the darkness that lies within the soul on a personal level—through relationships and life's pursuits—and purge and transform it to a higher plane. The scorpion is the symbol for this sign. The fifth bestial figure we are to meet in the zodiac is the lowest form of this sign. The phoenix, the legendary bird that rose from its own ashes to live again, is the highest, implying that Scorpio must face darkness that lies within the personality and transcend to a soul level. Pluto, lord of the underworld, rules this sign and, through the myth of Persephone, conjures up a mythic tale of rape and pillage. There is the potential for great strength and power in Scorpio, once the individual rises, like the phoenix, above personality issues to the realm of the soul. In addition to strength, you will note a secretiveness, a stubbornness, and a strong reserve in people with strong Scorpio influences and eighth-house planets in their birth charts.

SAGITTARIUS in symbol form appears to us as the centaur, half man and half horse. The glyph for this fiery sign is represented by the archer aiming an arrow toward the heavens, his four-footed bestial frame supporting him. This is the sign of perception of the higher mind or the search for wisdom that comes from experience. Pictorially this sign suggests man's struggle to release himself from his lower (bestial) nature. Mythology portrays Sagittarius as part immortal and part beast. The race of the centaurs was bred from the coupling of a goddess (Hera) and a mortal. Chiron, the king of the centaurs, was famed as a scholar and healer. Poisoned by a wound to the thigh, he could not die because he was immortal, but he could not live either because the poison had no antidote. This implies that an element of depression underlies the bright optimistic surface of Sagittarius, popularly cited for a friendly, optimistic, and extroverted approach to life. The function of the physical wound is to turn Sagittarius' outgoing and fiery spirit inward to the realm of the superconscious, wherein lie wisdom and knowledge beyond the grasp of the mere mortal. From this one can sense in this sign the duality that exists between the flesh and the spirit. An aversion to rigid rules and the expectations of others create in Sagittarius an overwhelming desire for freedom and independence which in turn makes for difficulties in relationships at times. Jupiter, as planetary ruler of this ninth-house sign, brings the gifts of spirituality, understanding, and forward movement—or progress into the future. You will notice that those who have many planets in Sagittarius, the ninth house, a strongly placed Sagittarian Sun, or Sagittarius rising love to be on the move, have some spiritual or philosophical leanings, and face life head-on with a smile and a buoyancy that looks forward to tomorrow.

CAPRICORN, ruled by the persevering mountain goat, is the tenth-house mid-heaven sign in the natural zodiac. This sector is associated with how others see you, your reputation, the business world, and your parents. A practical sign, Capricorn uses available assets to get the most from them. Capricorn marks the time of the winter solstice, when the days start to grow colder and the natural out-of-doors fire of summer is replaced by home and the heated hearth. The tone is more serious, less airy. Saturn rules this sign and is known as a cold, unfeeling planet. Material affairs and steady concentration of effort are more important to Saturn than is the realm of the feelings. The myth behind this sign involves, as it does with Aries, the confrontation between father and son—or the sacrifice of the king to give birth to fertility on the earth. In *The Astrology of Fate* Liz Greene says: "Capricorn almost always seems to find the personal father a disappointment, just as Leo does, for the father he seeks is nothing less than divine." Saturn, frequently called the lesson giver of the zodiac, is closely associated with the father. Its symbol or glyph is shaped like the sickle (which Father Time holds, as does the Grim Reaper). Capricorn's lessons involve the loss of faith and the limitations imposed on life. An interest in worldly success, material strength, ambition, persistence, and hard work are part of the Capricorn ethic, and you will notice these traits or qualities among your friends who are strongly Capricornian—either through tenth-house planets, a strong Sun in Capricorn, several planets in the sign, or Capricorn rising.

AQUARIUS is known as the water bearer but is, in fact, an air sign. It is the fourth and last of the human representations in the zodiac. The symbol for this sign depicts a human figure pouring water from an urn onto the earth, symbolizing the dissemination (or communication) of ideas from one individual (the single container) to all humanity (the fertilization by water of the earth). Communication, then, is a keyword for Aquarius, as it is for all the air signs, but for this air sign there is more of a sense of altruism and an involvement of the collective in the dispersal of knowledge and information. The fast-moving and forward-thrusting planet Uranus rules this sign. Aquarius is interested in progress and the future. This inventive and socially minded sign has a great concern with the group, or humankind as a collective, rather than an individual, being. Mythology emphasizes this group orientation and the need to help others in the story of Prometheus, who saved humankind from darkness by stealing fire from the gods, thus bringing light (science/progress) to earth. But revenge, guilt, and suffering enter the myth, for this deed did not go unpunished. Accompanying a genuine wish to spread goodwill among humankind are a self-doubt and an impulse toward self-punishment in the background of Aquarius. Those with many planets in Aquarius or the eleventh house, a strong Aquarius Sun, or Aquarius rising are often experienced as forward thinkers, somewhat detached emotionally, rebellious, and highly individualistic. The struggle in this sign involves Uranus (liberation) and Aquarius' co-ruler Saturn (discipline). When these two primarily incompatible forces are integrated within the individual, there is great potential for spiritual evolvement.

PISCES rules the feet in the human body and, under an astrological parallel, bottoms out the natural cycle of the zodiac by virtue of its placement as the twelfth and final sign. Pisces' search is for inner spiritual peace. The bestial symbol for this sign is the fish, and the symbol for Pisces features two fishes swimming in opposite directions. One swims toward the realm of the soul, and the other toward the world of the personality. One frequently hears that if the spiritual inclinations of this sign do not overpower and conquer the personality dimensions of the Pisces individual, then there is much suffering in the life. Indeed, Pisces, holding domain over the twelfth sector in the natural zodiac, is identified with suffering, just as is the tie-in of the twelfth house in astrology, for only through suffering is the spirit released from bondage to the personality. Neptune, the planet representing fantasy or that which is not real, is the ruler of this sign. Pisces is sensitive, compassionate, and emotional and has a feeling connection to all life-forms, and its mythic role is either to save and redeem humankind through selfless service or to identify with the role of victim and dissolve into chaos. This duality is embodied in the figure of Dionysus, god of the vine and the grape (hence drunkenness), who was called upon to travel annually to visit the underworld (the unconscious) and be born again. This helps somewhat to explain the connection of Pisces and the twelfth house to the realm of solitude. Pisces needs to escape from the world, to retreat from time to time, and to overcome a sensual response to life. Shyness, sweetness, sensitivity, a sense of separateness, and sacrifice—these are all parts of the person who has planets in Pisces, the twelfth house, the Pisces Sun, and Pisces rising.

This very brief journey through the zodiac is meant to set the flavor and tone for the journey that lies ahead in the pages of this book. Learning about your own birth chart is a thrilling experience, for it holds the key to what your life is all about. It is not a rare occurrence to hear someone bemoan his or her personal birth chart. "Oh, I wish I had a chart like yours," your friend may say to you, or, "What I wouldn't give to have a chart like his!" But the true fact is the only chart that is right for you is the one you were born with.

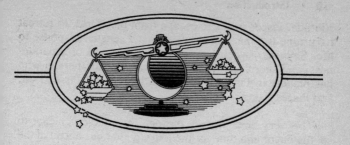

Libra

SEPTEMBER 24—OCTOBER 23

ASTROLOGY THROUGH THE CENTURIES

No one knows exactly when the notion of divining by the stars caught hold of the human mind. In every part of the world, in every culture and clime, the Sun, Moon, planets, and stars have played some part in the mythological scheme of human society. It is inevitable that this should be so, for what is more breathtaking than the sunrise? What is more awesome than the countless beads of starlight? It is no wonder that primitive people revered them.

Although societies have generally delegated some significance to astrology, not all of them have ascribed an astrological meaning to the planets and the signs of the zodiac. The earliest records we have of a belief in astrology were unearthed in Mesopotamia. The stellar art began developing into its "modern" form around 4000 B.C., when the first temples were built along the banks of the Euphrates River in honor of the Sumerian star gods. These ingenious people were adept in many branches of divinatory practices, including a technique of interpreting the patterns of oil poured into a bowl of water, observing the flight of birds, and studying the entrails of sacrificed animals. They were the first to devise a primitive astroscopy that involved the observation of the Sun, Moon, and planets, without, however, taking note of their relative positions in the zodiac.

The Sumerians were later to develop the twelve-house system of horoscopy in combination with the twelve signs of the zodiac, which were then identified with the constellations of the ecliptic. Dating from about 2870 B.C., during the reign of Sargon of Agade, documents have been found involving predictions based upon the positions of the Sun, Moon, and the five known planets, also including such phenomena as comets and meteors. At this time astrology had already begun to acquire a distinctively modern flavor.

In 3000 B.C. the house system was already described in the same fashion as that used in contemporary astrology: first house—self-assertiveness; second—poverty/riches, finances; third—brothers, sisters, communications; fourth—parents, home life; fifth—children, creativity; sixth—illness/health, work; seventh—wife/husband, marriage; eighth—death, sex; ninth—religion, education; tenth—dignities, career; eleventh—friendship, hopes; and twelfth—enmity, restrictions, subconsciousness.

With the spread of Sumerian culture, astrology became of central importance to early civilized humankind. From the Mesopotamian mythogenetic zone, astrology, the religion and science of the priestly cult, spread into Egypt, Persia, and India. From there it eventually crossed into Europe and to the East, encountering the primitive civilizations of China and Japan, and finally into Central and South America. Astrology had so great an influence on the beginning of technological humankind that the finest, most beautiful, and long-lived architectural works of the ancient world were none other than temples to the planetary deities, to the wanderers, places of worship that were also used as observatories. The priests ruled their people with absolute authority and were felt to be in touch with the very source of nature itself (in their eyes) and able to predict exactly what would befall their people.

There was no direct communication between the Sumerians and the builders of Stonehenge in England, but that marvelous work of primitive architecture was, in fact, a megalithic computer, begun sometime around 2500 B.C. The gigantic stones of this pre-Druidic temple are situated so that the rising and setting of the solstitial Sun and Moon, plus solar and lunar eclipses throughout the year, could be seen between two of the strategically placed colossal standing stones.

Astrology entered India at least as early as 3000 B.C.,

and even now the stellar science plays an all-important role in the lives of most Hindus. The main difference between Oriental and Occidental horoscopy today is that, in the East, an actual sidereal zodiac is the rule, observing the positions of the planets in relation to the constellations. In the West, however, the position of the Sun on the first day of spring is taken to be the first degree of Aries; because of the precession of the equinoxes, the Western "Aries" is now almost into the constellation Aquarius, marking the beginning of a new eon or "great year."

Soon after astrology was introduced in India from Sumerian sources, it was carried by way of trade routes into China, where it was received, as usual, with reverence. The Chinese themselves elaborated to some extent on the Indian form of astrology, combining it with the indigenous Taoist religion and the philosophy of the *I Ching*. Correlating the five elements, the cardinal points and the zenith, the five known planets, colors of the spectrum, emotional dispositions, and so forth, the Chinese evolved a highly complex system of divination that resembles the Hebrew Kabbalah in many ways. In association with native religion, astrology was successful as an aid in the ruling of the Chinese Empire for thousands of years.

The Chinese signs of the zodiac were not placed on the ecliptic, as are the signs of Indian and Western astrology, but on the equator. Each of the twelve signs ruled a two-hour period of the day, one of the months of the year, and one entire year during a twelve-year cycle. Therefore, it can be said that one was born in the Year of the Rat or the Year of the Monkey, and these animals would convey a particular astrological significance. The Chinese names for the signs of the zodiac are as follows: Dog, Boar, Rat, Ox, Tiger, Hare, Dragon, Snake, Horse, Goat, Monkey, and Cock.

In the seventh century before the Christian Era, King Ashurbanipal of Assyria built a great library in the city of Nineveh and furnished it with thousands of astrological cuneiform tablets, some dating from around 4000 B.C. In the year 612 B.C. Nineveh was conquered by the Chaldeans and the library was destroyed. The assailants, however, were soon to become masters of stellar divination themselves, and the name Chaldean was later synonymous in the West with an adept of the occult arts.

Astrology entered the Hellenic world at least as early as the Alexandrian wars, when hosts of Greek warriors fought their way to the banks of the Indus River and came under the influence of Egypt, Persia, and Babylonia, on the one hand, and of the mystical, introspective philosophies of India and the Far East, on the other. Astrological works said to have been written by the pharaoh Nechepso and the priest Petosiris were translated into Greek around 150 B.C. and became the cornerstone of pre-Christian European astrology.

As the Roman Republic was gradually infiltrated by Asian religious and philosophical thought, its citizens turned to astrology as the central theme of this new consciousness. The star-minded prophets of Baal and Ishtar were evicted from Rome in 139 B.C. along with the Jews, but as the Eastern cults gained massive public support over the years, the Roman government could eventually do nothing but tolerate the existence of various astrological sects. During the time of the Roman general Pompey (106–48 B.C.), the senator Nigidius Figulus wrote a textbook on the science in Latin. More influential were the studies of Posidonius of Apamea, written at the end of the republic.

With the founding of the Roman Empire in 27 B.C. and the subsequent official adoption of Oriental cults, astrology was accepted by nearly everyone. The emperor Tiberius turned from the worship of the elder gods in favor of the new science, which everywhere manifested itself more as a religion than as the pure mathesis (science) it is. It was thought then, as it is sometimes believed today, that the planets and signs (being representatives of theological and exalted paganism that replaced the old, stale forms of Roman religion) controlled events on earth. Astrology gained such a hold on Rome that the nation's citizens did nothing without consulting its oracles. According to one report, the Romans would not even take a bath without the assurance that it would be astrologically profitable.

The Alexandrian scholar Claudius Ptolemaeus, or Ptolemy, wrote the famous treatise on astrology entitled *Tetrabiblos* during the second century A.D., probably drawing on Egyptian and Babylonian sources. With the aid of such eminent minds as this, astrology became ingrained in the people's thinking to such an extent that virtually all philosophy and scientific thought in this period were dependent on its precepts. *The Dream of Scipio* by Cicero, written some two hundred years before Ptolemy's treatise, speaks of the heavenly spheres in much the same way as the medieval Kabbalists describe their system of *sephiroth,* and it was this type of occultism that continued to inspire the best minds in the West well past the fall of the Roman Empire and served as a foundation for modern-day astrology.

When astrology was still quite new to Europe, many Greek philosophers were doubtful of the accuracy of its forecasts. Carneades, before the advent of the Roman Empire, posed the question, "Are all the men that perish together in a battle born at the same moment because they have the same fate?" Of course, there was also the argument concerning the destinies of twins. The Chaldeans were able to answer all of the objections to their science, noting the effect of the Sun on the seasons of the year, the effect of the Moon on the ocean's tides, not to mention the more complicated evidence revealed in natal horoscopy. Nobody could refute this logic, and because their testimony proved true year after year and their personality analysis quite exact, astrology conquered the West with little difficulty. The skeptics refused to accept it, rejecting it along with all other learning. The Stoics, who believed in the omnipotence of fate, accepted astrology wholeheartedly. By the end of the second century anyone who would dare contest the validity of sidereal divination would have been considered idiotic.

To the early Christians, though, excluding those wonderfully bizarre Gnostic sects, astrology was undeniably interwoven with the paganism they abhorred. Polemics against the science were launched, using the language of the Greek dialecticians who had argued against the art when it first entered the Hellenic sphere. The same arguments that had been proved false by the early stellar prophets were used, but in the frenzy of Christian conversion the astrologers were condemned along with the rest of European paganism. The library at Alexandria, containing many thousands of astrological textbooks, was burned to the ground; the ancient monuments were destroyed or turned into Christian churches. In the fourth century of the Christian Era (the Piscean Age), Theodosius the Great outlawed all forms of paganism under penalty of death. A bloodbath, resembling the horrible autos-da-fé of the later Inquisition, ensued. Thousands of Roman citizens fled their native lands because of the terrible cruelty of their new "enlightened" rulers. Many went to India, where a cultural flowering occurred, signaling the beginning of the Indian golden age.

With the reign of Theodosius and the forbidding of the traditional European forms of religion as well as the Asian cults, the ghastly thousand-year journey of the Dark Ages began. It is at this point that the history of astrology in the West comes predominantly under the sphere of the Arabs. In Rome the papacy rejected astrology as a pagan (i.e., evil) practice. In Byzantium, however, it was recognized to some degree that astrology and Christianity were not incompatible, for many accepted Scriptures implied a belief in stellar significance ("And God said, Let there be lights in the firmament of the heaven to divide the day from the night; and let them be for signs, and for seasons, and for days, and years" [Genesis 1:14]. There are numerous Kabbalistic/astrological references all through the Old and New Testaments, primarily in the ultimate book, Revelation.). St. Augustine had declared that astrology was a fraud and that even if its predictions were accurate, they were obviously made under the influence of evil spirits.

With the appearance of Islam and the sudden emergence of the Arab empire in the seventh century A.D., astrology was saved from a state of ignominy. Damascus became a center of occult learning. Al-Mansur established a grand observatory in Baghdad. In the ninth century

Albumazar wrote *Introductorium in Astronomiam*, a textbook of astrological theory. By way of Spain, Arab scientific knowledge revived the faltering European educational centers.

Throughout the Middle Ages in Europe there was a raging controversy about whether astrology should be accepted as a science or as a "black art." By the thirteenth century, following the example of St. Thomas Aquinas, academicians generally accepted that the stars were the cause of all that took place on earth. The University of Bologna established a chair of astrology in the year 1125. Dante found astrology to be a source of inspiration in the writing of *The Divine Comedy* in the fourteenth century—for example, when the poet hero visits the angels of the planetary spheres.

By the fifteenth century even the papacy was using astrology to make important decisions. Pope Sixtus IV was himself an astrologer of repute, and Julius II recognized the need for astrological counsel. Johann Müller drew up horoscopes for the pope, established the first European observatory in Nuremberg, and published a thirty-year ephemeris on his own printing press. Copernicus (1473–1543), renowned for his discovery that the Earth is not the center of the solar system, was an astrologer. It is peculiar that modern anathemas against astrology use his discovery as a tool for contradicting astrological theory, but the founder of modern astronomy himself proclaimed that stellar divination was not in the least affected by his then-controversial deductions.

Michel de Notredame (Nostradamus) was one of the foremost astrologers of his time and the author of a book called *Centuries,* a collection of prophecies that remains popular to this day. In 1556 he was hired to compute the horoscopes of the royal children of the French court. Queen Catherine de Médici's honored him all his life after she discovered that his interpretations concerning the fate of her children were correct.

The Danish astrologer Tycho Brahe, the Englishman Francis Bacon, and the Italian Tommaso Campanella all helped to keep astrology alive through the sixteenth and seventeenth centuries. The Elizabethan court astrologer John Dee (1527–1608) was also a professional alchemist and magician. It was he who believed he had conversed with angels, leading him to discover a system of "Enochian" keys, or calls, that could unlock the worlds of the five elements and the thirty aethyrs. After experimentation with these magical methods, he was forced to retract what he had declared concerning their sanctity, for the content of the visions they produced clearly ran counter to the Christian code of ethics.

It remained for Aleister Crowley in the twentieth century to take up the thread of Dee's magical (or psychological) research by invoking the thirty aethyrs in the desert of North Africa. Crowley left behind a record of spiritual achievement unparalleled in the rationalistic West, entitled *The Vision and the Voice*. Within these "aethyrs," or psychic substrata, exist various combinations of astrological "powers," though it is difficult to say whether they are objective astral phenomena or subjective dreamlike experiences.

In the seventeenth century Johannes Kepler and William Lilly were representative of their age's astrological thought. The former, a mathematician, had definite doubts about the accuracy of astrological delineation as he knew it but expressed a belief that an authentic science of the stars could be developed if serious-minded men put it to the test. The latter, Lilly, was a prodigious writer and a leading horoscope maker in England. He predicted the Great Fire of London in 1666.

In more recent years Alan Leo and Dane Rudhyar both have tried to bring their chosen profession into line with current scientific trends, giving it a new, more intellectual framework. During World War II Karl Ernst Krafft was employed by the Nazis to translate the teachings of Nostradamus, which, it was felt, could be used profitably as propaganda. On the British side, Louis de Wohl was convinced that the Germans were using astrology in their effort to win and that the British should use the same means. The government agreed, and de Wohl became the official astrological mouthpiece of the Allies.

While the West has been growing ever more divorced from its mystical beginnings, the East (namely, India and its neighboring countries) has retained its age-old belief in astrology and, in many instances, the primitive magic associated with it. In the non-Communist countries of the Far East, astrological practices have remained virtually unchanged. The Buddhist priests of Sri Lanka perform a ceremony with the intention of invoking planetary forces in the curing of disease, fever, and poverty; Chandra (the Moon), Buddha (Mercury), Shukra (Venus), Kuja (Mars), Guru (Jupiter), Shani (Saturn), Rahu (North Node), and Ketu (South Node) all represent spiritual powers which, when adverse, produce diseases and misfortune analogous to the Westerner's analysis of each planet's negative effects.

In present-day Europe and America astrology is once again gaining a place in the universities, and surprisingly enough, psychology is investigating its uses in therapy. Sigmund Freud, ever loath to lend any credence to astrology, stated shortly before his death that he did hold a masked interest in the occult. Carl Jung, the most influential psychologist since Freud, used horoscopes to aid him in diagnosing the causes of his patients' illnesses. His studies have done much to validate astrology's claim to be a science, not a parlor game for the superstitious.

The theories of sidereal effects have become more sophisticated with the passing of the centuries. Radiation, cosmobiological impulses, subatomic conscious forces (a euphemism for "gods") have all been put forth as explanations of astrological accuracy. Perhaps the most convincing argument presented by modern science is that of Carl Jung. He propounded a theory that divinatory arts such as astrology, the tarot, and the *I Ching* are examples of a universal principle that he called "acausal synchronicity." The significance of this hypothesis is that it states, in effect, that there are no influences whatsoever acting upon the daily life of humanity originating in the position of the planets but rather that the planets portray a pattern of events synchronized to the life of the individual or group of individuals (such as a nation). This seems much more suitable than the theory of cosmic radiation, for no matter how much radiation exists in the earth's atmosphere, it cannot account for all the aspects of human life that astrology can accurately predict.

Acausal synchronicity does, to some extent, account for psychological analysis by the way of the natal chart, but many predictions would be impossible according to this theory. It may account for changes within the individual organism, but it is difficult to explain how planetary vibrations can cause events to happen to an individual, events that could be accurately predicted by ordinary horoscopy. To recognize the fact that every aspect of the universe acts in conformity with the remainder of the universe is only to extend the concept of ecology one step further. One can find significance in every aspect of the physical world. Astrology happens to be the most logical, mathematically determined divinatory science we have developed thus far. The fact is that the stars do not have a *causal* effect on the Earth, but a connection between the planets and individuals that is rooted in astrological meaning does much to alleviate it from the age-old objections to its validity.

As for the spiritualistic theory of cosmic effects, there is no evidence to support it which cannot be explained by more practical hypotheses. This does not mean that it is necessarily false, but it lowers the probability of its being true. The theory of acausal synchronicity presents a cleaner, more efficient astrological theory and explains how the planets can actually describe every detail of human experience without being the direct cause. They are an abstraction of our daily activities. If the spiritualistic theory were, in fact, true, then the *causal* arts of magic (i.e., the omnipotence of the magician in controlling his universe through controlling spiritual noumena) must be granted. Here one begins to fall into the trough of uncertain, difficult, and pretentious metaphysics—difficult to prove and impossible to integrate with the truths of physical existence. It may be that astrology and magic are examples of psychic causality. If so, everything we know is *wrong*! Not only that, but natural laws are thrown topsy-turvy, *psychological facts are disgraced as mere fables*, and we become the victim of a rampaging solipsism. In the years to come, we may see science turn its attention to problems such as these, and the outcome may be very surprising.

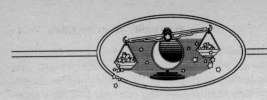

PERSONALITY TRAITS FOR LIBRA

Your Place in the Sun. Librans are the zodiac's beautiful people—being naturally charming, gracious, and outgoing. Yours is the seventh sign of the natural horoscope, which rules the house of partnership, marriage, and legal matters. This shows that you're a romantic with a need for close companionship, and a peacemaker and perfector of human relations whose main gifts are sensitivity and an ability to adapt and compromise. As an air sign, you are intelligent, communicative, and sociable. As a cardinal sign, you have executive ability and like to set things into motion. You especially enjoy bringing opposites together to form a new synthesis; thus, you may excel as an artist, diplomat, matchmaker, or lover! Harmony is your aim.

The Significance of Your Ruling Planet. Your ruler is Venus—symbol for the energy of harmony, adjustment, evaluation. Under its influence, you are kindhearted, sweet-tempered, and active in initiating smooth relations with others. You also have an excellent artistic sense, which shows in your attractive personal appearance and in your appreciation of music, form, and color. In general, you are nourished by all that is cultured, refined, and beautiful—becoming dispirited when subjected to ugly surroundings or a prosaic style of life. Your ideal occupation is in the field of art, music, fashion, hairdressing, cosmetology, human relations (counselor, lawyer, mediator, hostess, teacher, or writer).

The Meaning of Your Symbol. Your symbol is the scales, showing your sense of balance. You long for peace, poise, and equilibrium and strive for these continually in your life-style, expression, and personal relationships. You have a well-developed sense of give and take and are just and impartial in dealing with others. You also prefer a well-rounded development to anything one-sided—either mental, emotional, or physical. Intellectually, you have excellent powers of reason and comparison and tend to weigh, measure, and evaluate before you act. The scales also show your sense of proportion in artistic matters where, instinctively, you know about spacing, placement, how much is too much, and what goes with what for overall perfection.

Qualities to Stress. You have much talent, but you will have to commit yourself to a specific goal and awaken your power of will if you are to develop fully. Your instinctive tendency is to be easygoing, perhaps because natural gifts and a cheerful, lovable temperament make good things come your way more readily than they do to most. Be that as it may, consistent effort and application are still the only way to any deeper growth and development. Unless you take this route, you are apt to wind up a dilettante with only surface successes to your credit. To work against this, why not set aside a period of time each day to work on your chosen goals? Even a half hour persistently will pay off in the long run. Once in the habit, you'll enjoy it.

Weaknesses to Overcome. Your main problem is lack of independence. You have too strong a need to placate others and tend to look to them for approval in cases where your own inner voice should be the sole guide. You're also overly sensitive to inharmony and shy away from turbulent situations—including those where it may be vital to take a firm and even undiplomatic stand. Other weaknesses are laziness, vanity, flirtatiousness, insincerity. You can be overly idealistic, unable to accept the realities of imperfect humanity and daily married life. Another negative is vacillation. You have great difficulty making a decision. Even when you do, you are given to looking back and wondering if it was right. Try to overcome this habit, for you are just wasting precious time.

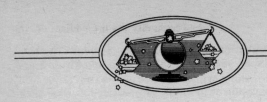

SUN SIGNS
AROUND THE ZODIAC

The Sun stands at the center of the zodiac, as the focal point of our charts. Just as the heart pumps lifeblood throughout our bodies, so, too, is the sun the life-force energy that ignites our beings, expressing itself as our identities, how we define ourselves in the world. The Sun also describes our conscious self-expressions, what we know ourselves to be and how we project that to others. It is the creative thrust of energy that moves us forward. Placement and aspects to the Sun describe the issues we struggle with on our path' to fulfilling the map laid out by our charts. How we solve these challenges is the free-will aspect of astrology, as we ourselves determine exactly how our Sun Sign energy gets expressed.

It is said that the Sun is the soul or the self, that aspect of us central to our being which involves the smooth running of our inner and outer lives. Our ability to take hold of whatever thought, desire, or wish we have and move it into a conscious place is described by our Sun Sign. How we take the inner pieces of our personality and integrate them and then reflect them to others—creatively and interpersonally—is another function of that core part of us.

Our purpose in life is also signified by the Sun Sign under which we were born. Understanding our Sun Sign can help us define our mission, issues, aims, goals, and life task as well. The Sun represents that central place inside us from which is shed the light of consciousness on other parts, struggles, and pieces. In defining some of our obstacles, clarity and growing self-awareness enable us to over-come barriers to expressing our inner strength and essence.

Finally, the Sun represents our joy in life, the path which by its right nature in our lives successfully leads us to "follow our bliss." In turning in toward a center of ourselves that we know feels right, we can move out into the world in the best way possible. Then, contributing our greatest talents, we make it a more joyful and fulfilling place for those around us as well, extending as far as the heart can see.

The more successful we are in finding and fulfilling ourselves, the more readily, easily, and helpfully we can reach out and shine the light on the paths of others. Our Sun stands symbolically as that beacon, illuminating our own path to self-understanding and self-mastery.

Aries

 Aries is the first sign of the zodiac and as such is associated with leadership, the head, and being first. Aries individuals are known for their spontaneity and assertive-ness and, unless negatively aspected, a certain natural leadership ability. Idealism, too, is part of the Aries heritage. With the energy and motivation to stand up for matters of principle, Aries is the champion of the fight for individual freedom for the self and of the fight for others.

Aries is motivated by action, by taking charge in a situation and moving forward in it. This core of inner self therefore often involves a life of removing obstacles to the expression of an overt and straightforward energy. In the struggle to assert themselves, Aries people are often in-volved with dealing with issues of anger and aggression, learning how to channel or even make a career of those characteristics—as criminal lawyers, boxers, politicians, or warriors on the path to peace, truth, or justice.

A sense of humor is often the trademark of such indi-viduals, who have been through the school of hard knocks long enough to realize that the head is often smarter and faster than the hand. The wise Aries learns that a quick quip can do much more than a clenched fist to forward his or her aims.

Taurus

Taurus is reputed to be the most stubborn, determined, and stable sign because it is associated with the earth and money, as well as with creativity, sensual pleasure, and fertility. These characteristics all relate to the material or physical aspects of life, of which Taureans are notoriously aware and to which they are quite sensitive.

Comfort is a basic aspiration of such members of the zodiac. Taurus is very much aware of basic needs and what feels good. Sensualists and even hedonists, Taureans are no less practical when it comes to seeing to it that all the necessities are taken care of before the pleasure begins.

The energy of creativity made manifest in some tangible form often leads Taurus people into the field of art or some related endeavor. Expressing a unique aesthetic sensibility, these materially minded artists often find lucrative outlets for their talents.

With a particularly acute sense of timing, Taurus is able to attune to knowing exactly when and how to get a job done and then brilliantly see it through to completion. Security is the impetus that keeps Taurus' nose to the grindstone. Otherwise she or he surely would be dissolved somewhere in a puddle of sensual delight.

Gemini

Gemini is the sign most directly expressing our basic duality as human beings: how every issue has two sides (at least) and how each moment of life has a myriad of possibilities for action, passivity, philosophical distance, and emotional reaction. The complexity of this awareness makes Gemini the first of the mental signs, and communication and thought are keys to the Gemini personality. Writing and study are some of the skills applied in making the bridges that Gemini builds between the self and others.

Gemini is also known for a great diversity of charms and talents, taking on a plethora of projects and commitments and a multileveled and reflective awareness that makes for a rather self-contradictory quality evident in interactions. When directed, the energy of the Sun Sign person can be brilliant and productive, often in the field of literary endeavors or the media.

The awareness that members of this sign have of the many details that constitute existence results in a fascinating personality, an inspiring conversationalist, and an interesting companion. Life is incredibly entertaining to Gemini, and as much as you are a part of his or her audience, you are also part of the show.

Cancer

 Cancer is the Sun Sign most clearly associated with the home, nurturing, and that inner part of ourselves that is still a child in sensitivities and needs to be taken care of. Most often this need does not get directly expressed and instead emerges as a very mothering, directive energy—often by a Cancer who has walled off an incredibly deep vulnerability that goes wanting inside.

Developing emotional security and finding a place of safety in life are the driving forces of this Sun Sign individual. Often Cancer people use money or intellect—or neurotic worry—as shields against their fantastic psychic attunements to the feelings of others, reflecting their own sensitive selves.

The quality of knowing intuition can make Cancer individuals a success in just about any field chosen. The driving emotional needs, however, make monetary success or even fame too often an unsatisfying substitute for that deeper striving to be truly nurtured that is sought throughout their lives.

The most secure, rewarding, and emotionally fulfilling

employment this sign can undertake involves taking care of others—neighborhood police surveillance work, perhaps—or attaining a level of expertise in a field where compassion, understanding, and nurturing are needed.

Leo

 Leos shine when happy and then reflect to others their own finest qualities, encouraging and inspiring them with tireless enthusiasm. On the other hand, keeping a Leo happy takes a lot of energy and usually requires an entire audience of admirers.

This need for attention is expressed in negative ways, however, only when there isn't a creative outlet, an arena in which Leo is known to stand out. This lack can make for a whiny, self-centered, narrowly focused, and dominating character with little to share but complaints.

Leo may as a child have been deprived of the love and recognition that one needs to develop into a secure, confident adult. Dignity can become overly dramatic histrionics and a sense of confidence can degenerate into an overbearing pride when Leo has not learned to bolster self-esteem so that each sensation of vulnerability need not be so devastating.

The ego must be honed to keep Leo on his or her best behavior. Skills and talents need to be cultivated so that there is always a place for Leo to go that feels like a platform for well-deserved adulation. Once in the comfortable position of leading and advising others, Leo can move on to lend that golden glow to the rest of a fun-filled, creative, and loving life.

Virgo

 These hardworking and most sensitive members of the zodiac know just what they can do to serve you, and most often they deliver that promise modestly, completely, and well. Virgos are ever alert to any physical needs that are as yet unfulfilled, and their well-developed gifts—especially those involving the use of the hands or particular analytical or other mental abilities—are always efficiently directed.

The almost driving perfectionism of members of the sign, however, needs to be tempered by an acceptance and toleration for what is—for their own and others—human limitations. Otherwise, a sadly cynical, frustrated, and/or depressed person is the result. A more fruitful direction for the discriminating talents of Virgo is the purification in some way of the environment or some system that connects to the betterment of our physical world for us all to live healthier and simpler lives.

An overwhelming sensitivity—to others, to allergens, to disorder, tension, pain, etc.—drives Virgo into a kind of intellectual retreat or one that involves the manipulation of others in order to avoid revealing a deeper side of self, although a wealth of tender responsiveness is there for the asking by the right person, at the correct time, in the appropriate way.

Libra

Libra is the only sign represented by neither an animal nor a human symbol. Instead, the scales represent the rather abstract quality of Librans. Equality, justice, and a sense of fairness are what members of this sign are driven by in arriving at and fulfilling their life purposes. As such, they need to find a balance between their own needs and those of others, their desires and direction in life—as opposed to the ones they have been following in order to please or pacify others. Problems can develop when Librans give with the expectation of getting, rather than just seeing to it that their own needs are taken care of before giving anything of themselves to others.

Librans are always involved in some kind of relationship, so that they can see the mirrors of their own inner selves in others. Partnership can be quite crucial to them because they have trouble defining themselves alone or apart from others.

Above all, Librans seek harmony, usually manifested in a sensitivity to the aesthetic surroundings in which they live and work. The deeper peace they seek, however, lies within themselves, where they struggle with anything that gets in the way of experiencing serenity. Once in touch with their own inner beauty, however, they easily bring it out in others.

Scorpio

 Scorpio is the sign that governs transformation—that is, conscious change, acknowledging and taking responsibility for some inner negativity and turning it into a constructive force. It may seem to members of this sign that life is filled with task after task of this kind. Indeed, emotional challenges of the most arduous variety are often Scorpio's lot in life. Surviving and moving through such difficulties, however, result in a highly developed character, furthered through a concentration of positive power.

Within the psyche of these magnetic and strong individuals is an indomitable strength which, when not correctly channeled, can become an unscrupulous force for domination and even brutality over others. The driving nature of a Scorpio who has not come to terms with a great inner power can be manifested in destructiveness to the self and to others or in the cultivation of disease.

Once Scorpio has discovered the miraculous power of turning that negativity around and making it part of everyday life, healing on all levels becomes one of many precious gifts the Scorpio individual possesses—to be performed on the self as well as conveyed to others. A profession aligned with the positive expression of such energies satisfies the Scorpio soul, helps others, and turns the energy around.

Sagittarius

 Sagittarians are often known as the wanderers of the zodiac because they may never really seem to land or plant themselves firmly anywhere—in a relationship, career, or home—for very long. Should you find a happy Sagittarian who has seemingly given up that overt striving for freedom, you may have found one who knows the true secret of the sign: that life is but a journey to be lived out, the process being even more important than the goal, how you love and work as much as who and what and how much.

Sagittarians are philosophical travelers with an insatiable curiosity and zest for life. They thrive on the new and, with lively enthusiasm, bring great joy and excitement into the lives of others. All people are potential friends to a Sagittarian, who is a citizen of the world, at home everywhere.

Sagittarians get into quandaries about what direction to take—they are easily diverted—when other parts of their personalities demand fulfillment. The answer lies in seeing even a life-binding commitment as but a deeper path to explore, enjoy, and move along down the path of life.

Good careers for Sagittarians range from judges to space explorers, philosophers, teachers, or writers. Any profession undertaken is pursued with joy and satisfaction so long as it involves the exploration of life and being with people.

Capricorn

Capricorn is traditionally that hardworking sign of the zodiac that takes responsibility for all that goes on, sees to it that everything necessary gets completed successfully and well, and has a rather serious view of life. This typically describes the early attitude of members of this sign, who have usually emerged from childhoods that leave them deprived of some significant aspect of youth and mature before their time. Responsible to a fault, they often enter adulthood motivated mostly by a fear for their own survival and for that of those in their charge as well.

Capricorns derive a sense of purpose and satisfaction from taking good care of either a large number of people or a significant area of expertise or materials of some value. Always up for a good challenge, they can be strong adversaries and staunch supporters of others, their ideas, their work—whatever serves the well-being of the group.

Usually because they have taken strict good care of their physical selves throughout their lives, Capricorns live long and relatively healthy lives, active and employed well into old age. With arduous lives behind them, their later years are often dotted with the delight of a childlike and life-loving existence they didn't get to enjoy when young.

Aquarius

Aquarius is a rather challenging sign, with issues and struggles that all of us in this Aquarian Age are now learning about. Aquarians especially are dealing with coming to terms with the scientific and the artistic needs within us all, allowing for full expression of both. Another way of viewing this dilemma is the need to reconcile the dreamer (Aquarians are filled with magnificent and sometimes grandiose ideas for the future) with the pragmatist, knowing that the priority is to get things done now so that the greatest number of people can immediately benefit.

Many Aquarians feel the pull of these conflicting drives their entire lives, while others sacrifice one aspect of their natures for another. The larger truth that can serve to help the Aquarian fulfill his or her purpose is that he or she heeds the guiding intuitive voice within that can lead him or her to a successful and peaceful integration of those various parts of self.

Members of this sign are especially successful in

professions in which they can channel their uniqueness and talent into helping others recognize their own gifts and cultivate self-sufficiency in them. Because they thrive on being of service, they automatically do well.

Pisces

 As members of the last sign of the zodiac, Pisceans are in touch with the temporal nature of reality, with the fact that everything is finite and that nothing endures. Pisceans do not find themselves attached to the future, to plans or to material gain—let alone to any profession that seeks to structure or organize resources, people, or time to the destruction of the human spirit. Pisces thrives on a creative flow that involves spontaneity, artfulness, and the ability to tap into an abundant emotional and spiritual reservoir within. Conflicts Pisceans experience often involve a choice between acting toward something new and staying with the known; all their lives involve building bridges, most often between the inner selves and the outer world of others.

With the gift of magically understanding the value of every human and other sentient being, each moment and every feeling, Pisceans fulfill themselves often by being there for others and by supporting friends and family, clients and customers through the travails of everyday life. Pisceans possess a magnificent intuitive ability to extend the self as needed, when needed in just the right way to be of help to others.

HOW TO MAINTAIN GOOD HEALTH

If you were born from September 24 to October 3, Venus rules your decan. Being one of the most gregarious of all the signs, you love to socialize and party. However, in so doing, you are inclined to put on some extra pounds. You may also have difficulty metabolizing carbohydrates, which can overtax your kidneys. Cutting down on desserts and alcohol will help keep the weight off and place less strain on these vital organs. In addition, drinking eight glasses of water helps flush out harmful wastes from your system. Niacin, found in liver, lean meat, fish, eggs, and whole wheat, helps the body burn off carbohydrates more efficiently. And if you are over forty, eat more leafy greens and drink more milk in order to keep your kidneys functioning normally. Exercise is essential for your figure and fitness; try dancing with your special beau.

If you were born from October 4 to October 13, Uranus rules your decan. Because a harmonious environment is so necessary to your well-being, stressful situations can easily upset your equilibrium. Therefore, retreating to a quiet place to meditate for a few minutes a day can do wonders for your body and soul. You may be subject to spasms and cramps in your lower back. Therefore, always remember to bend your knees when lifting heavy objects. Visiting a chiropractor periodically can help keep your spine in proper alignment. Massages can also relax the back muscles and ease mental tension as well. Including plenty of milk and dairy products as well as sardines, salmon, and green vegetables ensures that you are getting enough calcium in your diet, which is essential for keeping your spine strong and flexible. Yoga stretching exercises are beneficial.

If you were born from October 14 to October 23, Mercury rules your decan. You place a high premium on your intellect. However, mental work late at night can cause insomnia. Therefore, it's best to just relax and unwind during the evening hours. A cup of warm milk or chamomile tea before bedtime can do wonders for a restful night's sleep. Your veins and venous circulation also need special care. To help the veins retain their elasticity and to keep that youthful beauty, foods rich in Vitamin E should be included in your diet. The best sources for this nutrient are soybeans, leafy green vegetables, whole grains, and eggs. You should also use cosmetics containing Vitamin E. Since proper breathing is very important to your physical well-being, exercise in the fresh air as much as possible.

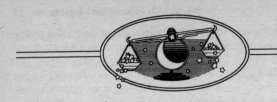

YOUR GUIDE TO FRIENDS AND LOVERS

How You Relate

Because yours is the sign of partnership, you would rather have an alliance with a friend or lover than go it alone. In fact, love is so important to you that you don't feel really complete without it. Yet because you also need your own space, you can, at times, be somewhat detached.

Libra with Aries: Because Aries is your opposite sign, you are strong where the other is weak and vice versa. You can help your Aries friend be more diplomatic and Aries can show you how to be more assertive. You are magnetically drawn to your Aries lover. Through a mutual give-and-take, this can be a fine combination.

Libra with Taurus: With your combined appreciation for the arts, your friendship with Taurus can be most fulfilling. Your Taurus lover is romantic, sensual, and very caring. You both are fond of the "good life," and Taurus can provide the financial means to obtain it. However, in return, you may have to give this possessive individual your undivided attention. All in all, it can be well worth it.

Libra with Gemini: Having similar interests and philosophical viewpoints makes for an intellectually stimulating friendship with Gemini. Your Gemini lover can sweep you off your feet with romantic words. And Gemini's many-faceted personality can always continue to keep you intrigued. However, although Gemini can give you the space you need, a commitment will be harder to come by.

Libra with Cancer: Even though you operate at cross purposes from time to time, you admire your Cancer friend's emotional sensitivity and caring nature. This goes doubly for your Cancer lover. You love to socialize, while Cancer prefers to stay at home. And if possessive Cancer should catch you flirting with another, the ensuing emotional outburst can really upset your delicate balance.

Libra with Leo: Since you both are outgoing, you and your Leo friend can be quite a social asset to each other. Your Leo lover can also be your very best friend, since you are perfectly in tune together. In addition, lovemaking can be really grand. You may not get as many compliments as you'd like from this sometimes self-absorbed individual, but still, it's a worthy match.

Libra with Virgo: Sharing intellectual and artistic tastes can cement a friendship with Virgo. You enjoy your Virgo lover's earthy sensuality. However, this individual's frugality can clash with your love of luxury. You thrive on flattery, but Virgo can be overly critical toward you. This duo has a better chance of working if you learn and grow with each other.

Libra with Libra: Because you are both so companionship-oriented, an association with another Libra should be quite satisfying. You also share a love of art, music, and cultural activities. You and your Libra lover make a most attractive couple. This can be an equal, give-and-take relationship. And because you complete each other, you two can be as close as two peas in a pod.

Libra with Scorpio: You admire your Scorpio friend's determination and decision-making capabilities. As a lover, Scorpio is intense, passionate, and possessive. These qualities can enthrall you until Scorpio throws a jealous scene because of an innocent flirtation on your part. You will have to make most of the concessions in order for this relationship to work.

Libra with Sagittarius: Your Sagittarius friend is exciting and fun to be with. In addition, you share a love of travel and social events, and a sense of fair play. Sexual attraction and compatibility enhance a love relationship with a Sagittarius. And this freedom-loving soul also respects your space.

Libra with Capricorn: Your Capricorn friend can teach you to be more responsible, and career-oriented Capricorn can learn to let go and relax a little in your presence. Though Capricorn can be sexually satisfying as a lover, you desire an equal relationship, while Capricorn demands to be the boss. Compromise is definitely needed.

Libra with Aquarius: There is a meeting of the minds with your Aquarius friend. In addition, because you are both people-oriented, you share an enjoyment of participating in group activities. As a lover, Aquarius is inventive, spontaneous, and won't make heavy emotional demands on you. Although flattery (which you love to hear) is not one of Aquarius's strong suits, this union should still be happy.

Libra with Pisces: You and your Pisces friend can enjoy creative activities. In addition, Pisces can help you grow on an emotional and spiritual level. Your super-romantic Pisces lover can melt your heart. However, when the first glow wears off, you may find Pisces's extreme dependency hard to deal with.

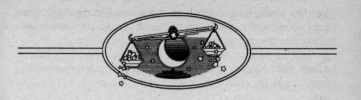

CAREER-WEALTH POTENTIALS

Are You in the Right Job? Three houses of a birth-chart are significant in determining your career potentials—the tenth (general field of work), the third (mental skills and aptitudes), and the sixth (capacity for work; conditions related to employment; relationships with co-workers, employees, etc.) A dream job for you would be one in plush but tasteful surroundings, where you would meet elegant and fascinating people and could utilize your special talents in both an enjoyable and lucrative manner. That would indeed be a dream job for you, but it just might not always be available. If you are a positive-type Libran, you are quick to see opportunities—can even create them for yourself in your own subtle way. In general, you are attracted to a career that brings you into contact with other people rather than to one in which you work in solitude, for relationships of varying kinds are important to you. Your ability to communicate your ideas is shown by Sagittarius on your solar third house, an indication of your enthusiasm and persuasiveness in projecting them to others. People tend to listen with respect because you speak with authority and knowledge. With Pisces on your solar sixth house, you have an appreciation of artistic and cultural matters and often have creative talent in these areas as well. Cancer on your solar tenth house gives you a special flair for dealing with the public, whether by personal contact or through an awareness of just what people will or will not buy. The combination of your Libra Sun Sign with these signs on your solar third, sixth, and tenth houses shows that you would be at your best in the fields of hotel, motel, or restaurant management, personnel work, counseling (Cancer); writing, teaching, advertising, law, foreign enterprises (Sagittarius); art, music, drama, photography, social service, creative writing (Pisces).

Are You Aware of Your Wealth Potentials? In a birth-chart, the second house signifies personal property, possessions, financial connections, investments, ability to increase income, valuable ideas, monetary prowess, ambitions, personal belongings, earnings, and all forms of money (gold, jewels, bonds, securities, stocks, etc.). Scorpio, your money house, is ruled by Mars and co-ruled by Pluto. This house is between Libra, ruled by Venus, and Sagittarius, ruled by Jupiter. The house opposite your money house is Taurus, ruled by Venus. This combination makes you a resourceful, energetic, and willful earner; you may sometimes be able to save money, but generally you become a spendthrift. You have good ability to increase your income, but your mixed attitude toward saving and spending may not allow you to hold all that you can amass. Sometimes you may be impulsive and rash in spending. However, you do possess a good economic outlook and valuable ideas to earn money. You are ambitious in money-making and probably strongly believe that it is necessary to spend money in order to make money. You do not lack the necessary courage to take bold steps in investments. Furthermore, you have fine financial connections and excellent business prowess. If you are not extremely careful, you are likely to create disharmonious relations with fellow workers, superiors, and subordinates. The way in which you perform your work may be good, but you tend to interfere with others' business. You must try to overcome this tendency so that you do not put yourself in a bad light in your dealings with others. By nature, you like to have everything around you running on an even keel, but you must realize that you have to do your part if you want this congenial atmosphere to prevail in your working surroundings. Many valuable ideas enter your head, and you have the resourcefulness to make them pay off well. You may be put in a position of authority where business secrets and policy-making may be concerned. You should also have good contacts with top people. However, there may be some delays or obstacles in getting the promotions you feel you deserve or in attaining the success you have planned so carefully to achieve.

HOBBIES FOR FUN AND PROFIT

What do you do with your leisure time? Many psychologists say that from the answer to this question they can tell even more about your personality than they can from complete knowledge of your vocation. Although most people have far fewer hours to spend on hobbies than they must give to daily routine, the way those free hours are spent reveals much concerning the individual's chance for happiness and progress.

Like a poet, you say, "A thing of beauty is a joy forever." Nothing gives you greater pleasure than creating something of lasting loveliness. This may be a painting, sculpture, delicately molded vase or bowl, wood carving, or hammered cooper plaque. No matter what you choose to make, you will see that it has exquisite lines and harmony of color. In the matter of colors and contrasts, your sense for the beautiful will direct you to make the best choice. Interior decorating could be the proper career for channeling these creative desires.

Alluring scents have as great an appeal to you as expressions of beauty through the sense of touch and sight; you may want to make a collection of perfumes or experiment in making cosmetics. To grow a garden of fragrant flowers would give you delight.

As Libra stands for balance, there is a practical as well as an artistic side to your nature. This could find expression in the rejuvenation of old objects to increase their value for resale. It might be surprising what your own attic holds that could be thus utilized, and there are always secondhand shops and church rummage sales. The search for salvageable objects in itself can be an interesting hobby.

Since routine chores are not as distasteful to you as they are to some, you find pleasure in organization work with specifically assigned duties. Your method of discharging these is often an inspiration to those with whom you work, and it is certain that you will win respect and prestige by your participation in community-welfare service.

The opportunity to win admiration and gratitude in more personal relationships is also yours, for you may often be consulted for advice in the emotional problems of your associates. Guidance can be a very satisfying hobby for you and may lead to other interesting avocations.

Your spare-time activities should be chosen with cosmic influences in mind if you are to derive the most satisfaction and relaxation for yourself. Wise use of leisure also enables you to give the maximum pleasure and help to your associates. The position of the Sun at the time of your birth inclines your choice of hobbies in certain directions. To ignore these forces and swim against the tide, so to speak, is to hold yourself back from development—emotionally and spiritually, often even physically.

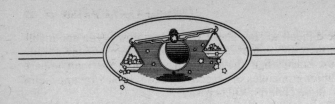

STELLAR TIPS FOR PARENTS

Fire, Earth, Air, or Water Element. While an element has a common mold, each sign falling under it has individual characteristics. The fire signs are Aries (March 21–April 20), Leo (July 24–August 23), and Sagittarius (November 23–December 21); the earth signs are Taurus (April 21–May 21), Virgo (August 24–September 23), and Capricorn (December 22–January 20); the air signs are Gemini (May 22–June 21), Libra (September 24–October 23), and Aquarius (January 21–February 19); the water signs are Cancer (June 22–July 23), Scorpio (October 24–November 22), and Pisces (February 20–March 20). Here is the way to place children in their own particular environment.

Libra Parents with Fire Children. You are often amazed at the unending store of energy that fire-sign children seem to possess. While you may not be fond of exercise, it is necessary to make a concerted effort to include physical activities in their daily routine. Exercise provides a means for these offspring to release excess energy, and as a result of it, you will be less apt to be plagued by hyperactive devilkins who constantly get into mischief. While you tend toward a mental approach to life, carefully planning things and weighing decisions with great deliberation, these youngsters boldly plunge into projects, complete them, and immediately look for something else to do. Still you can be a source of serenity for fire-sign children, who live a life of hurried pace and little organization. Though it may

34

be difficult to slow these youngsters down, you can instill in them the importance of thinking before rushing ahead. Just start when they are very young. You can impart Libran principles of objectivity and fair play by appealing to these children's generosity.

Libra Parents with Earth Children. You appreciate children who are polite and well behaved. It shouldn't be too difficult to teach earth-sign children correct attitudes and behavior since they need structure and organization. Once such principles are made an integral part of the family's life-style, these children will develop a reasonably cooperative personality. Through the years, they will come to view understanding, objectivity, and a sense of fair play as important parts of your Libran nature and sources of strength to be relied upon. When difficulties arise, your calmness and swift, decisive action represent security. However, if you consistently take too long in your deliberations, these children will think it represents an inability to make decisions and, further, a lack of strength. They will then turn such situations into an opportunity to gain advantage. Use your intellectual skills to impart love of knowledge to these pragmatic offspring, who are apt to develop an interest only in subjects that have practical value and yield tangible results.

Libra Parents with Air Children. A Libran parent shares many traits of personality and temperament with air-sign children. The basic approach to life in your household is a mental one. Communication skills dominate. Rarely will there be misunderstandings, as it is an easy matter to talk problems out. Though planning and theorizing may be high on the list of activities, make sure that these children see projects through to completion and that problems are resolved in some tangible way. In general, there may be a lack of attention paid to the physical side of life. Good dietary habits and regular exercise must be religiously adhered to by air-sign people, though these matters often take a low place on their list of priorities. As a result, health is jeopardized. These children must learn that fresh air and sunshine are just as necessary as reading and writing. Walking places is better than riding. And socializing is just as easily done while in an exercise class or playing tennis as it is while sitting in chairs drinking tea.

Libra Parents with Water Children. Be careful that your tendency to approach everything on an intellectual basis is not viewed by sensitive water-sign children as a lack of warmth or caring. You may be able to remain emotionally removed from problems, but these youngsters will tend to take them in a personal way. When difficulties occur, don't give a lecture when you should be listening. Remember to give them a hug first; then you can ask questions. Help these offspring to realize there is a lesson to be learned from every disappointment, and that experiencing failure makes us grow strong in character and understanding. Your serene behavior will go far to allay the unreasonable fears water-sign children are prone to experience. However, don't think one explanation will suffice. These emotionally oriented children need constant reassurance of your affection for them.

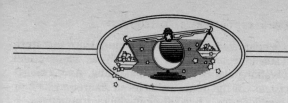

YOUR BIRTHDAY'S PLANETARY RULER

Planetary Rulerships. The system of planetary rulership of the days was evolved by the Egyptians, under Greek influence. The system spread over the entire then-known world and resulted in the days of the week being named after the planetary rulers. The planetary ruler of the day you were born exerts a powerful influence on your life. You can determine the planetary ruler on your birth day using the tables on pages 39–40. Find the year in question on Table 1. On the same line, to the right, note the key number under the month you were born. Add the key number to your date of birth (i.e., the day of the month); find the total in Table 2. On that line, to the left, will be found the day of the week you were born.

Born on Sunday/the Sun. You're daring, with a strong sense of romance and adventure. You're well liked by others and are social. Though confident, you have an inner need to live up to the best of your potentials. You give a lot to life and expect a lot in return. Arrogance could lead to problems.

Born on Monday/the Moon. You know how to get along with others but can be moody and self-centered. At times you hurt people without realizing it. You love home but may feel confined by domesticity. Nervous tension may interfere with your fulfilling your potentials, though these are great, especially in art.

Born on Tuesday/Mars. You have strong desires and are a fighter. Undoubtedly you will do your own thing, come what may. Individuality brings you success, but you need more tact and consideration for others. Your energy often keeps the midnight oils burning, for you keep going longer than most.

Born on Wednesday/Mercury. You have many irons in the fire but may only skim the surface. You're too often quick to abandon a project if success isn't immediate. Restlessness can interfere with study, which you need to be successful. Be less judgmental. Your versatility leads to achievement in such areas as medicine, writing, science, and theater.

Born on Thursday/Jupiter. You'd make a good fighter for a cause. You're quite independent in your outlook on life and have your own definition of honor. A love of ideas can make you overlook the human factor. Luck is with you, but don't overplay your hand. Though personable, you appear detached.

Born on Friday/Venus. You like life's finer things and spend freely on what you want. Though anxious to please others, you're not always considerate of their feelings. An artistic or professional career can lead you to popularity with the masses. Your sex appeal will bring you many admirers.

Born on Saturday/Saturn. You're ambitious but do better on your own among strangers than in the family milieu. You must like your work for you to succeed. You can easily rise to the heights, though you may resent authority. You need to learn when to be passive and when to be aggressive in timing in order to fulfill your potentials. Patience is your ally.

TABLE 1

			Jan.	Feb.	Mar.	Apr.	May	June	July	Aug.	Sept.	Oct.	Nov.	Dec.
1918	1946	1974	2	5	5	1	3	6	1	4	0	2	5	0
1919	1947	1975	3	6	6	2	4	0	2	5	1	3	6	1
*1920	*1948	*1976	4	0	1	4	6	2	4	0	3	5	1	3
1921	1949	1977	6	2	2	5	0	3	5	1	4	6	2	4
1922	1950	1978	0	3	3	6	1	4	6	2	5	0	3	5
1923	1951	1979	1	4	4	0	2	5	0	3	6	1	4	6
*1924	*1952	*1980	2	5	6	2	4	0	2	5	1	3	6	1
1925	1953	1981	4	0	0	3	5	1	3	6	2	4	0	2
1926	1954	1982	5	1	1	4	6	2	4	0	3	5	1	3
1927	1955	1983	6	2	2	5	0	3	5	1	4	6	2	4
*1928	*1956	*1984	0	3	4	0	2	5	0	3	6	1	4	6
1929	1957	1985	2	5	5	1	3	6	1	4	0	2	5	0
1930	1958	1986	3	6	6	2	4	0	2	5	1	3	6	1
1931	1959	1987	4	0	0	3	5	1	3	6	2	4	0	2
*1932	*1960	*1988	5	1	2	5	0	3	5	1	4	6	2	4
1933	1961	1989	0	3	3	6	1	4	6	2	5	0	3	5
1934	1962	1990	1	4	4	0	2	5	0	3	6	1	4	6
1935	1963	1991	2	5	5	1	3	6	1	4	0	2	5	0
*1936	*1964	*1992	3	6	0	3	5	1	3	6	2	4	0	2
1937	1965	1993	5	1	1	4	6	2	4	0	3	5	1	3
1938	1966	1994	6	2	2	5	0	3	5	1	4	6	2	4
1939	1967	1995	0	3	3	6	1	4	6	2	5	0	3	5
*1940	*1968	*1996	1	4	5	1	3	6	1	4	0	2	5	0
1941	1969	1997	3	6	6	2	4	0	2	5	1	3	6	1
1942	1970	1998	4	0	0	3	5	1	3	6	2	4	0	2
1943	1971	1999	5	1	1	4	6	2	4	0	3	5	1	3
*1944	*1972	*2000	6	2	3	6	1	4	6	2	5	0	3	5
1945	1973	2001	1	4	4	0	2	5	0	3	6	1	4	6
1901			2	5	5	1	3	6	1	4	0	2	5	0
1902			3	6	6	2	4	0	2	5	1	3	6	1
1903			4	0	0	3	5	1	3	6	2	4	0	2
*1904			5	1	2	5	0	3	5	1	4	6	2	4
1905			0	3	3	6	1	4	6	2	5	0	3	5
1906			1	4	4	0	2	5	0	3	6	1	4	6
1907			2	5	5	1	3	6	1	4	0	2	5	0
*1908			3	6	0	3	5	1	3	6	2	4	0	2
1909			5	1	1	4	6	2	4	0	3	5	1	3
1910			6	2	2	5	0	3	5	1	4	6	2	4
1911			0	3	3	6	1	4	6	2	5	0	3	5
*1912			1	4	5	1	3	6	1	4	0	2	5	0
1913			3	6	6	2	4	0	2	5	1	3	6	1
1914			4	0	0	3	5	1	3	6	2	4	0	2
1915			5	1	1	4	6	2	4	0	3	5	1	3
*1916			6	2	3	6	1	4	6	2	5	0	3	5
1917			1	4	4	0	2	5	0	3	6	1	4	6

*Leap Year.

TABLE 2

Sunday	1	8	15	22	29	36
Monday	2	9	16	23	30	37
Tuesday	3	10	17	24	31	
Wednesday	4	11	18	25	32	
Thursday	5	12	19	26	33	
Friday	6	13	20	27	34	
Saturday	7	14	21	28	35	

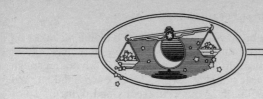

YOUR MOON SIGN

Moon. The Moon in your horoscope rules your emotional life. It is your desires, as opposed to willpower and ego; your emotional needs, as opposed to what expediency or reason dictates. It indicates how you are likely to react to the various situations and experiences you encounter. To a certain extent it rules your body's physical and mental functions as well as the functions and routine of daily life. When you are emotionally troubled, all these normal functions will be correspondingly interrupted. The Moon also indicates your actual residence and all aspects of your domestic life. It indicates your relationships with babies and young children in your life, and it rules women in general and your mother in particular.

Moon in Aries. You want to turn your feelings into physical experiences. When you want something (or someone), you don't always stop to think whether it's practical or whether it will involve a deeper or longer emotional commitment than you're willing to give. You are an eager participant in life and will soon lose interest in people who don't demonstrate the same passionate enthusiasm that you do. Your adventurous spirit can make it hard to settle down and accept responsibilities and daily routine unless you have other outlets that keep you happy and stimulated. You are easily insulted but can just as easily be persuaded to forget an incident if you receive an apology. A quick temper can get you into trouble at times, but fortunately you are also quick to forget your anger. You are meant to be master of your own successes or failures. You may relish this kind of challenge or may be all too willing to blame mistakes on everyone else. Resentful of authority, you may find it difficult to take direction or advice from anyone. Though you are capable of being self-indulgent, overconfident, and just plain foolhardy, your courageous and dynamic spirit can turn you into an inspired leader. Others will greatly admire your passion and tireless efforts. Magnanimous generosity wins you many friends, though this generosity can be diminished by your sometimes careless disregard for the feelings of others. Women with an Aries Moon may be unflatteringly aggressive in romance, but they are emotionally well suited to conquer many other types of situations that would destroy less hardy types. Men with an Aries Moon expect too much and give too little in romance but are emotionally well suited to pursue other matters with an enterprising, often clever and original approach.

Moon in Taurus. You require tangible proof of affection from others. Though there is a conservative element in your nature, you have very strong physical appetites and don't hesitate to gratify desires. Material comforts and the advantages material wealth can bring are important to you, and in pursuit of such things you can become overly concerned with social status. You need the solid structure of home and family, but you are not necessarily a homebody and can spend a lot of time on other pursuits instead of taking care of routine household or family chores. It is likely that you have artistic or musical talent, certainly an appreciation of beauty in all forms, and a desire for an attractive, well-decorated home. You don't like to be rushed or forced into emotional commitments. However, once you have made a commitment, you doggedly hang on forever. You have a great sense of humor about most things but can get very upset with people who do not keep their promises to you or prove unreliable in other matters. It is hard for you to accept when things go wrong, and it may take you a long time to make necessary changes or adjustments. Your calm temperament has a stabilizing influence on others, but it can also give you an aura of self-containment that makes you appear too proud or aloof. Your memory may be excellent, but sometimes it is too long for your own good and you waste time bearing grudges that should have been forgotten. Women with a Taurus Moon are independent and self-reliant. They often gain materially through marriage. Men with a Taurus Moon are diplomatic in social relationships and sensual romantic partners. Though hedonistic, they are usually unselfishly devoted to their children.

Moon in Gemini. You may give the impression of emotional coolness because of your analytical approach to emotional experiences. Sometimes this intellectual approach goes too far and robs you of the actual physical enjoyment of things. You are very talkative, alert, and innately curious about everything. You have a wide range of interests and may have trouble limiting yourself to one thing at a time. Always looking for intellectual stimulation, you are easily bored. You love intrigue and gossip and sometimes pay too much attention to what everyone else is doing instead of tending to your own business. News and information seem to come to you, and to others it appears you always know what's going on. As eager to share information as you are to receive it, you are very good in all areas of teaching and communication; however, you don't always take the time to get all the facts straight before repeating them. You instinctively understand what others want to hear and how to please them, but you can be very secretive about your own feelings. An emotional duality in your character allows you to say or do one thing even though you really think or feel something else. Though outwardly bright and optimistic, you can harbor an inner loneliness that others don't suspect. To keep happy and productive, you need a variety of tasks and a frequent change of scene. Women with a Gemini Moon are often skilled with their hands. Though they can be very efficient and organized, they are usually not very domestic. Men with a Gemini Moon are charming, with a wide variety of interests and many friends. They are not particularly suited to sustained passion in themselves or to putting up with emotional hysteria in others.

Moon in Cancer. You need to feel there is depth to your emotional involvements or at least that there is the potential for a real commitment. You are intuitive, though at times it gets entangled with self-serving needs. Creative and talented, you are vulnerable to the influence of those with whom you spend the most time, and it is sometimes hard to tell when you are expressing your own opinions or reflecting those of someone else. You can be extremely passive even in unhappy situations. Though you may eventually take on a more satisfying relationship, emotional insecurity can make you possessive and unwilling to let go of the unhappy relationship. You hate to throw anything away, whether material possessions or relationships, and if you are not careful, your life can become cluttered with useless things. Lack of motivation can seriously sabotage your personal growth and success since it can result in laziness, disorganization, and sloppiness. There are contradictory elements in your emotional makeup. For instance, you can be quite shy but also very aggressive, very warm and loving but also selfish and demanding. A nurturing instinct makes you hospitable and philanthropic. You have strong identification with home and family and domestic skills that can make you an excellent cook or gardener. You tend to treat everyone as family and often use this as a successful ploy in gaining the cooperation of others. Women with a Cancer Moon are vulnerable and emotionally dependent while at the same time intuitive and clever; much depends on their backgrounds. Men with a Cancer Moon are domestic and usually have a close relationship with their mother or a physical resemblance to her. It is hard for men with a Cancer Moon to act with emotional certainty or sustained aggressiveness.

Moon in Leo. You are magnanimous and passionate with a strong need for instant physical gratification. Your enthusiasm and tendency for exaggeration are great in some circumstances but can lead to being what others may consider insincere. Aroused by the excitement of a particular moment, you may later forget what you said or promised in your enthusiasm even though you were being sincere at the time. Stubborn pride is often your downfall, and your unwillingness to admit when you are wrong can put a severe strain on relationships. It's hard for you to separate emotions from ego, and your ego prompts you consciously or subconsciously to dominate relationships. Though you can be extremely stubborn, you can also demonstrate such inspired purpose and determination that it makes you a natural leader. Your people-oriented personality wins many friends and can make you an excellent fund-raiser as well as extremely effective in public relations. Strongly idealistic, you are capable of great personal sacrifice. You are very assertive when it comes to protecting not only your own freedom but also the rights and freedom of others. In romantic attachments you can be jealous though you may not be particularly possessive. You are likely to have artistic talent or at least a great interest in art, architecture, and design. Women with a Leo Moon have forceful emotional natures. If disappointed in love, they are not anxious to repeat an unflattering failure. They can be too materialistic and preoccupied with status, but they accept responsibilities as a matter of pride. Men with a Leo Moon can be braggarts who always need to have the last word. They actively seek the good things in life, but their emotional natures also include a willingness to share their good fortune generously.

Moon in Virgo. You are guarded about your feelings and consciously or subconsciously put up invisible barriers, perhaps tangible impediments, for those who want a relationship with you. In most cases, however, you really hope others will view these barriers as a challenge to be overcome. It is difficult for you to lose inhibitions. Though not lacking in passion, you lean more to compassion, which makes you a victim in relationships you would like to terminate but feel guilty about ending lest you hurt your partner's feelings. You have a good sense of humor, but your critical eye can direct your humor toward sarcasm. Though serious-minded with common sense about most things, you can be surprisingly unrealistic at times. Your creativity has a practical element, and if you are a writer

or an artist, you usually stick to what you know best. You
know what it takes to make others feel better, and your
sympathetic nature makes you valuable as a friend but also
makes you vulnerable to exploitation. You are fond of
books and writing, and your intellectual curiosity gives
you a penchant for gathering information, a tendency that
can develop into serious research or turn out to be an
indulgence for gossip. You are mentally and emotionally
stimulated by travel, communication in all forms, and the
idea that what you do serves a definite and helpful purpose
not only for your own good but for the good of others.
Women with a Virgo Moon may encounter sorrow through
marriage or marry men with serious problems. They can
be dreadful nags or themselves victims of nagging spouses.
Men with a Virgo Moon tend to idealize their wives but
not be very passionate toward them. Their quiet emotional
natures tend toward domesticity but often hide desires for
intrigue and flamboyancy.

Moon in Libra. In spite of a certain analytical detachment
in emotional situations, you are loving and loyal in relationships. You have a romantic nature, if not an overly passionate approach. Hurt when emotionally compromised, you
would prefer not to hang on to a relationship if your partner
is unwilling. However, when you are guilty of an emotionally compromising situation, you may rationalize why such
deception was necessary since above all, you hate confrontation and hurting the feelings of others. You are disin-
clined to live alone, preferring attachment of some sort
even if it is not marriage. Your accomplishments are often
motivated by (and even dependent upon) stimulation you
get from interaction with others, so it is in your best
interests to be out in public. You are better at planning
maneuvers than at carrying them out. It isn't that you are
not capable of carrying them out; it's just that you can rely
on your considerable ability to enlist the cooperation of
others, and it is they who perform the actual execution of
projects while you step back to supervise the job. Though
you can be quite good at planning and problem solving,
you can be very impractical about personal matters. You

are apt to have aesthetic tastes, which can be seen in a fondness for dressing well, an interest in art and music, and a desire for an attractive home. Women with the Moon in Libra have temperaments more suited to finances, gaining social status, and pursuing intellectual matters than to raising children or taking care of mundane household chores. Men with a Libra Moon have a streak of domesticity that may show up as an interest in cooking, home design or furnishings, and gardening. If their mates are unable to keep them mentally stimulated, their attentions tend to wander.

Moon in Scorpio. Your actions are primarily led by strong emotional needs, but you may not be open about revealing those needs to others. You have powerful sexual energy that can be sublimated into attaining many goals having nothing to do with sex. A Scorpio Moon in the horoscope often indicates wide mood swings, which, with maturity, you can learn how to control properly. Though you don't like being forced into emotional commitments, once they are made, you hang on forever. You have a keen competitive spirit that can make you a formidable opponent. There is almost nothing you can't accomplish if you develop your incredible willpower and amazing ability to overcome all kinds of adversity. Just when everyone thinks you're down, you'll find a way to come back better and stronger than ever. Intense concentration is another factor in your success, but one mistake you can make is being so intent on controlling others that you never learn self-control. Though secretive yourself, you have a keen interest in others because of a genuine interest in human nature and also because it gives you an emotional advantage, a conscious or subconscious sense of being in control. When you develop undesirable habits, the stubborn quality of your nature makes it difficult to break them. Your relationships suffer from jealousy and possessiveness whether on your part or that of your partner's. Women with a Scorpio Moon can be shrewdly ambitious. Their ambition is not so much wanting to acquire greath wealth as a desire to gain positions of power. Men with a Scorpio Moon can be driven to distraction by situations that offer no solution and by people who refuse to tell them anything. Their emotional natures are best suited to dealing with resources, especially human resources.

Moon in Sagittarius. You are idealistic and romantic. Your risk-taking, adventurous spirit and magnanimous generosity are a curse as well as a blessing. They can leave you vulnerable to those who exploit your generosity, but they are also the combination needed for success, especially in enterprises that more cautious people would avoid. Your open, honest personality, while appreciated by some and certainly by those who know you well, can nevertheless be too candid at times, making you seem rude or tactless rather than merely truthful. Impatience can be your biggest stumbling block to success unless you learn to control it. Knowledge will play a significant role in your destiny. No matter how scholarly you may or may not be, you will be required to have increasing knowledge and expertise in your particular field, and that is what makes you successful. A duality in your nature can make you fickle and emotionally insecure but also readily adaptable to changing circumstances and stable relationships. Social and business associations with powerful and educated people are the way you are likely to approach learning and personal advancement, two of your main goals in life. If this approach is taken too far, however, you may become pseudointellectual and an incurable snob. For you, the best opportunities are likely to involve writing, teaching, performing, or any area dealing with sales, entertainment, art, education, and communication. Women with a Sagittarius Moon often make better friends than lovers, though their restlessness may lead to sexual adventures. Friendship is very important to them. Their natures are not well suited to domestic life. Men with a Sagittarius Moon are inveterate chasers of the ideal woman. Their natures tend toward selfishness and personal freedom, but they have a sense of loyalty and a prophetic intuition.

Moon in Capricorn. Practical by nature and fearing rejection, you do not spontaneously act on your emotions or openly declare your feelings unless you feel you're on solid ground. Your outward formality or reticence can be deceiving since in private you can be a very passionate sexual partner. Though willing to fulfill responsibilities connected with relationships, you may be unable or unwilling to understand what others actually want or need. It is hard for you to relate to those who do not share your views or values. Capricorn's influence on your Moon is demonstrated in your constant worry and in your desire for formality and structure. Anything vague or unspecified, whether in business or personal relationships, makes you feel insecure; you must know where you stand. Ambitious and strong-willed, you are more than capable of accomplishing a lot for others, though you are primarily directed to seek your own advancement. You have a great respect for knowledge and are probably quite bright. You are apt to be given or voluntarily to assume heavy family responsibilities, in the care of your children or your parents when they are older. A tendency to harbor anger and resentment inside can result in physical maladies or mental depression or both. It is hard to confide emotional problems, though you are interested in and very helpful dealing with the problems of others. Female relationships are likely to be problematical and inhibited in some way. Women with a Capricorn Moon can be ambitious at the expense of their emotional lives. However, they are interested in preserving traditional family structures and are excellent administrators. Men with a Capricorn Moon are often rugged individualists who demand attention and respect. They are apt to be either too close to or too distant from their mothers.

Moon in Aquarius. You are sympathetic without being sentimental. If you are rarely beset with moodiness (as is likely), you may fail to pay attention to it in others, giving the impression you don't care. You are idealistic, optimistic, and friendly. Your highly social nature attracts many friends, and as far as you're concerned, it's the more, the merrier since it is hard to focus your attention on one person. Your orientation to people makes you a good social mixer or organizer. Even if you are a bit eccentric or erratic, or perhaps because of it, you have a calming effect on those who are mentally disturbed or hysterical. Although you don't like being rushed into emotional commitments, once you have made them, you are extremely loyal and will doggedly pursue, protect, and hang on to relationships. Strong individualism can make marriage difficult especially if your spouse is not as strong as you, and if, in addition, you both have to make determined efforts to make the relationship successful. Once you have formed attitudes, interests, and behavior patterns, marriage and raising a family are not likely to change anything. You tend to remain independent in views and attitudes, which may turn out to be fairly traditional. You are likely to have talent for or a very strong interest in art, entertainment, or public relations. Your unflappable nature is not often surprised or repelled by what others consider strange or abnormal. In fact, you may deliberately say or do bizarre things for their shock value. Women with an Aquarius Moon are better companions than mothers to their children. Men with an Aquarius Moon display little possessiveness in romance, which is sometimes interpreted by their parents as lack of love. Their mental abilities are keener than their interest in material wealth.

Moon in Pisces. You need to establish solid relationships and values that can provide you with an underlying strength you do not naturally possess. It may be very difficult for you to see the reality of many situations especially if you are emotionally involved in any way, and it may be even harder for you to accept reality if it happens to disagree with your concept of how things should be. Shy and vulnerable to the influence of others, you can be an easy prey to the demands of stronger personalities. Easily wounded, you do not do well in relationships with those who are emotionally independent and demand personal freedom. You may do very well if your home is near the ocean or some other body of water. Romantic and idealistic, you have a vivid imagination. Your remarkable sensitivity can make you a gifted writer, actor, musician, or illustrator. These traits may also be demonstrated in a gift for promotion, though you may not always be aware of how much actual substance is in your various schemes. Yours is an addictive nature, if you do not exercise great care from an early age, you may find yourself waging a lifelong battle against overindulgence of every kind. While your analytical abilities can be remarkably imaginative and farsighted, your major flaw is either lack of practicality or clarity or both. Women with a Pisces Moon are psychic, likely to be artistic, and prone to anxiety complexes. Their emotional natures are well suited to the comfort of domestic life, though they may not be efficient householders. Men with a Pisces Moon are vulnerable to victimization in their own relationships, while at the same time they still manage to have strength and wisdom to handle the affairs of others ably.

Your Moon Sign Nature

How to Find Your Moon's Sign and Degree

This is the simplest and briefest table that has been devised for getting the Moon's place on any date over a great many years, and if you follow carefully the directions below, you will have a part of your individual horoscope that heretofore has been available only to those who knew how to use an ephemeris or were able to have individual charts drawn up for them. If you follow the simple directions, you get not only the sign occupied by the Moon but also the actual degree, correct within 1½ degrees, for any hour of any date between 1880 and 2000 inclusive.

HOW TO FIND YOUR MOON'S PLACE

1. Note your birth year in the tables (pages 56–79).
2. Run down the left-hand column and see if your date is there.
3. IF YOUR DATE IS IN THE LEFT-HAND COLUMN, move across on this line till you come to the column under your birth year. Here you will find a number. This is your BASE NUMBER. Write it down, and go directly to the part of the directions below, under the heading "What to Do with Your Base Number."
4. IF YOUR BIRTH DATE IS NOT IN THE LEFT-HAND COLUMN, get a pencil and paper. Your birth date falls between two numbers in the left-hand column. Look at the date closest *after* your birth date; move across on this line to your birth year. Write down the number you find there, and label it "TOP NUMBER." Having done this, write directly beneath it on your piece of paper the number printed just above it in the table. Label this "BOTTOM NUMBER."
   Subtract the bottom number from the top number. If the top number is smaller, add 360 to it and then subtract. The result is your DIFFERENCE.

5. Go back to the left-hand column and find the date next *before* your birth date. Determine the number of days between this date and your birth date by subtracting. Write this down, and label it "INTERVENING DAYS."

6. In the Table of Difference below, note which group your DIFFERENCE (found through Step 4) falls in.

Difference	Daily Motion
80–87	12°
88–94	13°
95–101	14°
102–106	15°

Note: If you were born in leap year *and* use the difference between February 26 and March 5, use the special table following:

Difference	Daily Motion
94–99	12°
100–108	13°
109–115	14°
116–122	15°

Write down the DAILY MOTION corresponding to your place in the proper Table of Difference above.

7. Multiply this daily motion by the number labeled "INTERVENING DAYS" (found through Step 5).

8. Add the result of Step 7 to your BOTTOM NUMBER (under 4). The result of this is your BASE NUMBER. If it is more than 360, subtract 360 from it and call the result your BASE NUMBER. Now turn to the table of Base Numbers on page 55.

WHAT TO DO WITH YOUR BASE NUMBER

LOCATE YOUR BASE NUMBER in the table on page 55. At the top of the column you will find the SIGN your MOON WAS IN. At the left you will find the DEGREE (°) your Moon occupied at: 7:00 A.M. of your birth date if you were born under eastern standard time, 6:00 A.M. of your birth date if you were born under central standard time, 5:00 A.M. of your birth date if you were born under mountain standard time, 4:00 A.M. of your birth date if you were born under Pacific standard time.

IF YOU DON'T KNOW THE HOUR OF YOUR BIRTH, accept this as your Moon's sign and degree.

IF YOU DO KNOW THE HOUR OF YOUR BIRTH, get the exact degree as follows:

If you were born *before* 7:00 A.M., EST (6:00 A.M. CST, etc.), determine the number of hours before that time that you were born. Divide this by two. *Subtract* this from your base number, and the result in the table will be the exact degree and sign of the Moon on the year, month, date, and hour of your birth.

If you were born *before* 7:00 A.M., EST, (6:00 A.M. CST, etc.), determine the number of hours before that time that you were born. Divide this by two. *Subtract* this from your base number, and the result in the table will be the exact degree and sign of the Moon on the year, month, date, and hour of your birth.

TABLE OF BASE NUMBERS

	♈	♉	♊	♋	♌	♍	♎	♏	♐	♑	♒	♓
0°	0	30	60	90	120	150	180	210	240	270	300	330
1°	1	31	61	91	121	151	181	211	241	271	301	331
2°	2	32	62	92	122	152	182	212	242	272	302	332
3°	3	33	63	93	123	153	183	213	243	273	303	333
4°	4	34	64	94	124	154	184	214	244	274	304	334
5°	5	35	65	95	125	155	185	215	245	275	305	335
6°	6	36	66	96	126	156	186	216	246	276	306	336
7°	7	37	67	97	127	157	187	217	247	277	307	337
8°	8	38	68	98	128	158	188	218	248	278	308	338
9°	9	39	69	99	129	159	189	219	249	279	309	339
10°	10	40	70	100	130	160	190	220	250	280	310	340
11°	11	41	71	101	131	161	191	221	251	281	311	341
12°	12	42	72	102	132	162	192	222	252	282	312	342
13°	13	43	73	103	133	163	193	223	253	283	313	343
14°	14	44	74	104	134	164	194	224	254	284	314	344
15°	15	45	75	105	135	165	195	225	255	285	315	345
16°	16	46	76	106	136	166	196	226	256	286	316	346
17°	17	47	77	107	137	167	197	227	257	287	317	347
18°	18	48	78	108	138	168	198	228	258	288	318	348
19°	19	49	79	109	139	169	199	229	259	289	319	349
20°	20	50	80	110	140	170	200	230	260	290	320	350
21°	21	51	81	111	141	171	201	231	261	291	321	351
22°	22	52	82	112	142	172	202	232	262	292	322	352
23°	23	53	83	113	143	173	203	233	263	293	323	353
24°	24	54	84	114	144	174	204	234	264	294	324	354
25°	25	55	85	115	145	175	205	235	265	295	325	355
26°	26	56	86	116	146	176	206	236	266	296	326	356
27°	27	57	87	117	147	177	207	237	267	297	327	357
28°	28	58	88	118	148	178	208	238	268	298	328	358
29°	29	59	89	119	149	179	209	239	269	299	329	359

♈ Aries
♉ Taurus
♊ Gemini

♋ Cancer
♌ Leo
♍ Virgo

♎ Libra
♏ Scorpio
♐ Sagittarius

♑ Capricorn
♒ Aquarius
♓ Pisces

56

MOON SIGN TABLES

	1880	1881	1882	1883	1884	1885	1886	1887	1888	1889
Jan. 1	144	294	67	190	315	105	238	359	127	276
8	240	32	152	278	52	202	323	89	224	12
15	341	116	239	18	151	286	49	190	321	96
22	67	202	342	113	236	13	153	284	46	185
29	154	302	77	198	325	113	248	8	136	285
Feb. 5	250	41	161	286	63	211	331	97	235	20
12	349	124	248	29	159	295	58	200	329	104
19	75	212	351	122	244	24	161	293	59	196
26	163	311	86	207	334	122	257	16	144	294
Mar. 5	275	49	170	294	88	218	340	105	260	28
12	10	133	257	38	180	303	69	209	350	112
19	94	222	359	132	264	34	169	302	74	205
26	185	320	95	215	356	133	265	25	166	305
Apr. 2	286	57	179	303	98	226	349	114	270	36
9	18	141	267	47	189	311	79	217	359	120
16	102	232	7	141	272	43	178	311	83	214
23	194	331	103	224	4	143	273	34	175	315
30	297	65	187	312	108	235	357	124	279	45
May 7	28	149	278	54	198	319	89	225	8	128
14	111	241	17	149	281	52	108	319	92	223
21	202	342	111	233	13	154	281	43	184	325
28	306	73	195	323	117	243	5	155	288	54
June 4	37	157	288	63	207	327	99	234	17	137
11	119	250	27	158	291	60	199	327	101	231
18	211	352	119	241	22	164	289	52	194	335
25	315	82	203	333	126	252	13	145	296	63

MOON SIGN TABLES

July 2	46	165	297	72	216	336	108	244	26	146
9	129	258	37	165	299	69	209	335	110	240
16	220	2	127	250	32	173	298	59	204	343
23	323	91	211	344	134	261	21	155	304	72
30	54	174	306	82	224	345	117	254	34	156
Aug. 6	138	267	48	174	309	78	219	343	119	250
13	231	11	136	258	43	181	307	68	215	352
20	331	100	220	354	142	270	30	165	313	80
27	63	184	314	93	232	355	125	265	42	165
Sept. 3	147	276	58	182	317	88	228	352	127	260
10	242	19	145	266	54	190	316	76	226	359
17	340	109	229	3	152	278	40	173	323	88
24	70	193	323	103	239	4	134	275	50	174
Oct. 1	155	286	67	191	325	99	237	1	135	271
8	252	27	154	274	64	198	324	85	236	8
15	350	117	238	11	161	286	49	181	332	96
22	78	202	332	113	248	12	144	284	58	182
29	163	297	75	200	333	110	245	10	143	282
Nov. 5	262	36	163	263	74	207	332	94	245	18
12	359	124	248	19	171	294	59	190	342	104
19	87	210	342	122	257	20	154	292	67	190
26	171	308	83	208	341	120	253	18	152	292
Dec. 3	271	45	171	293	82	216	340	104	253	27
10	10	132	257	28	181	302	67	199	351	112
17	95	218	353	130	265	28	165	300	76	198
24	179	318	91	217	351	130	262	26	162	301
31	279	55	179	302	89	226	348	113	261	37

MOON SIGN TABLES

	1890	1891	1892	1893	1894	1895	1896	1897	1898	1899
Jan. 1	49	170	298	87	220	340	109	258	30	149
8	132	259	37	183	303	69	209	352	114	240
15	221	2	131	266	32	174	301	76	203	335
22	323	94	215	357	135	265	25	169	305	76
29	58	178	307	96	229	348	117	268	39	157
Feb. 5	141	267	47	190	312	78	219	359	122	249
12	230	12	140	274	42	162	310	84	214	353
19	332	103	223	7	143	274	34	179	314	84
26	67	187	315	106	236	357	125	278	46	168
Mar. 5	150	276	72	198	321	87	243	8	130	259
12	241	20	161	282	52	190	331	92	225	1
19	340	113	244	17	152	283	55	188	323	93
26	75	196	337	117	244	6	148	289	54	177
Apr. 2	159	285	81	206	329	97	252	17	138	269
9	251	28	170	290	63	198	340	100	235	9
16	350	121	253	25	162	291	64	196	333	101
23	83	204	346	127	252	15	157	299	62	185
30	167	295	89	215	337	108	261	25	146	280
May 7	261	36	179	299	73	207	349	109	244	19
14	0	129	262	33	172	299	73	204	344	108
21	91	213	355	137	261	23	167	308	71	193
28	174	307	98	224	345	119	269	34	155	291
June 4	271	46	188	308	81	217	357	119	253	29
11	11	137	272	42	182	307	82	213	354	117
18	99	221	6	146	269	31	178	316	80	201
25	183	317	106	233	353	129	277	43	164	300

MOON SIGN TABLES

July 2	278	56	195	317	89	227	5	128	261	39
9	21	145	281	51	192	315	91	223	3	125
16	108	229	17	154	278	39	189	324	89	209
23	192	327	115	241	2	138	286	51	173	309
30	287	66	203	327	99	237	13	138	269	49
Aug. 6	31	153	289	62	201	324	99	234	11	134
13	117	237	28	162	287	48	200	332	97	219
20	201	336	124	250	12	147	296	59	183	317
27	295	76	211	336	108	247	21	146	279	58
Sept. 3	39	162	297	72	209	333	107	245	19	143
10	125	246	38	171	296	57	209	341	105	228
17	211	344	134	257	22	155	305	67	193	326
24	305	86	220	345	118	256	29	155	290	67
Oct. 1	47	171	305	83	217	341	116	256	27	151
8	134	256	47	179	304	67	218	350	113	238
15	220	352	144	265	31	164	315	75	202	335
22	315	94	228	352	128	264	39	162	301	75
29	55	179	314	94	225	350	125	266	36	160
Nov. 5	142	265	56	189	312	77	226	359	121	248
12	229	2	153	274	40	173	324	84	210	346
19	327	102	237	0	139	272	47	171	311	82
26	64	188	323	103	234	358	135	275	45	167
Dec. 3	149	275	63	198	320	86	235	9	129	257
10	237	12	162	282	47	184	332	93	218	356
17	338	110	246	9	149	280	56	179	321	91
24	72	196	333	112	243	5	145	282	54	175
31	158	284	72	208	328	95	244	18	138	265

MOON SIGN TABLES

	1900	1901	1902	1903	1904	1905	1906	1907	1908	1909
Jan. 1	280	55	188	308	76	227	358	119	246	39
8	21	149	272	37	179	32u	82	208	350	129
15	112	234	2	141	270	43	174	311	81	213
22	195	327	101	234	353	138	273	44	164	309
29	288	66	196	317	83	238	6	128	255	50
Feb. 5	31	158	280	46	188	328	89	219	359	138
12	121	241	12	149	279	51	184	319	89	221
19	204	335	111	242	2	146	283	52	173	317
26	296	76	204	326	92	248	13	136	264	59
Mar. 5	40	166	288	57	211	334	98	229	21	147
12	130	249	22	157	300	59	194	328	110	230
19	213	344	121	250	24	154	293	59	195	325
26	305	86	212	334	116	258	22	144	288	69
Apr. 2	49	175	296	68	219	345	106	240	29	156
9	138	258	31	157	309	69	202	338	118	239
16	222	352	132	258	33	163	304	68	204	334
23	315	96	220	342	127	267	31	152	299	77
30	57	184	304	78	227	354	114	250	38	164
May 7	177	268	40	177	316	78	210	348	126	249
14	231	1	142	266	42	172	313	76	212	344
21	325	104	229	350	138	275	40	160	310	85
28	65	193	313	87	236	3	124	259	47	172
June 4	155	277	48	187	324	88	219	358	134	259
11	239	11	151	275	50	182	322	85	220	355
18	336	112	238	359	149	283	48	169	320	93
25	74	201	322	96	245	11	133	267	57	180

MOON-SIGN TABLES

July 2	163	286	57	197	333	97	228	8	142	267
9	248	21	160	283	58	193	330	94	228	6
16	347	121	247	7	159	291	57	178	330	102
23	84	209	332	105	255	19	143	276	66	188
30	171	295	66	206	341	105	239	17	151	275
Aug. 6	256	32	168	292	66	204	338	103	237	17
13	357	130	255	17	168	301	65	188	339	111
20	94	217	341	113	265	27	152	285	76	196
27	179	303	77	215	350	113	250	25	160	283
Sept. 3	264	43	176	301	75	215	346	111	246	27
10	6	229	263	27	176	310	73	198	347	121
17	103	225	350	123	274	35	161	294	85	206
24	188	311	88	223	358	122	261	33	169	292
Oct. 1	273	53	185	309	85	224	355	119	256	36
8	14	149	271	36	185	320	81	207	356	130
15	113	233	359	133	283	44	169	305	93	214
22	197	319	99	231	7	130	271	42	177	301
29	283	62	194	317	95	233	5	127	266	44
Nov. 5	22	158	279	45	193	329	89	216	5	139
12	121	242	6	144	291	53	177	316	101	223
19	206	328	109	239	15	140	281	50	185	311
26	293	70	203	325	105	241	14	135	276	52
Dec. 3	31	167	288	54	203	338	98	224	15	147
10	129	251	14	155	299	61	185	327	109	231
17	214	338	118	248	23	149	289	59	193	322
24	303	78	213	333	115	249	23	143	286	61
31	41	176	296	61	213	346	107	232	26	155

MOON SIGN TABLES

		1910	1911	1912	1913	1914	1915	1916	1917	1918	1919	1920
Jan.	1	168	289	57	211	337	100	228	23	147	270	39
	8	252	20	162	299	61	192	332	110	231	5	143
	15	346	122	251	23	158	293	61	193	329	103	231
	22	84	214	334	119	256	23	145	290	68	193	316
	29	175	298	65	221	345	108	237	32	155	278	49
Feb.	5	259	31	170	308	69	203	340	118	249	16	150
	12	356	130	260	32	167	302	70	203	338	113	239
	19	94	222	344	128	266	31	154	298	78	201	325
	26	184	306	75	231	353	116	248	41	164	286	60
Mar.	5	267	42	192	317	77	214	2	127	248	26	172
	12	5	140	280	41	176	311	89	212	346	123	259
	19	105	230	5	136	276	39	176	308	87	209	346
	26	192	314	100	239	2	124	273	49	173	294	85
Apr.	2	276	52	200	326	86	223	10	135	257	35	181
	9	13	149	288	51	184	321	97	232	355	133	267
	16	115	238	14	146	286	48	184	318	96	218	355
	23	201	322	111	247	11	132	284	57	181	303	96
	30	285	61	208	334	96	232	19	143	267	43	190
May	7	21	160	296	60	192	331	105	231	4	142	275
	14	124	246	22	157	294	56	192	329	104	227	3
	21	209	331	122	255	20	141	294	66	190	312	105
	28	294	69	218	342	106	240	29	151	277	51	200
June	4	30	170	304	69	202	341	114	249	14	151	284
	11	132	255	30	167	302	65	200	340	112	235	11
	18	218	340	132	264	28	151	304	74	198	322	114
	25	304	78	228	350	115	249	59	159	286	60	209

MOON SIGN TABLES

July 2	40	179	312	78	212	349	122	248	25	159	293
9	140	264	38	178	310	74	209	350	120	244	21
16	226	349	141	273	36	161	312	84	206	332	123
23	314	87	237	358	125	258	48	168	295	70	218
30	51	187	321	86	223	357	131	256	36	167	302
Aug. 6	148	272	48	188	319	82	219	359	129	252	31
13	234	359	149	282	44	170	320	93	214	342	131
20	323	96	246	6	133	268	57	177	303	81	226
27	62	195	330	94	234	5	140	265	46	175	310
Sept. 3	157	281	57	198	328	90	229	8	138	260	41
10	242	9	158	292	52	180	329	102	222	351	140
17	331	107	255	15	141	279	65	186	312	91	234
24	73	204	339	103	244	13	149	274	56	184	319
Oct. 1	166	289	68	206	337	98	239	17	148	268	51
8	250	18	167	301	61	189	338	111	231	359	150
15	339	118	263	24	149	290	73	195	320	102	242
22	83	212	347	113	254	22	157	284	65	193	326
29	176	296	78	214	346	106	250	25	157	276	61
Nov. 5	259	27	177	309	70	197	348	119	240	7	161
12	347	129	270	33	158	300	81	203	329	112	250
19	91	221	355	123	262	31	164	295	73	202	334
26	185	305	88	223	355	115	259	34	165	285	70
Dec. 3	268	34	187	317	79	205	359	127	249	16	171
10	356	138	279	41	168	310	89	211	340	120	259
17	99	230	3	134	270	40	172	305	81	211	343
24	194	313	97	232	4	124	267	44	173	294	78
31	277	42	198	325	87	214	9	135	257	25	181

MOON SIGN TABLES

	1921	1922	1923	1924	1925	1926	1927	1928	1929	1930
Jan. 1	194	317	80	211	5	127	250	23	176	297
8	280	41	177	313	90	211	349	123	260	22
15	4	141	275	41	175	312	86	211	346	123
22	101	239	3	127	272	51	172	297	83	221
29	203	325	88	222	13	135	258	34	184	306
Feb. 5	289	49	187	321	99	220	359	131	269	31
12	14	149	284	49	185	320	95	219	356	131
19	110	249	11	135	281	59	181	305	93	230
26	211	334	96	233	21	144	266	45	191	314
Mar. 5	297	58	197	343	107	230	8	153	276	41
12	23	157	294	69	194	328	105	238	6	139
19	119	258	19	157	292	68	189	327	104	238
26	219	343	104	258	29	153	275	70	199	323
Apr. 2	305	68	205	352	115	239	16	163	284	51
9	33	166	303	77	204	337	114	247	14	149
16	130	266	28	164	303	76	198	335	115	246
23	227	351	114	268	38	161	285	79	208	331
30	313	78	213	1	123	250	25	172	292	61
May 7	42	176	313	85	212	348	123	255	23	160
14	141	274	37	173	314	84	207	344	125	254
21	236	359	123	277	47	169	295	88	217	339
28	321	88	222	11	131	259	34	181	301	70
June 4	50	186	321	94	220	358	131	264	31	171
11	152	282	45	182	324	92	215	354	135	263
18	245	7	134	285	56	177	305	96	226	347
25	329	97	232	20	139	268	44	190	310	78

MOON SIGN TABLES

July 2	58	197	329	103	229	9	139	273	40	181
9	162	291	54	192	333	101	223	4	144	272
16	254	15	144	294	65	185	315	104	236	355
23	338	106	242	28	148	276	54	198	319	87
30	67	208	337	112	238	20	147	282	49	191
Aug. 6	171	299	62	202	341	110	231	15	152	281
13	264	24	153	302	74	194	324	114	244	4
20	347	114	253	36	157	284	65	206	328	95
27	76	218	345	120	248	29	156	290	59	200
Sept. 3	179	309	70	213	350	119	239	25	161	290
10	273	32	162	312	83	203	332	124	252	13
17	356	122	264	44	166	293	75	214	337	105
24	86	227	354	128	258	38	165	298	70	208
Oct. 1	188	318	78	223	358	128	248	35	169	298
8	281	41	170	322	91	212	340	134	260	23
15	5	132	274	52	175	303	85	222	345	115
22	97	235	8	136	269	46	174	306	81	216
29	196	327	87	233	7	137	257	44	179	307
Nov. 5	289	50	178	332	99	221	349	144	268	31
12	13	142	283	61	183	313	93	231	353	126
19	107	243	12	144	279	54	183	315	91	225
26	206	335	96	241	17	145	266	52	189	314
Dec. 3	297	59	187	343	106	230	359	154	276	39
10	21	152	291	70	190	324	101	239	1	137
17	117	252	21	153	289	63	191	324	99	234
24	216	343	105	249	28	152	275	59	199	322
31	305	67	197	352	115	237	9	162	285	47

MOON-SIGN TABLES

	1931	1932	1933	1934	1935	1936	1937	1938	1939	1940
Jan. 1	61	196	346	107	231	8	156	277	41	181
8	162	294	70	193	333	104	240	5	145	275
15	257	20	158	294	68	190	329	105	239	0
22	342	108	255	32	152	278	67	202	323	88
29	68	207	353	116	239	19	164	286	50	191
Feb. 5	171	302	78	203	342	113	248	15	153	284
12	267	28	168	302	78	198	339	113	248	8
19	351	116	266	40	161	286	78	210	332	96
26	77	217	2	124	248	29	172	294	59	200
Mar. 5	179	324	86	213	350	135	256	24	161	306
12	276	48	177	311	87	218	348	123	257	29
19	1	137	277	48	170	308	89	218	340	119
26	87	241	10	132	258	53	180	302	70	223
Apr. 2	187	334	94	223	358	144	264	34	169	314
9	285	57	185	321	95	227	356	133	265	38
16	9	146	287	56	179	317	99	226	349	128
23	96	250	19	140	268	61	189	310	80	231
30	196	343	102	232	7	153	273	43	179	323
May 7	293	66	193	332	103	237	4	144	272	47
14	17	155	297	65	187	327	108	235	357	139
21	107	259	28	148	279	69	198	318	90	240
28	205	351	111	241	17	161	282	52	189	331
June 4	301	75	202	343	111	246	13	154	281	56
11	25	165	306	73	195	337	117	244	5	150
18	117	267	37	157	288	78	207	327	99	248
25	215	0	120	250	28	169	291	60	200	339

MOON-SIGN TABLES

July 2	309	83	211	353	119	254	23	164	289	64
9	33	176	315	82	203	348	125	253	13	160
16	126	276	46	165	297	87	216	336	108	258
23	226	8	130	258	39	177	300	69	210	347
30	318	92	221	2	128	262	33	173	297	72
Aug. 6	41	187	323	91	211	359	133	261	22	171
13	135	285	54	175	306	97	224	346	117	269
20	237	16	139	267	49	185	309	78	220	355
27	326	100	232	10	136	270	44	181	307	80
Sept. 3	50	197	331	100	220	9	142	270	31	180
10	144	296	62	184	314	107	232	355	125	279
17	246	24	147	277	58	194	317	89	228	4
24	335	108	243	18	145	278	55	189	316	89
Oct. 1	59	206	341	108	229	17	152	278	40	188
8	152	306	70	193	323	117	240	4	135	288
15	255	32	155	287	66	203	325	100	236	13
22	344	117	253	27	154	287	65	198	324	98
29	68	215	351	116	239	26	162	286	50	196
Nov. 5	161	316	78	202	332	126	248	12	145	297
12	264	41	163	298	74	212	333	111	244	22
19	353	126	262	36	162	297	74	208	332	108
26	77	223	1	124	248	34	172	294	59	205
Dec. 3	171	325	87	210	343	135	257	20	156	305
10	271	50	171	309	82	220	342	121	253	30
17	1	135	271	46	170	306	81	217	340	118
24	87	231	11	132	257	43	181	302	66	215
31	182	333	95	218	354	143	266	28	167	313

MOON SIGN TABLES

	1941	1942	1943	1944	1945	1946	1947	1948	1949	1950
Jan. 1	326	88	212	353	135	258	23	165	305	70
8	50	176	316	86	220	348	126	256	29	163
15	141	276	50	169	312	87	220	340	123	261
22	239	12	133	259	52	182	303	69	224	354
29	334	96	221	2	143	256	33	174	314	78
Feb. 5	57	186	324	95	227	358	134	265	37	173
12	150	285	58	178	321	96	228	349	132	271
19	250	20	142	267	62	190	312	78	234	2
26	342	104	231	11	152	274	43	182	323	86
Mar. 5	65	196	332	116	236	8	142	286	46	182
12	158	295	67	199	329	107	236	10	140	282
19	261	28	150	290	72	198	320	102	243	10
26	351	112	242	34	162	282	53	204	332	94
Apr. 2	74	205	340	125	245	17	152	294	55	191
9	166	306	74	209	337	118	244	19	148	292
16	270	36	158	300	81	206	328	112	252	19
23	0	120	252	42	170	290	64	212	340	103
30	83	214	351	133	254	25	163	302	64	199
May 7	175	316	82	218	346	128	252	28	158	302
14	279	45	166	311	89	215	336	123	260	28
21	9	128	262	50	179	299	73	222	349	112
28	92	222	1	141	263	34	173	310	74	207
June 4	184	326	91	226	356	137	261	36	168	310
11	287	54	174	322	98	224	345	134	268	37
18	17	138	271	60	187	308	81	231	357	122
25	102	231	12	149	272	42	183	318	83	217

MOON SIGN TABLES

July 2	194	335	99	234	7	145	270	44	179	318
9	296	63	183	332	106	233	353	144	276	45
16	25	147	279	70	196	318	90	241	5	132
23	111	240	21	157	281	52	192	327	91	227
30	205	343	108	242	18	153	278	52	190	327
Aug. 6	304	72	192	342	115	241	3	153	287	53
13	33	156	288	80	203	327	99	251	13	141
20	119	250	30	165	289	63	201	336	99	238
27	216	351	117	251	29	162	287	61	200	335
Sept. 3	314	80	202	351	125	249	13	162	296	61
10	41	166	297	90	211	336	108	260	21	149
17	127	261	39	174	297	74	209	345	107	249
24	227	0	125	260	39	171	295	71	210	344
Oct. 1	323	68	211	359	135	257	23	170	306	69
8	49	174	306	99	220	344	119	269	30	157
15	135	272	47	183	305	85	217	353	116	259
22	236	9	134	269	47	180	303	81	217	353
29	334	95	221	7	144	265	31	179	315	78
Nov. 5	58	182	317	107	229	352	130	277	39	165
12	143	283	55	192	314	94	226	1	126	269
19	244	18	142	280	55	190	311	91	226	3
26	343	104	229	17	153	274	39	189	323	86
Dec. 3	67	190	328	114	237	0	140	285	47	174
10	153	292	64	200	324	103	235	9	136	277
17	252	28	149	289	64	199	319	100	234	12
24	352	112	237	27	162	282	47	199	332	95
31	76	198	338	123	246	9	150	293	57	180

MOON-SIGN TABLES

	1951	1952	1953	1954	1955	1956	1957	1958	1959	1960
Jan. 1	193	335	115	237	5	146	285	47	178	317
8	296	66	198	331	106	237	8	143	277	47
15	29	150	293	70	199	320	104	241	9	131
22	113	239	35	161	283	51	207	351	93	222
29	204	344	123	245	16	154	284	54	188	325
Feb. 5	304	75	207	340	115	245	17	152	287	55
12	37	159	301	80	207	329	112	252	17	140
19	122	249	45	169	291	61	216	339	101	233
26	214	352	132	253	27	162	303	65	199	333
Mar. 5	313	96	216	349	125	265	27	180	297	75
12	45	180	309	90	215	351	121	248	25	161
19	130	273	53	178	299	86	224	548	109	258
26	225	14	141	261	37	185	311	72	308	255
Apr. 2	323	104	225	357	135	273	36	168	307	83
9	53	189	319	100	223	359	131	271	33	169
16	137	284	62	186	307	96	232	357	117	269
23	234	23	150	270	45	194	319	81	216	5
30	334	111	235	6	145	281	45	157	317	91
May 7	62	197	329	109	222	7	141	279	42	177
14	146	295	70	195	316	107	240	5	127	279
21	243	32	158	280	54	203	327	91	224	14
28	344	120	244	15	155	289	54	187	326	99
June 4	70	205	340	117	241	15	152	287	51	185
11	154	305	78	204	325	117	249	14	136	288
18	251	42	166	290	62	213	335	100	233	24
25	363	128	252	25	164	298	62	197	334	108

MOON SIGN TABLES

July 2	79	213	351	125	250	24	163	295	59	194
9	164	315	87	212	335	125	258	22	146	296
16	260	52	174	299	71	223	344	110	243	33
23	2	137	260	36	172	307	70	208	342	117
30	88	222	1	133	258	33	173	304	68	204
Aug. 6	173	323	97	220	345	134	268	29	156	305
13	269	61	182	307	81	232	352	118	253	42
20	10	145	269	47	180	316	79	219	350	126
27	97	231	11	142	266	43	182	313	75	214
Sept. 3	183	331	107	228	354	142	277	38	165	314
10	280	70	191	316	92	240	1	126	264	50
17	18	154	277	58	188	324	88	229	359	134
24	105	241	20	152	274	53	190	323	84	225
Oct. 1	192	340	116	236	3	152	286	46	174	323
8	290	78	200	324	105	248	10	134	275	58
15	26	162	286	68	197	332	98	238	8	142
22	112	252	26	161	270	63	190	332	92	235
29	201	350	125	245	11	162	295	35	182	334
Nov. 5	301	86	208	332	113	256	19	143	285	66
12	35	170	296	76	206	340	108	246	17	150
19	121	262	36	170	290	73	208	341	100	244
26	209	0	153	254	19	172	302	64	190	344
Dec. 3	312	94	217	341	123	264	27	153	293	74
10	45	178	307	84	216	348	119	254	26	158
17	129	271	45	179	299	81	217	349	109	252
24	217	11	140	263	27	183	310	73	198	252
31	321	103	225	352	132	273	34	164	302	355

MOON-SIGN TABLES

	1961	1962	1963	1964	1965	1966	1967	1968	1969	1970
Jan. 1	96	217	350	128	26	27	163	298	76	197
8	179	315	89	217	350	126	260	27	161	297
15	275	53	179	302	86	225	349	112	257	36
22	18	141	263	65	189	311	74	207	359	122
29	105	225	1	135	275	35	173	307	85	206
Feb. 5	189	323	98	225	0	134	270	35	171	305
12	284	64	187	310	95	234	357	121	267	45
19	26	149	272	46	197	320	81	218	7	130
26	113	234	11	144	283	45	182	314	93	156
Mar. 5	198	331	109	245	9	142	280	54	180	313
12	293	73	195	332	105	244	5	142	277	53
19	34	159	280	71	204	329	90	243	15	139
26	122	243	19	166	291	54	190	338	101	226
Apr. 2	208	340	119	253	19	151	290	63	189	323
9	304	82	204	340	114	252	14	150	288	61
16	42	167	289	81	213	337	99	252	23	147
23	130	253	28	176	299	64	198	347	109	235
30	216	349	128	261	26	161	298	71	197	333
May 7	315	90	212	348	127	260	23	158	299	70
14	51	176	298	91	222	345	109	261	31	155
21	137	263	36	185	307	74	207	357	117	245
28	225	359	136	270	35	172	306	81	205	344
June 4	325	98	222	355	137	268	31	168	309	78
11	60	184	308	99	231	353	119	270	42	163
18	146	272	45	195	315	82	217	6	126	253
25	233	10	144	279	43	183	315	89	214	355

MOON SIGN TABLES

July 2	336	106	230	6	147	276	40	178	318	87
9	70	191	318	108	241	1	129	278	51	171
16	154	281	54	204	324	91	227	14	134	261
23	241	21	153	288	52	193	323	98	223	335
30	345	115	239	16	156	286	47	188	327	97
Aug. 6	79	200	327	116	250	10	138	288	60	180
13	163	289	66	212	333	99	238	22	144	270
20	250	32	161	296	61	203	331	106	233	14
27	353	124	246	27	164	295	55	199	335	106
Sept. 3	88	208	336	126	259	19	147	297	68	189
10	171	297	77	220	342	108	249	30	152	279
17	259	41	170	304	72	212	340	114	243	22
24	1	134	254	37	173	304	64	208	344	114
Oct. 1	97	217	345	136	267	28	155	308	76	198
8	181	306	88	228	351	117	259	38	161	289
15	270	50	179	312	82	220	349	122	254	31
22	10	143	262	47	182	313	72	217	353	123
29	105	226	352	146	275	37	163	318	84	207
Nov. 5	189	315	97	237	359	127	268	47	168	299
12	281	58	188	320	93	228	358	130	264	39
19	19	151	271	57	191	321	82	225	3	131
26	113	235	1	157	282	45	173	308	92	215
Dec. 3	197	326	105	245	7	138	276	55	176	310
10	291	66	197	329	102	237	7	139	273	47
17	30	159	280	63	202	329	91	234	13	139
24	121	243	11	166	291	53	183	337	101	223
31	205	336	113	254	14	148	284	64	185	319

MOON SIGN TABLES

74

	1971	1972	1973	1974	1975	1976	1977	1978	1979	1980
Jan. 1	335	108	246	7	147	279	56	179	318	90
8	71	198	332	107	243	6	144	278	54	176
15	158	283	69	207	328	93	240	18	139	263
22	244	20	169	292	54	192	339	102	224	4
29	344	117	255	17	156	288	64	189	327	99
Feb. 5	81	204	342	115	253	14	153	287	63	184
12	167	291	79	216	337	101	251	26	147	271
19	252	30	177	300	62	203	347	110	233	14
26	353	126	263	27	164	297	72	199	334	109
Mar. 5	91	224	351	124	262	34	162	296	72	204
12	176	312	60	224	346	122	262	34	156	293
19	261	55	184	309	72	226	356	118	244	37
26	1	149	270	37	172	320	80	208	343	130
Apr. 2	100	233	359	134	270	43	170	307	80	213
9	184	320	101	232	354	131	273	42	164	302
16	271	64	194	317	82	235	5	126	254	45
23	9	158	278	47	181	329	88	217	352	139
30	109	242	8	145	278	52	178	318	88	222
May 7	193	329	111	240	3	140	282	50	173	312
14	281	73	203	324	92	243	14	134	264	54
21	19	167	287	55	191	337	97	226	3	147
28	117	251	16	156	286	61	187	328	96	231
June 4	201	339	120	249	11	151	291	59	180	323
11	291	81	153	333	102	251	23	143	273	63
18	29	176	296	64	201	346	106	234	13	155
25	125	260	25	167	294	69	196	338	105	239

MOON-SIGN TABLES

July 2	209	350	129	257	19	162	299	68	188	334
9	300	90	222	341	111	261	32	152	282	72
16	40	184	305	72	212	354	115	243	23	163
23	133	268	5	176	307	78	206	347	104	248
30	217	0	137	267	27	172	308	77	197	344
Aug. 6	309	99	230	350	120	271	40	161	290	83
13	51	192	314	81	222	2	124	252	33	171
20	172	276	45	185	312	86	217	356	123	256
27	225	10	146	276	36	62	317	86	206	353
Sept. 3	317	109	238	0	128	281	48	170	299	93
10	61	200	322	90	232	10	132	262	43	180
17	151	284	56	193	321	94	228	4	132	264
24	234	20	125	284	45	191	326	94	215	2
Oct. 1	325	120	246	9	137	291	56	179	308	103
8	70	238	330	101	241	19	140	273	51	189
15	160	292	36	201	330	102	238	12	140	273
22	243	28	165	292	54	199	336	102	225	10
29	334	130	254	17	146	301	64	187	318	112
Nov. 5	79	217	338	112	249	27	148	284	59	197
12	169	301	76	210	339	111	247	21	148	282
19	253	36	175	300	63	207	347	110	234	18
26	344	139	262	25	156	310	73	195	329	120
Dec. 3	86	226	346	122	257	36	157	294	67	206
10	177	310	83	220	347	121	255	31	156	292
17	261	45	185	308	12	216	356	118	242	28
24	355	148	271	33	167	318	81	203	340	128
31	95	228	354	132	265	44	166	303	76	217

MOON SIGN TABLES

	1981	1982	1983	1984	1985	1986	1987	1988	1989	1990
Jan. 1	227	350	128	261	36	162	299	72	206	333
8	315	88	225	346	126	260	36	156	297	71
15	52	188	309	73	225	358	120	243	37	168
22	149	273	35	176	319	82	206	347	130	252
29	235	0	136	270	44	172	307	81	214	343
Feb. 5	324	98	234	355	134	269	44	165	305	82
12	63	196	318	81	236	6	128	252	47	176
19	157	281	45	184	328	90	217	355	139	260
26	242	10	144	280	52	181	316	90	222	352
Mar. 5	332	108	243	15	142	280	52	186	313	93
12	74	204	327	103	246	14	137	275	57	184
19	166	289	55	207	337	98	227	18	148	268
26	251	19	153	301	61	190	325	111	231	0
Apr. 2	340	119	251	24	150	291	60	195	321	103
9	84	212	335	113	255	23	145	286	68	193
16	176	296	65	216	346	106	237	26	157	276
23	259	28	164	309	70	198	336	119	240	8
30	348	129	259	33	159	301	68	203	331	113
May 7	93	221	343	124	263	32	152	296	74	202
14	185	305	75	224	355	115	246	35	165	285
21	268	36	174	317	79	206	347	127	249	17
28	357	139	267	42	169	311	77	211	341	122
June 4	101	230	351	135	271	41	161	307	82	211
11	194	313	83	234	4	124	254	45	173	295
18	277	44	185	325	88	215	357	135	258	27
25	8	149	275	50	180	319	86	219	352	130

MOON-SIGN TABLES

July 2	109	239	359	145	280	50	169	317	91	220
9	202	323	92	244	12	133	262	55	181	304
16	286	53	195	333	96	225	7	144	266	37
23	18	157	285	58	191	328	95	227	3	138
30	118	248	8	154	289	58	178	326	101	168
Aug. 6	210	332	100	254	20	142	271	66	189	313
13	294	63	205	342	104	235	15	152	274	48
20	29	165	294	66	201	336	104	236	13	147
27	128	257	17	163	299	66	183	334	111	236
Sept. 3	218	341	109	264	28	151	281	75	198	321
10	302	74	213	351	112	246	23	161	282	59
17	39	174	302	75	181	345	112	245	22	156
24	138	267	27	171	309	74	197	342	121	244
Oct. 1	226	349	119	274	36	159	291	84	206	329
8	310	85	221	0	120	257	31	170	291	69
15	49	183	311	84	220	354	120	255	30	166
22	148	272	36	180	319	82	206	351	130	252
29	235	357	130	282	45	167	302	92	215	337
Nov. 5	319	95	229	8	129	267	40	178	300	78
12	57	193	318	94	228	4	128	265	38	175
19	158	280	44	189	329	90	184	1	139	261
26	244	5	141	290	54	175	313	100	224	345
Dec. 3	328	105	238	17	139	276	49	186	310	87
10	65	203	326	103	236	14	136	274	47	185
17	167	289	52	200	337	99	222	12	147	270
24	252	13	151	298	62	184	323	108	232	355
31	337	113	248	24	149	284	59	194	320	95

MOON SIGN TABLES

	1991	1992	1993	1994	1995	1996	1997	1998	1999	2000
Jan. 1	110	243	16	145	280	53	185	317	92	224
8	206	326	107	243	16	137	278	55	186	307
15	290	54	209	338	100	225	21	148	270	36
22	18	158	300	62	190	329	111	231	2	139
29	118	252	24	154	289	62	194	325	101	232
Feb. 5	214	335	115	254	24	146	286	66	194	316
12	298	63	219	346	108	235	30	156	278	47
19	28	166	309	70	200	336	120	239	12	147
26	127	261	332	163	299	71	203	334	111	240
Mar. 5	222	356	123	265	32	167	294	76	202	337
12	306	87	228	354	116	259	39	165	286	71
19	39	188	318	78	210	359	129	248	21	170
26	137	281	42	171	309	91	212	342	121	260
Apr. 2	230	5	132	275	40	175	304	86	210	345
9	314	98	236	4	124	270	47	174	294	82
16	48	197	327	87	219	8	137	257	30	180
23	148	289	51	179	320	98	221	350	132	268
30	239	13	142	284	49	183	315	94	219	353
May 7	322	108	244	13	132	280	55	182	303	92
14	57	197	335	96	227	18	145	267	38	190
21	158	297	60	188	330	106	230	0	141	277
28	247	21	153	292	58	191	326	102	228	1
June 4	331	118	253	21	141	290	64	191	312	101
11	65	217	343	105	235	28	153	276	47	200
18	168	305	68	198	339	115	238	10	150	285
25	256	29	164	300	67	199	336	111	237	10

MOON SIGN TABLES

July 2	340	128	262	29	151	299	193	199	321	110
9	73	227	351	114	244	38	161	285	56	210
16	177	314	76	209	348	124	246	21	158	294
23	265	38	175	309	75	208	346	119	245	19
30	349	136	272	37	160	307	83	207	331	118
Aug. 6	83	237	359	123	254	48	169	293	67	218
13	186	322	84	220	356	133	254	32	166	303
20	274	47	184	318	83	218	355	129	253	29
27	359	145	282	45	170	316	93	215	340	127
Sept. 3	93	246	8	131	265	56	178	301	78	226
10	194	331	92	231	4	141	263	43	174	311
17	282	57	193	327	92	228	4	138	261	39
24	8	153	292	53	178	325	103	223	348	137
Oct. 1	104	255	17	139	276	64	187	309	89	234
8	202	340	102	241	13	150	273	52	183	319
15	290	67	201	337	99	238	12	148	269	49
22	16	163	301	62	186	335	111	232	356	147
29	115	262	26	147	287	72	195	318	99	243
Nov. 5	211	348	111	249	22	158	283	60	193	327
12	298	76	210	347	107	247	21	157	278	58
19	24	173	309	71	194	346	119	240	4	158
26	125	270	34	157	297	80	204	328	108	251
Dec. 3	221	356	121	257	32	165	293	68	202	335
10	306	85	219	356	116	255	31	166	286	66
17	32	184	317	79	202	357	127	250	13	169
24	134	279	42	166	305	89	212	338	116	260
31	230	4	131	265	41	173	303	77	212	343

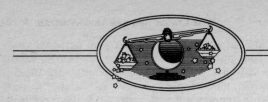

YOUR UNIQUE SUN AND MOON PORTRAIT

Since the luminaries are the most important bodies in any chart, the positions of the Sun and Moon, and their relationship to each other, furnish an important key to the understanding of human nature. The following exploration of these factors reveals the manner in which the individuality (Sun) is expressed through the personality (Moon).

Sun in Libra—Moon in Aries: The Moon in Aries indicates the presence of an aggressiveness that the Sun in Libra often lacks. Therefore, you may be adventurous and restless in thought and action. You may find it necessary, for your own safety, to curb your impulses and temper. The Sun in Libra and the Moon in Aries constitute a rather difficult combination. The peace-loving, equable Libran temperament is continually being upset by the active and sometimes violent Aries energy. There will be contention, even over matters that others may consider unimportant, unless you use a great deal of wisdom. You will find yourself impelled to fight, verbally or otherwise, for your concept of justice—and at the drop of a hat. You will attempt to correct anything and all that you consider unbalanced in the people who are around you. Your purpose is often admirable, but your method can be deplorable. If you exercise strength and wisdom, you are bound to be a fighter for the cause of justice.

Sun in Libra—Moon in Taurus: With the Moon in Taurus, you are inclined to be determined but courteous and reflective. You are not apt to change either your personal view-points or your purposes. Blended with the Sun in Libra, there is a capacity for stable relationships with others. Libra brings in, too, a sense of justice and balance in your determination to carry out your purposes in your relation-ships. If you do not stress the highest principles, however, these purposes may not be admirable, but you will remain fixed nevertheless. You will find yourself faithful to your hates as well as to your loves. Both Libra and Taurus are ruled by Venus. Hence, the concerns of this planet come to the fore. You possess a pleasant, even winning, person-ality, which will draw others to you. Birth and death, taxes and legacies, the financial matters of a partner will tend to occupy your mind. You will probably benefit from an inheritance or from an associate's money.

Sun in Libra—Moon in Gemini: With the Moon in Gemini, you possess an active, though sometimes superficial, men-tality. The natural restlessness of the Moon is accented not so much in the direction of the sensuous feelings as in the objective perception. You may take keen delight in litera-ture and science. However, unless you concentrate your efforts, you may merely skim the surface of things, being driven by your restless eagerness to cover as much terri-tory as possible. Combined with the Sun in Libra, a Gemini Moon will probably exhibit great skill in the use of words, particularly in argument or debate. Libra gives the ability to see both sides of a matter, while Gemini intensifies the mental interest and favors its expression. However, there is likely much changeability of mind and viewpoint. You may debate well and earnestly on one side of a question today—and take the opposite argument tomorrow. How-ever, with this combination of Sun and Moon, you sin-cerely perceive the truth of both sides. You are, therefore, quick-witted and versatile but lacking in stability.

Sun in Libra—Moon in Cancer: With the Moon in Cancer, you have a strongly developed protective instinct, a fond-ness for home and parents, an intense patriotism, change-able moods, and a restrained and affectionate disposition.

Cancer is the sign of the mother. It is ruled by the Moon, which is in harmony with the sign. Therefore, you tend to be emotionally contented and serene. Combined with the Sun in Libra (partnership, marriage), this emotional tranquillity is disturbed by any lack of balance. Harmonious relationships, particularly in the domestic sphere, are keenly desirable though not always obtainable. Any injustice is emotionally upsetting to you. In attempting to recover a balance, you may go to extremes. If you possess an active temperament, you may swing to the opposite extreme in your intensity, thus creating an unbalance or an unjust situation that you yourself may deeply regret. Frequently, you will be found defending or protecting something—the home, your partner, your party, your country, or your faith—against some real or imaginary opponent. Cancer indicates a certain defensive quality, while Libra denotes an unusual awareness of the other party or parties—the opponent. Your relationship to the public means a great deal to you.

Sun in Libra—Moon in Leo: In Leo, the Moon reveals some of its finest qualities. The Moon's natural restlessness and instability are held in abeyance by the fixed quality of Leo, while the Moon's emotional nature—illuminated by the heart sign Leo—is sublimated into more lasting love. There may be pridefulness, but you are tolerant and generous, especially in money matters. With the Sun in Libra, the Leo Moon constitutes an unusually harmonious combination. Leo is the sign of love, and Libra is the sign of marriage. With no afflicting factors, you will make one of the finest marriage partners. The Leo nature feels a great strength and energy within itself. Libra is continually seeking to obtain a balance in life. Consequently, the Libra–Leo combination draws from the reservoir of its own strength to compensate for the weakness of others. Like a monarch, you spread your beneficence over your associates, striving thus to establish a balance between yourself and them. With afflicting factors, a certain aggressiveness is shown, and you are inclined to force others under your power.

Sun in Libra—Moon in Virgo: With the Moon in Virgo, your mental faculties will be very alert, with a tendency toward a practical and analytical approach to any matter. You may have such an ideal conception of the way things should be that you continually criticize matters as they are. Nothing short of material perfection is your aim. The Moon in Virgo combined with the Sun in Libra indicates a potentially inharmonious condition unless you are living above the level of the emotions. The Libran love of balance and the Virgoan love of perfection do not blend well in merely personal, emotional relationships. You are under a continual tension because of your awareness of the imperfections existing in those with whom you associate. However, it is a fine combination for precision workers or those who gather statistics. The quest for truth—concrete and practical, rather than abstract—may be a motivating factor in your life. Your search is for facts—for proof. Anthropology or the sciences may hold a great deal of interest for you, particularly the material or practical sciences—chemistry, physics, or biology. You may also find that your attention, at some time or other in life, will turn to matters concerning hospitals, prisons, asylums, monasteries, and other places of confinement or exile.

Sun in Libra—Moon in Libra: With the Moon in Libra, the quality of balanced judgment is emphasized. Your senses report facts accurately, and these facts are weighed until a balanced conclusion is reached. The mental side of the Moon is strong in Libra, but you may find that you have a tendency to be indecisive. Any decision may call for a major effort on your part. In some cases, however, an almost superhuman wisdom may be present. You can be very charming—perhaps more so than the native of any other sign. On the negative side, there may be a great deal of dependence on others. The attempt to maintain peace in any association may become almost a mania. You may find yourself fighting in some way for the peace and harmony you wish to obtain. You can very well be a master strategist, for you have excellent judgment.

Sun in Libra—Moon in Scorpio: The Moon in Scorpio does not reveal its best qualities, for the emotional nature is emphasized—often to the point where you live only for your desires. It does incline toward an enterprising, forceful, and courageous personality—qualities that are very helpful if you are emphasizing the positive side of your nature, but dangerous if your moral nature is weak. You will not tolerate opposition or be swerved from your purpose. Combined with the Sun in Libra, the Scorpio tendency toward emotional extremes is conditioned by the Libra virtues. You may be quarrelsome. Scorpio is a jealous sign, and Libra rules the partner or the opponent. With the Moon in Scorpio, you will feel a natural power within yourself. Given an opportunity to express this power, you can be very fair and just. But if you are thwarted, the lower side of your nature may come to the surface. This may even give way to hatred and lead you to condone murder as justifiable. No one is more intense in carrying out his/her concepts of justice than you. You will be concerned with possessions—perhaps even opposing the theory of individual possession.

Sun in Libra—Moon in Sagittarius: The Moon in Sagittarius indicates a hopeful, frank, and generous nature. Your mind is philosophically inclined and very clear-sighted. You may be a natural-born teacher. This placement of the Moon added to the Sun in Libra makes for a rather fortunate combination. Sagittarius denotes an instinctive knowledge of law, whether it be the laws of nature or man-made laws. Libra, the sign of relationship, indicates awareness of responsibility to others. With this combination, therefore, you should have very high morals and a keen sense of right and wrong, combined with an almost prophetic ability to foresee the outcome, not only of your own actions, but also the actions of others. Many philosophers and scientists have combinations of planets in these two signs. Understanding the natural laws of relationship could be a major purpose in your life. If you express the negative side of your nature, however, you may become a lover of formal, conventional, or ceremonial matters—a set pattern of relationship becoming the symbol of law to you. Watch out for a tendency to let your mental faculties be stimulated to the point of danger.

Sun in Libra—Moon in Capricorn: The Moon in Capricorn is not favorable for personal happiness, for the cold austerity and sense of responsibility inherent in this sign tend to curb personal emotions. But it is excellent if you deal with the public or your work calls for concentration. Executive ability and leadership are clearly marked. However, in some cases, concentration can amount to obsession. Many of the world's great leaders have had the Moon in Capricorn. Combined with the Sun in Libra, this emphasizes the ability to concentrate on a plan or purpose. Cold, calculating, and patient in purpose, you adjust your relationship with others or govern the mutual relationships of others after your own concepts of balance. Your unusual administrative and executive abilities are especially helpful in circumstances where personal hopes and wishes, either your own or others', must be disciplined to carry out a larger program. However, you must watch out for a tendency to be cruel or intensely fanatical. But with all your faults, you will have the capacity to get things accomplished, even if it calls for great self-sacrifice. At some time in life, you may be called upon to organize a defense of your home, your parents, your occupation, or your country. You are a great believer of the view that each person must do his duty.

Sun in Libra—Moon in Aquarius: The Moon in Aquarius gives you a friendly, independent, and unconventional personality. Unusual, original, or eccentric subjects hold your attention. You probably have a wide range of interests. Consequently, in your emotional life, you are seldom long satisfied with the companionship of one individual but feel a friendliness toward everyone. Combined with the Sun in Libra (balance), a Moon in Aquarius emphasizes the intellectual side of your nature—Libra lending the stability to the mind that the restless Aquarius often lacks. On the whole, Aquarius–Libra is a very favorable combination, although you may not create a big name for yourself. Your mental ability is very keen, and you can converse intelligently on many and varied subjects. You have a great deal of sympathy for and understanding of others, for you hold that all have their appointed place in life. Intolerance and exclusiveness are two qualities you fail to understand. Love, romance, and the theater may hold a prominent place in your interests. You are generally inclined to favor music of the intellectual or classical type. A number of people whose careers are related to the stage or concert have this combination of Sun and Venus.

Sun in Libra—Moon in Pisces: With the Moon in Pisces, you possess an active imagination. You are generally kind and sympathetic—often too much so. A lover of beauty in all its forms, you are inclined to suffer greatly in an adverse environment or uncongenial surroundings. Lacking stamina, you may be too sensitive to maintain your emotional independence. Pisces is excellent for the poet, the dreamer, the musician, or the artist, but it is a difficult position for the Moon when one is faced with the realities of life. Combined with the Sun in Libra, a Moon in Pisces emphasizes the love of beauty—balanced form and color—but inclines more toward poetry than art or music. Libra tends to objective awareness—related to form and color, but Pisces is subjective and immensely conscious of the screen of imagination. Music provides no form and color, while art is too objective. Poetry, on the other hand, provides a word picture to be realized on the screen of your imagination. You may be incurably romantic, marriage being viewed idealistically in your imagination. You dream of perfect situations—and find objective life very disillusioning. Not finding material perfection in the objective world, you may become cynical or naggingly critical. You may hide your real self behind a mask. It is always well for you to remember to make a sincere effort to accept life as it is. Otherwise, you could just drift away into a world of unreality.

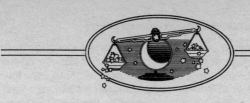

YOUR RISING SIGN AND SUN-SIGN COMBINATION

Your Sun Sign describes that core identity you possess, that source of your sense of self and the purpose that guides you through life. Your ascendant is the way in which that self gets expressed, the filter through which you see the world and through which the world sees you. Not only is each combination different, but every person has a unique way of manifesting it. As the length of days and nights varies in different latitudes, the guidelines below may be less than accurate, so try reading the message before or after the one suggested, to see if it is more helpful in deepening your understanding of how you manifest your unique self in the world.

If you were born between 4:00 A.M. and 6:00 A.M., you are a double-Libra individual. The impact of Venus on your life heightens your involvement in relationships, especially partnerships of both a romantic and business nature. Pleasing people in general is your instinctive response in interactions with others, which can make for a superficial harmony at first and, if performed at deeper levels, often brings a certain deceitfulness and instability to the unions you are trying to create. Avoid sacrificing the seemingly inharmonious parts of yourself that need to be expressed in your attempt to maintain the peace—or it may cost you the relationship you cherish so dearly.

If you were born between 6:00 A.M. and 8:00 A.M., you have a Scorpio ascendant. Despite the strength of the Libra

Sun-Sign and its goal of keeping the peace, a certain willfulness emanates from the rulership of Pluto over your rising sign. Still waters run deep here, as there is a tendency to withhold yourself in relationships and to manipulate others psychologically in order to get the effect you desire. Beware of undermining your own efforts, for as you create a structure or relationship founded on deception or an imbalanced desire to control, so will you destroy the very harmony and unity you are so desperate to create. Your psychological acumen and charm do much to promote your business success.

If you were born between 8:00 A.M. and 10:00 A.M., your ascendant is Sagittarius. Jupiter can be an uplifting influence on your personality and your way of cultivating relationships since it makes for a friendly and easygoing impact on other people. As relationships get a bit more involved, however, you may tend to be less than reliable or dependable as a mate or partner. You could also be rightly accused of creating a philosophy around whatever seems at the time to be agreeable to all parties, though it might not truly reflect your own deeper beliefs or be something you can remain faithful to for very long.

If you were born between 10:00 A.M. and noon, your ascendant is Capricorn. Strengthening the dependability of your nature, Saturn's influence here also ensures a certain professional way in handling matters of great importance to you. You are quite goal-oriented as well, and may choose to cultivate a partnership with one who shares similar aims or works in the same field as you do so that your union can be a productive professional collaboration as well as a personal venture. You are quite pragmatic in your approach to others and need to let more of your feelings through in order to cultivate more deeply rewarding relationships, ones that go beyond practical, well-run, businesslike endeavors.

If you were born between noon and 2:00 P.M., your ascendant is Aquarius. The level of unpredictability that Uranus brings to a chart is matched by its level of excitement. You are capable of cultivating some stimulating relationships, especially with people for whom predictability is not of great value. You might sometimes have to deal with a conflict between your desire to make things smooth and peaceful in relationships and that rebellious streak in you that is constantly upsetting things. Watch out for the impulse to always please others, which may undermine your own need for self-expression and lead to resentment and inner turmoil.

If you were born between 2:00 P.M. and 4:00 P.M., your ascendant is Pisces. Neptune is the ruler of your rising sign, adding a magical dimension to your effect upon others, as well as heightening your tendency to absorb and be receptive to those around you. The Libra Sun Sign tendency to give over your power to others is accentuated by the indecisiveness of a Pisces ascendant. You tend to obliterate your own personal self in an attempt to make the interactions around you pleasant, protecting your own inner sensitivities by focusing on others. Turn inward for renewal and refreshment of your inner self so that your intuitions are clear and strong.

If you were born between 4:00 P.M. and 6:00 P.M., your ascendant is Aries. The strength and passion of Mars ruling your rising sign attracts many others to you and reinforces your will to pursue your chosen mate. A conflict between wanting to pursue and wanting to attract a mate may arise for you. A certain combativeness, too, may distract you from the peace and harmony your Libra Sun Sign longs to cultivate in such unions. Also, your assertiveness may be less than welcome in some situations where a mate is trying to take the lead. Become aware of the impact you have on others in order to direct it toward your goal of balance with a partner and harmony in interactions.

If you were born between 6:00 P.M. and 8:00 P.M., your ascendant is Taurus. Venus then rules not only your Libra Sun Sign but your rising sign as well, bestowing added significance to beauty and satisfaction in your life. You are able to bring a kind of loving mutuality to your relationships if you remember that the focus of sensual pleasure need not always be on you. A Taurus ascendant could make for a certain complacency and material focus that does not serve to foster or strengthen unions. A stubborn streak could also make the cultivation of harmony more challenging. The caution you take, however, in choosing a mate will help you make the right long-term choice.

If you were born between 8:00 P.M. and 10:00 P.M., your ascendant is Gemini. The duality of this sign is heightened by your awareness of the wide variety of contradictory aspects in a situation. Mercury governs small things as well, so the confusion and conflicts you experience with a mate may all be petty ones, but upsetting nonetheless to the harmony you are trying to create. Your ability to understand both sides of an issue is very helpful in resolving any partnership conflict that arises; your inability to choose a side to be on and stick to your decision is not. Start to take responsibility for the impact of your ambivalence on your relationships.

If you were born between 10:00 P.M. and midnight, your ascendant is Cancer. The lunar influence on your rising sign, ruled by the Moon, heightens the impact of your emotions on your view of the world and how you see others. You can tend to be moody, reactive, and self-protective in ways that make you inaccessible to others who are trying to create some kind of connection with you. Your need for emotional security could make you quite demanding of others, though you are quite able to reciprocate, offering compassion that is soothing and comforting to others. You need to learn to maintain a balance between your own emotions and other aspects of the relationship your partner needs acknowledged.

If you were born between midnight and 2:00 A.M., your ascendant is Leo. You brightly attract many admirers to you, as noted by the Sun's rulership of your rising sign.

You may emanate an inordinate need for self-acknowledgment as well, placing demands on your partner that bring imbalance and disharmony to your relationship. You love being the center of attention at all times and resent the amount of shared focus that a truly mutual relationship requires. Any traces of a rigid or bossy attitude need to be eliminated in order to foster the loving rapport you desire. You learn best from a partner who has the strength and character to assert his or her own needs to you.

If you were born between 2:00 A.M. and 4:00 A.M., your ascendant is Virgo. Giving a practical focus to all the small details of life, Mercury governs your rising sign and has a strong impact on your view of the world and of others in relationship with you. A certain perfectionism could bring a hypercritical edge to your interactions, so you would do best to cultivate an appreciation of people and situations just as they are. This way you won't alienate others and discourage the kind of relationship building that attracts you. Do make sure, however, that your needs are served in relationship; don't just focus on what you can do to serve and please others.

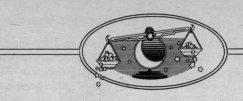

MERCURY: MIND OVER MATTER

Mercury is the planet governing the connections we make in the world. Communication is a part of how we reach out to other people. This includes our approach to putting ourselves forward in relationships. Our beliefs, attitudes, and all that governs just how we make that move to connect our inner world with what is going on around us are the domain of this planet.

Whether we choose to open up to others with words or some kind of nonverbal gesture, whether we find a strictly intellectual or formal way of making ourselves known or wait for others to notice, the varying styles of communication can be better understood by knowing the sign in which Mercury is placed in our charts.

Thinking is another aspect of ourselves that involves making connections—in this case, synthesizing the various parts of ourselves that make up the whole. What we think, how we think about ourselves, our attitudes toward others, and our beliefs about the world determine just what we want to put forward into it and how.

In a way Mercury acts as a filter through which we understand what is all around us. How we perceive and process what others put out to us affects our feelings, our interpretations, and our acts in relationships. The connections we make in our minds between events that occur influence our sense of self as well.

In other words, this little planet represents just how we connect all the diverse parts of our mind, impacting on not only the way we reach out but also the quality of our bond with others.

Sharing the knowledge, information, and feelings we have makes us part of a larger whole, more than just ourselves, now a small piece of the larger universe. Mercury points the way to how we deal with the human recognition that we are not alone in the world and to exactly what we do about this. The first inkling of a relationship starts with gestures and words and, even before that, the thoughts we have about others. So begin communication and the relations people forge with one another.

Mercury governs our understanding of and way of making that connection. As we read about our particular placement of Mercury in the chart, we are better able to see how the impact of our attitudes and thoughts affects other people and how we create some of the interactions and relationships we have in our everyday lives.

Mercury in Aries adds a lively, active tone to communications. The individual with this placement of Mercury is likely to take the lead in a conversation, even start one up without any kind of hesitancy or self-consciousness, and exudes a certain directness in ensuing dialogues. There may also be a serious flirtatiousness to interactions because the sign of Aries tends toward a passionate and directly sexual manner of engaging members of the opposite sex.

On the other hand, an Aries Mercury individual is often expressive in a rather combative way. Finding it easy to provoke disharmony, such a person could unintentionally start verbal arguments with others that lack any resolution or completion.

Lack of follow-through may be a bit frustrating in conversing with a Mercury in Aries individual. Many ideas will be communicated, and feelings conveyed, often without any sense of closure or even reciprocity. This person may be prone to asking questions and then not waiting until they are answered, starting a story and then interrupting himself or herself with another one, or perhaps just cutting someone off to say something that pops up and needs to be expressed immediately.

The thought processes and connections of this individual are intuitive, quick, and somehow magically provoked. An impatience about disclosure is expressed in a tendency to want to say things quickly. A marvelous wit and humor, however, take the edge off an omnipresent aggressiveness.

Mercury in Taurus denotes a certain deliberate, thoughtful, and cautious manner of expression and intellectual digestion of ideas and information. The almost scholarly seriousness with which even the most mundane conversation is received reflects the careful and conservative pacing of the Taurus Mercury individual's mind. A certain bluntness and conciseness are reflective of the Taurean respect for time and efficiency, moderation in using just the right number of words, and measured sensibility about communication in general.

These individuals are usually not the ones to initiate conversations, nor are they known for any particular adeptness in keeping one going. Their manner of conveying information is most often nonverbal—particularly physical—for words are not where Mercury in Taurus individuals feel most at home.

The thought processes of such people lend themselves to methodical and systematic presentation of ideas and even feelings. Frustration is in store for individuals seeking more philosophical or emotional exchanges because of the seeming lack of interaction that goes on. The truth is that Taurus Mercury people need time to take in fully what another person is telling them and then more time to formulate a response that is completely and concisely satisfying. Humor is a quality that presents itself almost as an antidote to the rather slow and serious manner of receiving and reacting to information.

Mercury in Gemini is quite a lively influence on one's manner of thought, understanding, and interaction with others. At home in its own sign, Gemini rules the communications aspect of the personality, which in such an individual may be dominant. Gemini Mercury people thrive on much interaction with others and may have serious issues about communication that need to be dealt with throughout life. Highly communicative, these people know just how to keep conversations going—not just leading or dominating them but facilitating equal participation.

Gemini individuals make connections everywhere they go—especially in the vicinity of their homes—with the mailman, the grocer, the sanitation worker, the gardener, learning all sorts of interesting tidbits about the way others live, think, work, and feel. This information is then readily shared with others, as Mercury in Gemini individuals forge links among people.

Gemini Mercury people are quick and adept at processing a lot of information at once. Alert to any small changes, these individuals bring their awarenesses to bear in almost every situation, sharing those awarenesses with others. If it seems there are always other things distracting these people while you converse with them, it's true. They always have thoughts pouring through them and, while in constant verbal motion, are simultaneously processing information and creating more.

Mercury in Cancer lends an emotional tone to an individual's manner of taking in and putting forth information, feelings, and ideas. With a pronounced lunar influence, feelings dominate the intellectual processes; the person may react emotionally to what is being said even before the words are fully understood. Responding to the tone rather than the message of another, such an individual knows exactly what you are really asking at the level beneath the actual question and may therefore have trouble responding directly to you.

The sensitivity of Mercury Cancer is matched only by their intuitive awareness. Communication with them is a double-edged sword. You can learn about the impact of your communication style on others by their reactions and profit from the wisdom of their intuitions. If you offend them, however, they tend to withdraw. As sharp communicators with strong psychic/intuitive edges, they may lead others out in conversation without really involving themselves in a personal way.

Thinking and feeling are closely aligned for Mercury in Cancer individuals. Despite the apparent detachment some of them cultivate as a defense, almost all that they say has some kind of emotional investment for them. They take in all levels of what you are saying in conversation and respond accordingly.

Mercury in Leo gives a dazzle and a shine to communications as well as a certain one-sidedness to interactions. The excitement of a Mercury in Leo individual's sharing some idea about which he or she is enthusiastic sparks the intellectual and emotional sensibilities. Sometimes, however, one may tire of hearing of the achievements of such an individual or any story that is so filled with excessive self-congratulatory airs that seem almost to negate the accomplishments of others. A certain inflexible, didactic, and dogmatic way of expression alternates with an entertaining, charming, and totally winning style that one could listen to and enjoy endlessly.

A fun sense of life—as well as language—makes for some remarkable and intriguing conversations with Leo Mercury people. Extroverts by nature, they may take a bit of time to warm up to new situations. Once into them, however, these individuals certainly know how to provide warmth, entertainment, and even inspiration to those with whom they interact.

The mental processes of Leo individuals usually start with "Well, what does this have to do with me?" in order to measure the worth of any interaction and just how much of the self Leo Mercury people need to invest in understanding and responding to it. These focused, purposeful individuals find a great satisfaction in the completion and appreciation of their thoughts and conversations as well as goals.

Mercury in Virgo indicates an awareness of and interest in the details that make up a situation, conversation, or thought. Though these individuals may seem a bit slow in responding to or comprehending what you say, they are really picking up on aspects even more exacting and detailed in what you are expressing than you yourself are likely to notice. You get a very thorough response when you ask these people questions.

As the ruler of the sign Mercury is at home in Virgo, where little things take on an importance all their own. These people truly believe that every particular aspect of life deserves attention, an attitude that centers them in the present, in the physical world to serve others best.

Virgo Mercury communicators may get mired in the practical aspects of reality, be less prone to go off on tangents, and be more likely to get into the how-to of things than most other individuals. Their awareness and ability to deal with mechanical things can be astounding—and quite a lifesaver—for fitting things together is part of the analytical nature of this kind of mind.

Those born with Mercury in Virgo use words with such exactitude that there is little ambiguity about their meaning. The only problem arises when you don't apply the same rules of perfection to your own communications.

Mercury in Libra denotes individuals whose prime concern in communication is making connections that foster harmony in relationships. Too often these may be people who let deeper feelings and truths slip by for that higher priority of peace in interaction. A conciliatory attitude or any kind of evasion of fact needs to be monitored. There is a sense of fairness in that they seldom dominate conversations. They may be too polite when *you* do to say so, but they are always able to hold their own. They often seem to have something nice or at least inoffensive to say which keeps the conversational ball rolling.

Libra Mercury individuals also tend to use words to make things better, lovelier, or easier to take. There is a kind of gentleness to the tones of those with this placement of Mercury, a way in which interaction is used truly to strengthen and beautify the bonds people have toward each other in relationships. The intent of these individuals is almost always, first, to promote good feelings between people, second, to communicate ideas or feelings.

The thought patterns of a Libra Mercury individual

may seem somewhat calculating in that they stem from the intention of propagating harmony among people. But with such positive motivation, what is the harm of a little bit of fiction mixed with fact?

Mercury in Scorpio can be an intensifying influence on the individual, manifested in a sharp, scathing, highly focused mentality. Interactions are very rarely of a light nature, nor are they usually detached or purely factual. The Scorpio influence on Mercury makes for a strongly felt undercurrent in interactions, so that even when the conversation seems to have little, if any, emotional content, something is going on under the surface.

There is rarely anything superficial going on in the mind of Mercury in Scorpio people—even concerning matters that don't seem to have much deeper significance. The seriousness and focus brought to bear upon ideas and interactions are matched only by the ability to penetrate the meaning of a situation and discern what is really being said underneath the words. Conversations with these people, therefore, are rarely boring and almost always impart some deeper insight to their listeners—about themselves, the Mercury in Scorpio people, or what is being discussed.

The mentality of these individuals brings a level of complexity, depth, and meaning to even the most superficial of subjects. Another aspect of Mercury in Scorpio people, aside from a scathing sense of black humor that even frightens some people away, is the power of Scorpio's silence.

Mercury in Sagittarius imparts a versatility and expansiveness to the mentality. The connections made are often general and perhaps superficial ones—offered to anyone who responds—with some philosophical ramifications which almost always engage someone in conversation. Spreading ideas is one of the activities at which these individuals feel most at home, so sharing information with others comes as second nature, as does putting others at ease in conversation. One may grow a bit tired of long-winded stories, but jokes, tidbits of juicy facts, humorous anecdotes, and assorted other ways of verbal sharing and fun are the forte of Sagittarius Mercury people. The ease and joy they impart in relating to others stem from their own enjoyment of friendly connections.

There may be a kind of slapdash quality, however, to how even important information is conveyed. Not the most organized of thinkers, Sagittarius Mercury types often miss a vital fact here or there—with such charm and wit that it is hard to pin them down to taking responsibility.

The mental outlook of these individuals is usually broadly philosophical. They take great delight in thinking and sharing, and their enthusiasm is readily imparted to their listeners. Mercury in Sagittarius people make great teachers, public speakers, or orators.

Mercury in Capricorn gives direction to the interactive focus of individuals, making for goal-oriented, factual, and dry manners of presentation. Small talk would be rather difficult for these people unless there were a lot of factual detail attached to a story that made it something solid to communicate, because real-life issues are the most comfortable subjects for conversation with Capricorn Mercury people. A certain seriousness pervades such interactions as well, the practical nature of the sign influencing how words get expressed, which are chosen, and what subjects will be discussed. You can totally rely on information from Mercury in Capricorn individuals, however, because they would be reluctant to impart less than accuracy, truthfulness, or verifiable information of a practical nature. You will not find a lot of emotional content in their interactions unless you are willing to look harder or plumb deeper. It's hard for these individuals even to touch on anything of an emotional nature because their factual, to-the-point natures often protect the deep and sensitive feelings hidden deep within.

The thinking process of a Capricorn in Mercury type is one of weeding out inessential thoughts so that there is little clutter, nothing to get in the way of the essentials of an interaction.

Mercury in Aquarius lends a touch of the offbeat to conversations and makes for fascinating interactions in which the focus is on other people. The Aquarian propensity for drawing others out and inspiring them to recognize their uniqueness is part of the motivation in any connections with an Aquarian Mercury type. Topics introduced range from factual situations or information to the most personal of emotional disclosures. These individuals are open to cultivating a conversation on any topic—as more of a supporter than participant, busy creating an environment wherein one feels that special attention one needs to recognize one's own particular importance and self-worth. As listeners Aquarians have an uncanny ability to focus. As communicators they can pick up on the most obscure aspects of an issue and elicit information or hold forth on it in most unusual ways.

The thought processes of Aquarians are erratic. At times they can match the depth of any other thinkers and even add to it with a particular gift of intuition. At other times their scan of a situation is rather superficial, catching all the details of a situation but missing the essential meaning, thereby distorting the whole thing. Emotional communication is difficult for Mercury in Aquarius individuals, as are comfortably knowing and experiencing their own negativity.

Mercury in Pisces imparts a magical quality to any interactions with such an individual. The intuitive way in which you are approached by this person meets you exactly where you are at that moment, drawing out whatever you need to say or share, putting you at ease with yourself, the conversation, and the person as well. It is often just the presence of the person that emanates a nonverbal acceptance and appreciation of your most sensitive inner self, allowing you to be and express any level of who you are.

A more difficult aspect of this placement of Mercury in Pisces is the individual's tendency to stick more to a global or inner truth about the temporal nature of reality than to the facts. In other words, despite an underlying consistency somewhat incomprehensible to the listener, on the surface of things this person seems constantly to change his or her mind. Though it may be the overwhelming emotional sensitivities of the Piscean Mercury person that makes for shifting awareness of what is important from moment to moment, there is difficulty in relying on any consistent opinion or reaction from one time to another.

This flexibility verging on variability of this person's mental focus is part of what causes the seeming inconsistencies in interactions. The mind of Pisces extends much farther than the bounds of any conversation, far beyond the facts and parameters of the present situation.

How to Find the Place of Mercury in Your Chart

Find your birth year in the left-hand column and read across the chart until you find your birth date. The top of that column will tell you where Mercury lies in your chart.

PLACE OF MERCURY—1880–1891

	ARIES	TAURUS	GEMINI	CANCER	LEO	VIRGO	LIBRA	SCORPIO	SAGITT.	CAPRI.	AQUAR.	PISCES
1880	3/5-5/11	5/12-5/27	5/28-6/10	6/11-6/27	6/28-9/3	9/4-9/19	9/20-10/7	10/8-10/29 11/25-12/12	1/10 10/30-11/24 12/13	1/11-1/30	1/31-2/16	2/17-3/4
1881	4/16-5/4	5/5-5/18	5/19-6/2	6/3-6/28 7/10-8/10	6/29-7/9 8/11-8/26	8/27-9/11	9/12-10/1	10/2-12/7	1/3 12/8-12/26	1/4-1/21 12/27	1/22-2/8	2/9-4/15
1882	4/10-4/26	4/27-5/10	5/11-5/28	5/29-8/3	8/4-8/18	8/19-9/4	9/5-9/27 10/23-11/10	9/28-10/22 11/11-11/30	12/1-12/19	1/14 12/20	1/15-2/1 2/26-3/17	2/2-2/25 3/18-4/9
1883	4/3-4/17	4/18-5/2	5/3-7/10	7/11-7/26	7/27-8/10	8/11-8/29	8/30-11/4	11/5-11/23	11/24-12/12	1/7 12/13	1/8-3/15	3/16-4/2
1884	3/26-4/8	4/9-4/30 5/13-6/13	5/1-5/12 6/14-7/2	7/3-7/16	7/17-8/2	8/3-8/25	8/26-9/16 10/10-10/27	9/17-10/9 10/28-11/15	11/16-12/4	1/21-2/14 12/5	1/2-1/20 2/15-3/7	3/8-3/24
1885	3/17-4/1	4/2-6/9	6/10-6/24	6/25-7/8	7/9-7/27	7/28-10/2	10/3-10/19	10/20-11/8	11/9-11/30 12/17	2/9 12/1-12/16	2/10-2/28	3/1-3/16
1886	3/9-5/15	5/16-6/1	6/2-6/15	6/16-7/1	7/2-7/28 8/7-9/8	7/29-8/6 9/9-9/24	9/25-10/12	10/13-11/1	11/2 12/17	1/13-2/3	2/4-2/20	2/21-3/8
1887	3/3-3/22 4/18-5/9	5/10-5/24	5/25-6/7	6/8-6/26	6/27-9/1	9/2-9/17	9/18-10/5	10/6-10/29 11/14-12/11	1/7 10/30-11/13 12/12-12/31	1/8-1/26	1/27-2/13	2/14-3/2 3/23-4/17
1888	4/14-4/30	5/1-5/14	5/15-5/30	5/31-8/7	8/8-8/22	8/23-9/8	9/9-9/28	9/29-12/4	12/5-12/23	1/1-1/19 12/24	1/20-2/5	2/6-4/13
1889	4/7-4/22	4/23-5/6	5/7-5/28 6/16-7/12	5/29-6/15 7/13-7/30	7/31-8/14	8/15-9/1	9/2-9/27 10/9-11/8	9/28-10/8 11/9-11/27	11/28-12/16	1/10 12/12	1/11-1/30 2/12-3/17	1/31-2/11 3/18-4/6
1890	3/31-4/13	4/14-4/30	5/1-7/1	7/2-7/22	7/23-8/6	8/7-8/26	8/27-11/1	11/2-11/19	11/20-12/9	1/4 12/10	1/5-3/12	3/13-3/30
1891	3/22-4/5	4/6-6/13	6/14-6/29	6/30-7/13	7/14-7/30	7/31-10/7	10/8-10/24	10/25-11/12	11/13-12/2	1/7-2/13 12/3	1/2-1/6 2/14-3/5	3/6-3/21

PLACE OF MERCURY—1892-1905

Year												
1892	3/13-3/30 4/20-5/15	3/31-4/19 5/16-6/5	5/29-6/11	6/6-6/20	7/5-7/25 8/30-9/9	7/26-8/29 9/10-9/29	9/30-10/16	10/17-11/4	1/3-1/13 11/5	1/2 1/14-2/7	2/8-2/25	2/26-3/12
1893	3/6-5/12	5/13-5/28	5/29-6/11	6/12-6/28	6/29-9/5	9/6-9/21	9/22-10/9	10/10-10/30 11/30-12/12	1/10 10/31-11/29 12/13-12/31	1/11-1/30	1/31-2/17	2/18-3/5
1894	4/17-5/5	5/6-5/20	5/21-6/3	6/4-6/26 7/18-8/10	6/27-7/17 8/11-8/28	8/29-9/13	9/14-10/2	10/3-12/8	1/1-1/4 12/9-12/28	1/5-1/23 12/29	1/24-2/9	2/10-4/16
1895	4/12-4/27	4/28-5/11	5/12-5/28	5/29-8/5	8/6-8/20	8/21-9/5	9/6-9/27	9/28-10/27 11/12-12/1	10/28-11/11 12/2-12/21	1/15 12/22	1/16-2/2 3/4-3/16	2/3-3/3 3/17-4/11
1896	4/4-4/18	4/19-5/3	5/4-7/10	7/11-7/26	7/27-8/10	8/11-8/29	8/30-11/4	11/5-11/23	11/24-12/12	1/8 12/13	1/9-3/15	3/16-4/3
1897	3/27-4/9	4/10-4/29 5/22-6/12	4/30-5/21 6/13-7/4	7/5-7/18	7/19-8/3	8/4-8/25 9/22-10/10	8/26-9/21 10/11-10/28	10/29-11/16	11/17-12/6	1/1 1/25-2/14 12/7	1/2-1/24 2/15-3/9	3/10-3/26
1898	3/19-4/2	4/3-6/10	6/11-6/25	6/26-7/10	7/11-7/27	7/28-10/4	10/5-10/21	10/22-11/9	11/10-11/30 12/22	2/10 12/1-12/21	2/11-3/1	3/2-3/18
1899	3/11-5/15	5/16-6/3	6/4-6/17	6/18-7/2	7/3-7/26	7/27-8/14 9/10-9/26	8/15-9/9 9/27-10/13	10/14-11/2	1/13 11/3	1/14-2/4	2/5-2/22	2/23-3/10
1900	3/4-3/29	3/30-4/16 5/11-5/25	4/17-5/10 5/26-6/8	6/9-6/26	6/27-9/2	9/3-9/18	9/19-10/6	10/7-10/29 11/19-12/12	1/8 10/30-11/18 12/13	1/9-1/28	1/29-2/14	2/15-3/3
1901	4/16-5/3	5/4-5/17	5/18-6/1	6/2-8/9	8/10-8/25	8/26-9/10	9/11-9/30	10/1-10/6	1/2 12/7-12/25	1/3-1/20 12/26	1/21-2/6	2/7-4/15
1902	4/9-4/24	4/25-5/9	5/10-5/28 6/26-7/12	5/29-6/25 7/13-8/2	8/3-8/17	8/18-9/3	9/4-9/27 10/16-11/10	9/28-10/15 11/11-11/29	11/30-12/18	1/13 12/19	1/14-2/1 2/19-3/18	2/2-2/18 3/19-4/8
1903	4/2-4/16	4/17-5/2	5/3-7/10	7/11-7/25	7/26-8/9	8/10-8/29	8/30-11/3	11/4-11/22	11/23-12/11	1/6 12/12	1/7-3/14	3/15-4/1
1904	3/24-4/7	4/8-6/13	6/14-7/1	7/2-7/15	7/16-8/1	8/2-8/27 9/8-10/8	8/28-9/7 10/9-10/26	10/27-11/14	11/15-12/4	1/1 1/14-2/14 12/5	1/2-1/13 2/15-3/6	3/7-3/23
1905	3/16-4/1 4/29-5/15	4/2-4/28 5/16-6/8	6/9-6/22	6/23-7/7	7/8-7/26	7/27-10/1	10/2-10/18	10/19-11/7	11/8-12/1 12/10	2/8 12/2-12/29	2/9-2/27	2/28-3/15

PLACE OF MERCURY—1906-1917

	ARIES	TAURUS	GEMINI	CANCER	LEO	VIRGO	LIBRA	SCORPIO	SAGITT.	CAPRI.	AQUAR.	PISCES
1906	3/8-5/14	5/15-5/31	6/1-6/14	6/15-6/30	7/1-9/7	9/8-9/23	9/24-10/11	10/12-11/1 12/7-12/12	1/12 11/2-12/6 12/13	1/13-2/1	2/2-2/19	2/20-3/7
1907	3/4-3/13 4/18-5/8	5/9-5/22	5/23-6/6	6/7-6/26 7/27-8/12	6/27-7/26 8/13-8/30	8/31-9/15	9/16-10/4	10/5-12/10	4/6 12/11-12/30	1/7-1/25 12/31	1/26-2/11	2/12-3/3 3/14-4/17
1908	4/13-4/29	4/30-5/13	5/14-5/29	5/30-8/6	8/7-8/21	8/22-9/11	9/8-9/28 11/2-11/11	9/29-11/1 11/12-12/13	12/4-12/22	1/18 12/23	1/19-2/4	2/5-4/12
1909	4/6-4/20	4/21-5/5	5/6-7/12	7/13-7/29	7/30-8/13	8/14-8/31	9/1-11/7	11/8-11/26	11/27-12/15	1/9 12/16	1/10-3/16	3/17-4/5
1910	3/29-4/12	4/13-4/30 6/2-6/11	5/1-6/1 6/12-7/6	7/7-7/21	7/22-8/5	8/6-8/26 9/29-10/11	8/27-9/28 10/12-10/31	11/1-11/18	11/19-12/8	1/3 1/31-2/15 12/9	1/4-1/30 2/16-3/11	3/12-3/25
1911	3/21-4/4	4/5-6/12	6/13-6/28	6/29-7/12	7/13-7/30	7/31-10/6	10/7-10/23	10/24-11/11	11/12-12/2 12/28	2/12 12/3-12/27	2/13-3/4	3/5-3/20
1912	3/12-5/16	5/17-6/4	6/5-6/18	6/19-7/3	7/4-7/25 8/21-9/10	7/26-8/20 9/11-9/27	9/28-10/15	10/16-11/4	1/14 11/5	1/15-2/6	2/7-2/24	2/25-3/11
1913	3/5-4/7 4/14-5/11	5/12-5/27	5/28-6/10	6/11-6/27	6/28-9/3	9/4-9/19	9/20-10/8	10/9-10/30 11/24-12/12	1/9 10/31-11/23 12/13	1/10-1/29	1/30-2/15	2/16-3/4 4/8-4/13
1914	4/17-5/4	5/5-5/18	5/19-6/2	6/3-8/10	8/11-8/26	8/27-9/12	9/13-10/1	10/2-12/7	1/3 12/8-12/27	1/4-1/22 12/28	1/23-2/8	2/9-4/16
1915	4/11-4/26	4/27-5/10	5/11-5/28	5/29-8/3	8/4-8/18	8/19-9/4	9/5-9/27 10/21-11/11	9/28-10/20 11/12-11/30	12/1-12/19	1/14 12/20	1/15-2/1 2/24-3/19	2/2-2/28 3/20-4/10
1916	4/2-4/16	4/17-5/2	5/3-7/10	7/11-7/25	7/26-8/9	8/10-8/28	8/29-11/4	11/5-11/22	11/23-12/11	1/7 12/12	1/8-3/14	3/15-4/1
1917	3/25-4/8	4/9-6/14	6/15-7/2	7/3-7/17	7/18-8/2	8/3-8/26 9/15-10/9	8/27-9/14 10/10-10/27	10/28-11/15	11/16-12/5	1/1 1/10-2/14 12/6-12/31	1/2-1/17 2/15-3/8	3/9-3/24

PLACE OF MERCURY—1918-1931

Year												
1918	3/17-4/2	4/3-6/9	6/10-6/24	6/25-7/8	7/9-7/27	7/26-10/2	10/3-10/20	10/21-11/8	11/9-12/1 ℞12/16	1/1-2/9 12/2-12/15	2/10-2/28	3/1-3/16
1919	3/9-5/15	5/16-6/1	6/2-6/15	6/16-7/1	7/2-9/8	9/9-9/25	9/26-10/12	10/13-11/2	11/3 ℞11/13	1/14-2/3	2/4-2/21	2/22-3/8
1920	3/3-3/19 4/18-5/8	5/9-5/23	5/24-6/6	6/7-6/26 8/3-8/9	6/27-8/2 8/10-8/31	9/1-9/16	9/17-10/4	10/5-10/30 11/11-12/10	℞10/31-11/10 12/11-12/30	1/8-1/27 12/31	1/28-2/13	2/14-3/2 3/20-4/17
1921	4/14-4/30	5/1-5/14	5/15-5/30	5/31-8/7	8/8-8/23	8/24-9/8	9/9-9/29	9/30-12/4	12/5-12/23	1/1-1/18 12/24-12/31	1/19-2/4	2/5-4/13
1922	4/7-4/22	4/23-5/6	5/7-5/30 6/11-7/13	5/31-6/10 7/14-7/31	8/1-8/14	8/15-9/1	9/2-9/30 10/5-11/8	10/1-10/4 11/9-11/27	11/28-12/16	℞1/11 12/17	1/12-2/1 2/9-3/17	2/2-2/28 3/18-4/6
1923	3/31-4/14	4/15-4/30	5/1-7/8	7/9-7/22	7/23-8/7	8/8-8/27 10/4-10/11	8/28-10/3 10/12-11/1	11/2-11/20	11/21-12/9	℞1/4 2/7-2/13 12/10	1/5-26 2/14-3/12	3/13-3/20
1924	3/22-4/5	4/6-6/12	6/13-6/29	6/30-7/13	7/14-7/30	7/31-10/6	10/7-10/24	10/25-11/11	11/12-12/2	1/1-1/13 12/3-12/31	2/14-3/4	2/26-3/13
1925	3/14-4/1 4/16-5/16	4/2-4/15 5/17-6/6	6/7-6/20	6/21-7/5	7/6-7/25 8/27-9/10	7/26-8/26 9/11-9/29	9/30-10/16	10/17-11/3	1/1-1/13 ℞11/6	1/14-2/6	2/7-2/25	2/26-3/13
1926	3/6-5/12	5/13-5/29	5/30-6/11	6/12-6/28	6/29-9/5	9/6-9/21	9/22-10/9	10/10-10/30 11/28-12/12	℞10/31-11/27 12/13-12/31	1/5-1/23 12/29	1/24-2/9	2/10-4/17
1927	4/18-5/5	5/6-5/20	5/21-6/4	6/5-6/28 7/14-8/11	6/29-7/13 8/12-8/28	8/29-9/13	9/14-10/2	10/3-12/8	12/9-12/28	1/1-1/16 12/29	1/17-2/2 2/29-3/17	2/3-2/28 3/18-4/10
1928	4/11-4/26	4/27-5/10	5/11-5/28	5/29-8/4	8/5-8/19	8/20-9/5	9/6-9/27 10/25-11/11	9/28-10/24 11/12-12/1	12/2-12/20	℞1/14 12/21	1/8-3/15	3/16-4/3
1929	4/4-4/18	4/19-5/3	5/4-7/11	7/12-7/27	7/28-8/11	8/12-8/29	8/30-11/5	11/6-11/23	11/24-12/13	℞1/1 12/14	1/23-2/15	1/8-3/15
1930	3/27-4/10	4/11-4/30 5/17-6/14	5/1-5/16 6/15-7/4	7/5-7/18	7/19-8/3	8/4-8/26 9/20-10/10	8/27-9/19 10/11-10/29	10/30-11/16	11/17-12/6	℞1/1 1/23-2/15 12/17	1/2-1/22 2/16-3/9	3/10-3/26
1931	3/19-4/3	4/4-6/10	6/11-6/26	6/27-7/10	7/11-7/28	7/29-10/4	10/5-10/21	10/22-11/9	11/10-12/1 ℞12/20	12/2-12/19	2/12-3/2	3/3-3/18

PLACE OF MERCURY—1932-1943

	ARIES	TAURUS	GEMINI	CANCER	LEO	VIRGO	LIBRA	SCORPIO	SAGITT.	CAPRI.	AQUAR.	PISCES
1932	3/10-5/15	5/16-6/2	6/3-6/16	6/17-7/1	7/2-7/27 8/10-9/8	7/28-8/9 9/9-9/25	9/26-10/13	10/14-11/2	↑1/14 11/3	1/15-2/4	2/5-2/22	2/23-3/9
1933	3/3-3/25 4/18-5/9	5/10-5/25	5/26-6/8	6/9-6/26	6/27-9/1	9/2-9/17	9/18-10/6	10/7-10/29 11/16-12/11	↑1/7 10/30-11/15 12/12	1/8-1/27	1/28-2/13	2/14-3/2 3/26-4/17
1934	4/15-5/2	5/3-5/16	5/17-5/31	6/1-8/9	8/10-8/24	8/25-9/9	9/10-9/30	10/1-12/5	↑1/1 12/6-12/25	1/2-1/19 12/26	1/20-2/6	2/7-4/14
1935	4/9-4/24	4/25-5/8	5/9-5/29 6/21-7/13	5/30-6/20 7/14-8/1	8/2-8/16	8/17-9/2	9/3-9/28 10/13-11/9	9/29-10/12 11/10-11/28	11/29-12/17	↑1/12 12/18	1/13-1/31 2/15-3/18	2/1-2/14 3/19-4/8
1936	3/31-4/14	4/15-4/30	5/1-7/8	7/9-7/23	7/24-8/7	8/8-8/27	8/28-11/1	11/2-11/20	11/21-12/9	↑1/3 12/10	1/6-3/12	3/13-3/30
1937	3/23-4/6	4/7-6/13	6/14-6/30	7/1-7/14	7/15-7/31	8/1-10/7	10/8-10/25	10/26-11/13	11/14-12/3	↑1/1 1/18-2/13 12/4	1/2-1/9 2/14-3/6	3/7-3/22
1938	3/15-4/1 4/24-5/16	4/2-4/23 5/17-6/8	6/9-6/22	6/23-7/6	7/7-7/26 9/3-9/10	7/27-9/2 9/11-9/30	10/1-10/18	10/19-11/6	↑1/7 1/7-1/12 11/7	↑1/6 1/13-2/8	2/9-2/26	2/27-3/14
1939	3/7-5/14	5/15-5/30	5/31-6/13	6/14-6/29	6/30-9/6	9/7-9/22	9/23-10/10	10/11-10/31 12/3-12/13	↑1/1 11/1-12/2 12/14	1/12-2/1	2/2-2/18	2/19-3/6
1940	3/4-3/7 4/17-5/6	5/7-5/21	5/22-6/4	6/5-6/26 7/21-8/11	6/27-7/20 8/12-8/28	8/29-9/13	9/14-10/2	10/3-12/9	↑1/5 12/10-12/28	1/6-1/24 12/29	1/25-2/11	2/12-3/3 3/8-4/16
1941	4/12-4/28	4/29-5/12	5/13-5/29	5/30-8/5	8/6-8/20	8/21-9/6	9/7-9/27 10/30-11/11	9/28-10/29 11/12-12/2	12/3-12/21	↑1/6 12/22	1/17-2/3 3/7-3/15	2/4-3/6 3/16-4/11
1942	4/5-4/20	4/21-5/4	5/5-7/12	7/13-7/28	7/29-8/12	8/13-8/30	8/31-11/6	11/7-11/25	11/26-12/14	↑1/9 12/15	1/10-3/16	3/17-4/4
1943	3/28-4/11	4/12-4/30 5/26-6/13	5/1-5/25 6/14-7/5	7/6-7/20	7/21-8/4	8/5-8/26 9/25-10/11	8/27-9/24 10/12-10/30	10/31-11/18	11/19-12/7	↑1/2 1/28-2/15 12/8	1/3-1/27 2/16-3/10	3/11-3/27

PLACE OF MERCURY—1944-1958

Year												
1944	3/19-4/3	4/4-6/10	6/11-6/26	6/27-7/10	7/11-7/28	7/29-10/4	10/5-10/21	10/22-11/9	11/10-12/1, 12/23	2/12, 12/2-12/22	2/13-3/2	3/3-3/18
1945	3/11-5/16	5/17-6/3	6/4-6/18	6/19-7/3	7/4-7/26, 8/18-9/9	7/27-8/17, 9/10-9/27	9/28-10/13	10/14-11/3	11/4-12/31, 1/13	1/14-2/4	2/5-2/22	2/23-3/10
1946	3/4-4/1, 4/17-5/11	5/12-5/26	5/27-6/9	6/10-6/27	6/28-9/3	9/4-9/19	9/20-10/7	10/8-10/29, 11/21-12/12	10/30-11/20, 12/13	1/10-1/28	1/29-2/15	2/16-3/3, 4/2-4/16
1947	4/16-5/3	5/4-5/18	5/19-6/2	6/3-8/10	8/11-8/26	8/27-9/10	9/11-10/1	10/2-12/7	12/8-12/26, 1/1	1/2-1/20, 12/27	1/21-2/7	2/8-4/15
1948	4/9-4/24	4/25-5/8	5/9-5/27, 6/29-7/11	5/28-6/28, 7/12-8/2	8/3-8/16	8/17-9/3	9/4-9/26, 10/17-11/9	9/27-10/16, 11/10-11/29	11/30-12/18, 1/13	1/13, 12/19	1/14-2/1, 2/20-3/17	2/2-2/19, 3/18-4/8
1949	4/2-4/16	4/17-5/1	5/2-7/9	7/10-7/24	7/25-8/8	8/9-8/28	8/29-11/3	11/4-11/21	11/22-12/11	1/5, 12/12	1/6-3/13	3/14-4/1
1950	3/25-4/7	4/8-6/14	6/15-7/2	7/3-7/16	7/17-8/1	8/2-8/27, 9/10-10/9	8/28-9/9, 10/10-10/26	10/27-11/14	11/15-12/4	1/1, 12/5-12/31	1/2-1/14, 2/15-3/7	3/8-3/24
1951	3/17-4/2, 5/2-5/15	4/3-5/1, 5/16-6/9	6/10-6/24	6/25-7/8	7/9-7/27	7/28-10/2	10/3-10/19	10/20-11/8	11/9-12/1, 12/13	1/1-1/29, 12/2-12/12	2/10-2/28	3/1-3/16
1952	3/8-5/14	5/15-5/31	6/1-6/14	6/15-6/30	7/1-9/7	9/8-9/23	9/24-10/11	10/12-11/1	11/2, 1/13	1/14-2/3	2/4-2/20	2/21-3/7
1953	3/3-3/15, 4/18-5/8	5/9-5/23	5/24-6/6	6/7-6/26, 7/29-8/11	6/27-7/28, 8/12-8/30	8/31-9/15	9/16-10/4	10/5-10/31, 11/7-12/10	11/1-11/6, 12/11-12/30, 1/6	1/7-1/25, 12/31	1/26-2/11	2/12-3/2, 3/16-4/17
1954	4/14-4/30	5/1-5/14	5/15-5/30	5/31-8/7	8/8-8/22	8/23-9/8	9/9-9/29, 11/5-11/11	9/30-11/4, 11/12-12/4	12/5-12/23	1/18, 12/24	1/19-2/4	2/5-4/13
1955	4/7-4/22	4/23-5/6	5/7-7/13	7/14-7/30	7/31-8/14	8/15-9/1	9/2-11/8	11/9-11/27	11/28-12/16	1/10, 12/17	1/11-3/17	3/18-4/6
1956	3/29-4/12	4/13-4/29	4/30-7/6	7/7-7/21	7/22-8/5	8/6-8/26, 9/30-10/11	8/27-9/29, 10/12-10/31	11/1-11/18	11/19-12/8	1/4, 12/9	2/3-2/15	3/12-3/28
1957	3/21-4/4	4/5-6/12	6/13-6/28	6/29-7/12	7/13-7/30	7/31-10/6	10/7-10/23	10/24-11/11	11/12-12/2, 12/29	2/12, 12/3-12/28	2/13-3/4	3/5-3/20
1958	3/13-4/2, 4/11-5/17	4/3-4/10, 5/18-6/5	6/6-6/20	6/21-7/4	7/5-7/26, 8/24-9/11	7/27-8/23, 9/12-9/28	9/29-10/16	10/17-11/5	11/6, 1/14	1/15-2/6	2/7-2/24	2/25-3/12

PLACE OF MERCURY—1959–1969

	ARIES	TAURUS	GEMINI	CANCER	LEO	VIRGO	LIBRA	SCORPIO	SAGITT.	CAPRI.	AQUAR.	PISCES
1959	3/6-5/12	5/13-5/28	5/29-6/11	6/12-6/28	6/29-9/5	9/6-9/21	9/22-10/9	10/10-10/31 11/26-12/13	↰1/10 11/1-11/25 12/14↰	1/11-1/30	1/31-2/17	2/18-3/5
1960	4/17-5/4	5/5-5/19	5/20-6/2	6/3-7/1 7/7-8/10	7/2-7/6 8/11-8/27	8/28-9/12	9/13-10/1	10/2-12/7	↰1/4 12/8-12/27	1/5-1/23 12/28-12/31	1/24-2/9	2/10-4/16
1961	4/10-4/25	4/26-5/9	5/10-5/27	5/28-8/3	8/4-8/17	8/18-9/3	9/4-9/26 10/22-11/9	9/27-10/21 11/10-11/29	11/30-12/19	1/1-1/13 12/20↰	1/14-1/31 2/24-3/17	2/1-2/23 3/18-4/9
1962	4/3-4/17	4/18-5/2	5/3-7/10	7/11-7/25	7/26-8/9	8/10-8/28	8/29-11/4	11/5-11/22	11/23-12/11	↰1/6 12/12↰	1/7-3/14	3/15-4/2
1963	3/26-4/8	4/9-5/2 5/10-6/13	5/3-5/9 6/14-7/3	7/4-7/17	7/18-8/2	8/3-8/25 9/16-10/9	8/26-9/15 10/10-10/27	10/28-11/15	11/16-12/5	1/1 1/20-2/14 12/6↰	1/2-1/19 2/15-3/8	3/9-3/25
1964	3/16-4/1	4/2-4/16	4/17-7/8	7/9-7/23	7/24-8/7	8/8-10/3	10/4-10/19	10/20-11/7	11/8-11/29 12/16↰	↰2/9 11/30-12/15	2/10-2/28	2/29-3/15
1965	3/9-5/14	5/15-6/1	6/2-6/15	6/16-6/30	7/1-7/30 8/3-9/7	7/31-8/2 9/8-9/24	9/25-10/11	10/12-11/1	↰1/6 11/2↰	1/7-2/2	2/3-2/20	2/21-3/8
1966	3/3-3/21 4/17-5/8	5/9-5/23	5/24-6/6	6/7-6/25	6/26-8/31	9/1-9/16	9/17-10/4	10/5-10/29 11/13-12/10	↰1/6 10/30-11/12 12/11↰	1/7-1/26	1/27-2/12	2/13-3/2 3/22-4/16
1967	4/14-4/30	5/1-5/15	5/16-5/30	5/31-8/7	8/8-8/23	8/24-9/8	9/9-9/29	9/30-12/4	12/5-12/23	1/1-1/18 12/24↰	1/19-2/5	2/6-4/13
1968	4/7-4/21	4/22-5/5	5/6-5/28 6/13-7/12	5/29-6/12 7/13-7/30	7/31-8/14	8/15-8/31	9/1-9/27 10/9-11/7	9/28-10/8 11/8-11/26	11/27-12/15	↰1/11 12/16↰	1/12-1/31 2/11-3/16	2/1-2/10 3/17-4/6
1969	3/30-4/13	4/14-4/29	4/30-7/7	7/8-7/21	7/22-8/6	8/7-8/26 10/7-10/8	8/27-10/6 10/9-10/31	11/1-11/19	11/20-12/8	↰1/3 12/9↰	1/4-3/11	3/12-3/29

PLACE OF MERCURY—1970—1980

1970	3/22-4/5	4/6-6/12	6/13-6/29	6/30-7/13	7/14-7/30	7/31-10/6	10/7-10/24	10/25-11/12	11/13-12/2	←2/12 12/3-12/31	2/13-3/4	3/5-3/21
1971	3/14-3/31 4/18-5/16	4/1-4/17 5/17-6/6	6/7-6/20	6/21-7/5	7/6-7/25 8/29-9/10	7/26-8/28 9/11-9/29	9/30-10/16	10/17-11/5	1/2-1/13 11/6←	1/1 1/14-2/6	2/7-2/25	2/26-3/13
1972	3/5-5/11	5/12-5/28	5/29-6/11	6/12-6/27	6/28-9/4	9/5-9/20	9/21-10/8	10/9-10/29 11/29-12/11	10/30-11/28	←1/10 12/12-12/31	1/31-2/17	2/18-3/4
1973	4/16-5/5	5/6-5/19	5/20-6/3	6/4-6/26 7/16-8/10	6/27-7/15 8/11-8/27	8/28-9/12	9/13-10/1	10/2-12/7	12/8-12/27	←1/3 12/28-12/31	1/23-2/8	2/9-4/15
1974	4/11-4/27	4/28-5/11	5/12-5/28	5/29-8/4	8/5-8/19	9/6-9/27 10/26-11/10	9/28-10/25 11/11-12/1	11/6-11/24	12/2-12/20	←1/15 12/21-12/31	1/16-2/1 3/2-3/16	2/2-3/1 3/17-4/10
1975	4/5-4/18	4/19-5/3	5/4-7/11	7/12-7/27	7/28-8/11	8/12-8/29	8/30-11/5	11/6-11/24	11/25-12/13	←1/7 12/14-12/31	1/8-3/15	3/16-4/3
1976	3/26-4/9	4/10-4/28 5/19-6/12	4/29-5/18 6/13-7/3	7/4-7/17	7/18-8/2	8/3-8/24 9/21-10/9	8/25-9/20 10/10-10/28	10/29-11/15	11/16-12/5	←1/1 12/6-12/31	1/2-1/24 2/15-3/8	3/9-3/25
1977	3/18-4/2	4/3-6/9	6/10-6/25	6/26-7/9	7/10-7/27	7/28-10/3	10/4-10/20	10/21-11/8	11/9-11/30	←1/12 12/1-12/20	2/10-3/1	3/2-3/17
1978	3/10-5/15	5/16-6/2	6/3-6/16	6/17-7/1	7/2-7/26 8/13-9/8	7/27-8/12 9/9-9/25	9/26-10/13	10/14-11/2	11/3-11/21	←1/17 12/12-12/31	2/4-2/21	2/22-3/9
1979	3/3-3/27 4/17-5/9	5/10-5/25	5/26-6/8	6/9-6/26	6/27-9/1	9/2-9/17	9/18-10/6	10/7-10/29 11/18-12/11	10/30-11/17 12/12←	←1/12	1/28-2/13	2/14-3/2 3/28-4/16
1980	4/14-5/1	5/2-5/15	5/16-5/30	5/31-8/8	8/9-8/23	8/24-9/9	9/10-9/29	9/30-12/4	12/5-12/24	←1/1 12/25-12/31	1/21-2/6	2/7-4/13

PLACE OF MERCURY—1981–1987

	ARIES	TAURUS	GEMINI	CANCER	LEO	VIRGO	LIBRA	SCORPIO	SAGITT.	CAPRI.	AQUAR.	PISCES
1981	4/8-4/23	4/24-5/7	5/8-5/27 6/22-7/11	5/28-6/21 7/12-7/31	8/1-8/15	8/16-9/1	9/2-9/26 10/13-11/8	9/27-10/12 11/9-11/27	11/28-12/16	1/1-1/11 12/17	1/12-1/30 2/16-3/16	1/31-2/15 3/17-4/7
1982	3/31-4/14	4/15-4/30	5/1-7/8	7/9-7/23	7/24-8/7	8/8-8/26	8/27-11/1	11/2-11/20	11/21-12/9	⌐1/4 12/10-12/31	1/5-3/12	3/13-3/30
1983	3/23-4/6	4/7-6/13	6/14-6/30	7/1-7/14	7/15-7/31	8/1-8/28 9/5-10/7	8/29-9/4 10/8-10/25	10/26-11/13	11/14-12/3	1/12-2/13 12/4⌐	1/1-1/11 2/14-3/5	3/6-3/22
1984	3/14-3/30 4/25-5/16	3/31-4/24 5/15-6/6	6/7-6/21	6/22-7/5	7/6-7/25	7/26-9/29	9/30-10/16	10/17-11/5	11/6-11/30 12/7⌐	⌐2/7 12/1-12/6	2/8-2/26	2/27-3/13
1985	3/6-5/12	5/13-5/29	5/30-6/12	6/13-6/28	6/29-9/5	9/6-9/21	9/22-10/9	10/10-10/30 12/4-12/11	⌐1/10 10/31-12/3 12/12⌐	1/11-1/31	2/1-2/17	2/18-3/5
1986	3/3-3/10 4/17-5/6	5/7-5/21	5/22-6/4	6/5-6/25 7/23-8/10	6/26-7/22 8/11-8/28	8/29-9/13	9/14-10/2	10/13-12/8	⌐1/4 12/9-12/28	1/5-1/23 12/29⌐	1/24-2/10	2/11-3/2 3/11-4/16
1987	4/12-4/28	4/29-5/12	5/13-5/28	5/29-8/5	8/6-8/20	8/21-9/6	9/7-9/27 10/31-11/10	9/28-10/30 11/11-11/22	12/3-12/21	⌐1/16 12/22⌐	1/17-2/2 3/11-3/12	2/3-3/10 3/13-4/11

Year												
1988	4/4-4/19	4/20-5/3	5/4-7/11	7/12-7/27	7/28-8/11	8/12-8/29	8/30-11/5	11/6-11/24	11/25-12/13	12/14 ↰1/9	1/10-3/15	3/16-4/3
1989	3/27-4/10	4/11-4/28 / 5/28-6/11	4/29-5/27 / 6/12-7/4	7/5-7/19	7/20-8/3	8/4-8/25 / 9/26-10/10	8/26-9/25 / 10/11-10/29	10/30-11/16	11/17-12/6	1/28-2/13 / 12/7 ↰1/1	1/2-1/27 / 2/14-3/9	3/10-3/26
1990	3/19-4/3	4/4-6/10	6/11-6/26	6/27-7/10	7/11-7/28	7/29-10/4	10/5-10/21	10/22-11/9	11/10-11/30 / 12/25 ↰1/13	12/11-12/24 ↰2/10	2/11-3/2	3/3-3/18
1991	3/11-4/15	4/16-6/3	6/4-6/18	6/19-7/3	7/4-7/25 / 8/19-9/9	7/26-8/18 / 9/10-9/26	9/27-10/14	10/15-11/3	11/4 ↰1/13	1/14-2/4	2/5-2/22	2/23-3/10
1992	3/3-4/2 / 4/14-5/9	5/10-5/25	5/26-6/8	6/9-6/26	6/27-9/2	9/3-9/18	9/19-10/6	10/7-10/28 / 11/21-12/11	10/29-11/20 / 12/12 ↰1/8	1/9-1/28	1/29-2/15	2/16-3/2 / 4/3-4/13
1993	4/15-5/2	5/3-5/17	5/18-5/31	6/1-8/9	8/10-8/25	8/26-9/10	9/11-9/29	9/30-12/5	12/6-12/25 ↰1/1	1/2-1/20 / 12/26 ↰1/1	1/21-2/6	2/7-4/14
1994	4/9-4/24	4/25-5/8	5/9-5/27 / 7/2-7/9	5/28-7/1 / 7/10-8/2	8/3-8/16	8/17-9/2	9/3-9/26 / 10/19-11/9	9/27-10/18 / 11/10-11/28	11/29-12/18	12/19 ↰1/12	1/13-3/17	3/18-4/8
1995	4/2-4/16	4/17-5/1	5/2-7/9	7/10-7/24	7/25-8/8	8/9-8/27	8/28-11/3	11/4-11/21	11/22-12/10	12/11-12/31 ↰1/5	1/6-3/13	3/14-4/1
1996	3/24-4/6	4/7-6/12	6/13-7/1	7/2-7/15	7/16-7/31	8/1-8/25 / 9/12-10/7	8/26-9/11 / 10/8-10/25	10/26-11/13	11/14-12/3	1/17-2/13 / 12/4 ↰2/4	1/1-1/16 / 2/14-3/6	3/7-3/23
1997	3/15-3/31	4/1-6/7	6/8-6/22	6/23-7/7	7/8-7/25	7/26-10/1	10/2-10/18	10/19-11/6	11/7-11/29 / 12/13 ↰1/11	11/30-12/12	2/9-2/26	2/27-3/14
1998	3/8-5/13	5/14-5/31	6/1-6/14	6/15-6/29	6/30-9/6	9/7-9/23	9/24-10/10	10/11-10/31	11/1 ↰1/11	1/12-2/1	2/2-2/19	2/20-3/7
1999	3/2-3/17 / 4/17-5/7	5/8-5/22	5/23-6/5	6/6-6/25 / 7/31-8/9	6/26-7/30 / 8/10-8/30	8/31-9/15	9/16-10/4	10/5-10/29 / 11/9-12/9	10/30-11/8 / 12/10-12/30	1/6-1/25 / 12/31 ↰1/17	1/26-2/11	2/12-3/1 / 3/18-4/16
2000	4/12-4/28	4/29-5/13	5/14-5/28	5/29-8/6	8/7-8/21	8/22-9/6	9/7-9/27 / 11/7-11/7	9/28-11/6 / 11/8-12/2	12/3-12/21	12/22-12/31 ↰1/17	1/18-2/4	2/5-4/11

YOUR MOST FREQUENT FAULT: ARIES—Haste; TAURUS—Stubbornness; GEMINI—Loquaciousness; CANCER—Inattention; LEO—Boastfulness; VIRGO—Timidity; LIBRA—Vanity; SCORPIO—Lack of sympathy; SAGITTARIUS—Sarcasm; CAPRICORN—Curiosity; AQUARIUS—Procrastination; PISCES—Self-immolation.

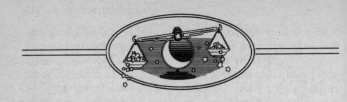

VENUS: LOVE AND ATTRACTION

Venus indicates how successfully (or perhaps unsuccessfully) your ego, emotions, and intellect are integrated to form your social attitudes and responses to other people, in your public as well as private relationships. Venus indicates what things you are likely to value and what you do not value, what you think is acceptable and adds to the quality of your life as well as what things are not acceptable and are to be avoided. It suggests the potential of your financial status and your luck in general.

Venus in Aries. You have a tendency to embrace enthusiastically relationships of all kinds for the sheer joy of energetic circulation. Unfortunately your penchant for undue haste when dealing with others can sometimes be interpreted as rudeness though you may have meant it as a sign of your passionate interest. You are friendly and, most of the time, attractively uncomplicated. Though you are not always discriminating in your values and relationships, your open eagerness is inspiring and contagious to those with shyer personalities, and even those who like to think they are superior may be attracted in spite of themselves to your guileless pursuit of their attentions. In some instances your lack of discrimination is more a case of not wanting to take the necessary time to make proper evaluations. You're not likely to seek a peaceful or mundane existence, preferring to be active and among people to find inspiration. Social groups you happen to be in are always a little livelier for your presence, and if you do happen to find yourself in a less than stimulating atmosphere and cannot do anything to animate this slow-moving society, you simply lose interest in the company. In more personal relationships your restlessness and impatience must be controlled, and you must learn to allow relationships to grow at their own pace, not at one that you dictate. You are an enthusiastic lover but can be very careless of your partner's feelings. Sometimes it is better to wait and find out what is wanted than to rush ahead and overwhelm others with what you think they need.

Venus in Taurus. You probably aren't the kind of person who rushes around in a social gathering slapping everyone on the back, spouting one-liners or the latest gossip. In fact, you are not likely to be very glib or talkative unless other factors in your natal chart support such behavior. You genuinely enjoy the society of others but most of the time prefer to keep a low but friendly profile. You have a somewhat pragmatic streak when it comes to other people and thus have a tendency consciously or subconsciously to make practical use of your social connections. However, your affections for the most part are deep and sincere. Friendships you establish usually last a lifetime unless a friend demonstrates serious reasons for you to lose trust in the relationship. You are not quick to lose your affection for someone, but once betrayed, you are not likely to forgive or forget. When it comes to forming close relationships, especially romantic partnerships, you don't like rushing into things or going against your instincts, and when you do, you are invariably disappointed at the outcome. You may feel more comfortable and be more successful if you take time and allow the relationship to form a solid base of mutual understanding and care slowly. You have a strong physical identification with life, and it makes you very fond of personal comfort, music, art, food, and fine wine, as well as all the other sensual delights. You not only love beautiful things for their own sake but have an appreciative eye for their monetary value as well.

Venus in Gemini. Consciously or subconsciously you are likely to be an accomplished flirt. It would be a mistake to accuse you of being emotionally shallow because other factors in your natal chart account for the depth of your emotional commitment. However, when it comes to purely social relationships, you are remarkably instinctive and adept at small talk and flattery. The influence of Gemini indicates that your physical pleasure in relationships is never as satisfying (at least in the long run) as the intellectual one you experience through interaction with others. Circulating and getting to know everybody and everything that is going on are far more to your liking than becoming too physically or emotionally intense. You derive a great deal of inspiration from having a wide variety of relationships with different kinds of people from vastly different backgrounds and experiences from your own. Anything or anyone new or different immediately gains your interest. You have a wonderful sense of humor and a sharp and ready wit, and you don't mind being teased, a good thing, too, because you're a big tease yourself. If other factors in your chart support it, you are also an excellent ad-libber or extemporaneous speaker. You're apt to have subscriptions to many magazines and more than likely can't pass a bookstore without at least going in to see what's on the sale table. You can develop your skills with people and become a superior organizer or networker for various groups. You are also likely to have talent in writing, teaching, sales, and all areas that involve communication and information.

Venus in Cancer. When it comes to socializing, you are likely to derive the most pleasure from family gatherings, and entertaining other people in your home is high on the list of your favorite ways to socialize. You are almost sure to place great value on and take interest in domestic and family life unless other factors in your natal chart interfere with this proclivity. Even if you prefer to remain unmarried, you will probably keep a cozy, well-managed home and will remain responsive to the needs and welfare of your parents or siblings even if you don't reside with them.

Venus in Cancer in your horoscope indicates good relationships with young children, primarily because you instinctively know how to amuse them and play games with them on their own level rather than as an adult. You are sensitive but not particularly shy in taking the initiative in establishing relationships with those who interest you for either personal or business reasons. And when you do want to connect personally with people, your usual approach is likely to be that of putting them at ease by treating them just like family members. You can sometimes go to extremes in your attitudes, but your normal response to others, especially to those close to you, is usually one of warmth and caring. You can also become too possessive and jealous at times, driving away the very people you care for the most. You like to collect things, especially household items and antiques, and you may have a special interest in history and genealogy.

Venus in Leo. It shouldn't take much to stimulate your interest and participation in being with others and, in the process, gaining many friends and acquaintances. The enthusiastic people-oriented qualities of Venus in Leo contribute some very outgoing, magnanimous elements to your social attitudes and behavior, and unless problems in your background and upbringing have seriously interfered with the development of these positive traits, life can be a grand adventure for you. It must not be forgotten that there is also sure to be a measure of ego involvement in the establishment of your social relationships. You may have a tendency to be overly impressed with status. Consciously or subconsciously you recognize a certain pecking order in social relationships and in social situations (and for the good of everyone concerned you had better not be placed at the bottom of the list). Whatever the social situation happens to be, you like to play a dominant role. However, no matter how gregarious or overdramatic you seem in superficial social situations, when it comes to personal relationships, you place great value on sincerity and loyalty. You have a generous, philanthropic attitude toward society in general and, given the opportunity, will achieve much for charitable and other worthwhile causes. You are likely to show special talent for or at least interest in art or design. You may also have a particular gift for public relations, promotion, fund-raising, and organization. Though you may be a bit of a spendthrift when it comes to personal finances, you may have a flair for economics, speculative ventures, and banking.

Venus in Virgo. You tend to be inhibited in social gatherings, especially when you are unfamiliar with all or most of the people. You are not particularly good at or perhaps even willing to engage in small talk or at spontaneously introducing yourself. However, you are by no means anti-social, and you respond positively to those who go out of their way to put you at ease and to those with similar interests or with whom you can quickly find some kind of personal identification, such as people who may also be shy or possess some other readily observable link to you. If you are unable to make any such personal contacts, you are likely to find yourself cleaning the ashtrays or reading the titles of books on a shelf while trying to think of a way to beat a hasty retreat. When confronted with intensely personal contacts, you're apt to withdraw immediately to a safe distance. Of course, if you are just as interested in connecting with someone as he or she appears to be in connecting with you, you hope the other person will understand that your facade of shyness is merely to gain some time to analyze the situation. When given such time, you are able to feel more comfortable and in control. It is then that matters can proceed to a more personal level. When it comes to friends, you tend to be a loyal and caring partner, but your sympathy leaves you vulnerable to being exploited. Knowing this leaves you little choice but to limit your close relationships to very few.

Venus in Libra. Relationships and interaction with others are important to you, and you tend to approach these matters with a certain intellectual interest and objectivity rather than a spontaneous emotional outpouring. You are not particularly shy, but whether or not you go out of your way to grab the social spotlight depends on the support of other factors in your natal chart. You may have a natural flair for knowing how to treat others and in the process get them to cooperate. However, you can sometimes be quite manipulative in going about selecting those with whom you wish to associate. It doesn't mean that your friendship when offered is insincere or shallow; it just means that you may have more than one motive for establishing associations with others and that you go about it in such a charming manner that other people may not always be aware of the true reason for your interest. The social graces and mannerisms that you develop are not likely to be so flirtatious as to be obvious but are probably flattering enough for you to be eagerly sought after by others. When it comes to close personal relationships, you have a very romantic nature, though you may not be consistently passionate. If you are unable to establish intellectual rapport with someone, you are not even likely to get to the romantic stage. You are very likely to have talent for music or art with natal Venus in Libra. You may also have interest in the law, literature, public relations, or design (particularly in the area of jewelry, home decoration, or flowers).

Venus in Scorpio. Your social attitudes and behavior are influenced primarily by emotional need rather than a sense of practicality or expediency, even though these factors are an important part of why you eventually hold on to or let go of relationships and associations. You are not usually shy and, in fact, may be quite gregarious, but how much public attention you actually seek is determined by other factors in your natal chart. It is likely, however, you'll be interested in controlling social groups and their activities more in a behind-the-scenes manner than by being an obvious leader. You have a strongly passionate nature that you must control if you wish to avoid letting possessiveness, obsessiveness, or jealousy destroy your personal as well as business associations. Even if you are outwardly easygoing, you may consciously or subconsciously try to control relationships. Most of your interactions with others, even fleeting or superficial ones, are tinged with a certain intensity. When people get your attention for any reason, you really tend to focus on them; that can be very disconcerting to some people while very flattering to others. Your social instincts and behavior are remarkably keen, direct, and purposeful. You are usually not one to mince words or engage in idle flattery unless you have some definite purpose. You are intrigued by people who radiate an aura of mystery about themselves, and you may enjoy creating the same type of illusion about your own public image. Secret societies, finance, research and investigation, use of resources, and psychology are areas that attract your interest and participation.

Venus in Sagittarius. Your social attitudes, behavior, and expressions are more than likely to exhibit the essential honesty that is traditionally associated with Sagittarius. However, it is also possible that your sense of social tact and diplomacy is sadly missing at times. When thinking that you're just being truthful, you blurt out statements that could have been softened by a little more discreet phraseology. However, those who know you well will sooner or later accept a certain bluntness as part of your charm and perhaps even come to appreciate the honesty with which your words were intended rather than object to the way they were phrased. Not only are you yourself likely to be very honest, but honesty and sincerity are two traits you value highly in others. You are friendly and outgoing and can easily win many friends and acquaintances. You are idealistic and can be easily hurt by others who fail to respond to a relationship in the same way you do. For this reason, uncomplicated friendships are easier for you to handle than deeply passionate entanglements that, more often than not, leave you feeling hurt and confused. Your idealism makes you passionate to a certain extent, but how much sustained physical action that passion translates into will depend on other factors in your natal chart. You have a good sense of humor and a quick wit. You are apt to be interested in religion, politics, publishing, higher education, and international travel. Some of your best friends as well as your marriage partner may be from a race or culture different from your own.

Venus in Capricorn. You will often encounter the restrictive influence of Venus in Capricorn in dealing with various romantic entanglements. Either you have some inhibition or reservation, or your partner may be afflicted with some impediment, but more often than not, something comes along to restrict the emotional freedom in your romantic relationships. Nor can your social attitudes and behavior be said to be altogether glib or spontaneous, even though you may truly enjoy social gatherings. Perhaps you are shy, or perhaps your cautious nature makes you feel more comfortable in situations and relationships in which social intercourse is rather formal, purposeful, and to some extent, calculated. Whether or not you consciously realize it, this type of restricted societal approach helps remove the possibility of any sort of rejection, which is something you wish to avoid at all cost. No matter how easygoing or strong your outer personality may appear, it is likely that underneath, you harbor a certain amount of personal insecurity when it comes to interacting with others. It is possible that you will marry someone older or more mature than you or that you will marry rather late in life. Whether or not you actually intend this to be so, you nevertheless want to make some practical use of your social connections—that is, to realize some personal advancement. However, you are not totally self-serving in this respect since you may be just as willing to help a friend in the same way. In fact, you can be a reliable source of mutual favors and benefits to your friends.

Venus in Aquarius. You have wide-ranging social attitudes and behavioral patterns. For you, a restricted code of social acceptability does not exist, and you eagerly accept all types of people into your social circle. As a matter of fact, as far as you are concerned, it's a case of the more, the merrier and perhaps the more different, the better, for you have such an eclectic social nature that you truly appreciate and value the uniqueness of those of different cultures or backgrounds. You are a people-oriented individual who would suffer if denied access to a telephone and who has no trouble attracting many friends and acquaintances. Though you tend to have a less than passionate approach to relationships, no one denies your fierce loyalty. As a romantic partner you may not demonstrate sustained passion, but your interest will be steady and faithful. It's difficult to predict whether your attitude toward love and marriage will be traditional or you will rebel against accepted practices. Either attitude would be perfectly within the framework of Venus in Aquarius. You may marry suddenly or unexpectedly, and your choice of marriage partner may be considered (at least by others) somewhat out of the ordinary. It is also possible you will end up marrying a friend. Your passions may be confined to dealing with life on a higher plane. You get very concerned, for example, when aroused by humanitarian principles or spiritual zeal. You are apt to be a good fund-raiser and organizer and excellent at public relations and to have a facility for international finance or diplomacy.

Venus in Pisces. You will interact with others according to your emotional background, and though you can try to overcome any negative influence from childhood, it will be especially difficult to do so if that influence was sustained throughout your developing years. Your social attitudes and behavior are also profoundly influenced by your emotional state at any given time, so that when you are unhappy, you are apt to retreat, while at other times you can be open and gregarious. Though the Piscean influence generally indicates a certain natural shyness, you are apt to love having lots of other people around. However, it must be said that you are vulnerable to those around you and, as a result, need to spend a certain time alone or have a private spot to retreat to in order to restore your equilibrium and sort out the various influences you have encountered each day. You can be severely hurt if a relationship does not go well, and as a result, you may be more than a little timid when it comes to attempting new associations. Discrimination in selecting relationships can be difficult for you because of your compassionate, idealistic nature. You effortlessly seem to attract a lot of people, who then proceed to take advantage of you. You have an active imagination and can become a fantastic storyteller or writer. You are sensitive to (and perhaps talented in) music and art and may be especially fond of dance and theater. It is also possible that your marriage partner may be in one of these fields.

How to Find the Place of Venus in Your Chart

Find your birth year in the left-hand column and read across the chart until you find your birth date. The top of that column will tell you where Venus lies in your chart.

PLACE OF VENUS—1880-1891

	ARIES	TAURUS	GEMINI	CANCER	LEO	VIRGO	LIBRA	SCORPIO	SAGITT.	CAPRI.	AQUAR.	PISCES
1880	4/14-5/7	5/8-6/1	6/2-6/25	6/26-7/20	7/21-8/13	8/14-9/6	9/7-9/30	1/1-1/4 10/1-10/25	1/5-1/30 10/26-11/18	1/31-2/24 11/19-12/13	2/25-3/19 12/14-12/31	3/20-4/13
1881	2/3-3/3	3/4-7/7	7/8-8/5	8/6-9/1	9/2-9/27	9/28-10/21	10/22-11/14	11/15-12/8	12/9-12/31		1/1-1/7	1/8-2/2
1882	3/15-4/7	4/8-5/2	5/3-5/26	5/27-6/20	6/21-7/15	7/16-8/10	8/11-9/6	9/7-10/6	1/1 10/7-12/31	1/2-1/25	1/26-2/18	2/19-3/14
1883	4/28-5/22	5/23-6/16	6/17-7/11	7/12-8/4	8/5-8/29	8/30-9/22	9/23-10/16	10/17-11/9	11/10-12/3	2/5-3/6 12/4-12/27	3/7-4/1 12/28-12/31	4/2-4/27
1884	2/15-3/10	3/11-4/5	4/6-5/4	5/5-9/7	9/8-10/7	10/8-11/3	11/4-11/28	11/29-12/22	12/23-12/31		1/1-1/20	1/21-2/14
1885	3/30-4/22	4/23-5/16	5/17-6/10	6/11-7/4	7/5-7/29	7/30-8/23	8/24-9/16	9/17-10/12	10/13-11/6	1/17-2/9 11/7-12/4	2/10-3/5 12/5-12/31	3/6-3/29
1886	5/7-6/3	6/4-6/29	6/30-7/25	7/26-8/19	8/20-9/12	9/13-10/7	10/8-10/31	11/1-11/23	11/24-12/17	12/18-12/31	1/1-1/6 2/19-4/1	1/7-2/18 4/2-5/6
1887	2/28-3/24	3/25-4/17	4/18-5/13	5/14-6/8	6/9-7/6	7/7-8/11 9/19-11/5	8/12-9/18 11/6-12/8	12/9-12/31		1/1-1/10	1/11-2/3	2/4-2/27
1888	4/13-5/7	5/8-5/31	6/1-6/25	6/26-7/19	7/20-8/12	8/13-9/6	9/7-9/30	1/1-1/4 10/1-10/24	1/5-1/29 10/25-11/18	1/30-2/23 11/19-12/12	2/24-3/19 12/13-12/31	3/20-4/12
1889	2/3-3/4	3/5-7/7	7/8-8/5	8/6-9/1	9/2-9/26	9/27-10/21	10/22-11/14	11/15-12/8	12/9-12/31		1/1-1/6	1/7-2/2
1890	3/15-4/7	4/8-5/1	5/2-5/26	5/27-6/20	6/21-7/15	7/16-8/10	8/11-9/6	9/7-10/7	1/1 10/8-12/31	1/2-1/25	1/26-2/18	2/19-3/14
1891	4/27-5/22	5/23-6/16	6/17-7/10	7/11-8/4	8/5-8/28	8/29-9/21	9/22-10/15	10/16-11/8	1/1-2/5 11/9-12/2	2/6-3/5 12/3-12/26	3/6-4/1 12/27-12/31	4/2-4/26

PLACE OF VENUS—1892–1906

1892	2/14-3/9	3/10-4/4	4/5-5/4	5/5-9/7	9/8-10/7	10/8-11/2	11/3-11/27	11/28-12/22	12/23-12/31				1/1-1/20	1/21-2/13
1893	3/29-4/22	4/23-5/16	5/17-6/9	6/10-7/4	7/5-7/28	7/29-8/22	8/23-9/16	9/17-10/11	1/1-1/15 10/12-11/6	1/16-2/8 11/7-12/4			2/9-3/4 12/5-12/31	3/5-3/28
1894	5/5-6/2	6/3-6/29	6/30-7/24	7/25-8/18	8/19-9/12	9/13-10/6	10/7-10/30	10/31-11/23	11/24-12/17	12/18-12/31			1/1-1/8 2/13-4/2	1/9-2/12 4/3-5/4
1895	2/28-3/23	3/24-4/17	4/18-5/12	5/13-6/7	6/8-7/6	7/7-8/13 9/13-11/6	8/14-9/12 11/7-12/8	12/9-12/31				1/1-1/10	1/11-2/3	2/4-2/27
1896	4/13-5/6	5/7-5/31	6/1-6/24	6/25-7/19	7/20-8/12	8/13-9/5	9/6-9/29	1/1-1/3 9/30-10/24	1/4-1/29 10/25-11/17	1/30-2/23 11/18-12/12			2/24-3/18 12/13-12/31	3/19-4/12
1897	2/2-3/4	3/5-7/7	7/8-8/5	8/6-8/31	9/1-9/26	9/27-10/20	10/21-11/13	11/14-12/7	12/8-12/31				1/1-1/6	1/7-2/1
1898	3/14-4/6	4/7-5/1	5/2-5/25	5/26-6/19	6/20-7/14	7/15-8/10	8/11-9/6	9/7-10/7 12/17-12/26	10/8-12/16 12/27-12/31	1/1-1/24			1/25-2/17	2/18-3/13
1899	4/27-5/21	5/22-6/15	6/16-7/10	7/11-8/3	8/4-8/28	8/29-9/21	9/22-10/15	10/16-11/8	1/1-2/5 11/9-12/2	2/6-3/5 12/3-12/26			3/6-3/31 12/27-12/31	4/1-4/26
1900	2/14-3/10	3/11-4/5	4/6-5/5	5/6-9/8	9/9-10/8	10/9-11/3	11/4-11/28	11/29-12/22	12/23-12/31				1/1-1/19	1/20-2/13
1901	3/30-4/22	4/23-5/16	5/17-6/10	6/11-7/4	7/5-7/29	7/30-8/23	8/24-9/16	9/17-10/12	1/1-1/15 10/13-11/7	1/16-2/9 11/8-12/5			2/10-3/5 12/6-12/31	3/6-3/29
1902	5/7-6/3	6/4-6/29	6/30-7/25	7/26-8/19	8/20-9/12	9/13-10/7	10/8-10/30	10/31-11/23	11/24-12/17	12/18-12/31			1/1-1/11 2/13-4/4	1/12-2/14 4/5-5/6
1903	2/28-3/23	3/24-4/17	4/18-5/13	5/14-6/8	6/9-7/7	7/8-8/17 9/7-11/8	8/18-9/6 11/9-12/9	12/10-12/31				1/1-1/10	1/11-2/3	2/4-2/27
1904	4/13-5/7	5/8-5/31	6/1-6/25	6/26-7/19	7/20-8/12	8/13-9/6	9/7-9/30	1/1-1/4 10/1-10/24	1/5-1/29 10/25-11/18	1/30-2/23 11/19-12/12			2/24-3/19 12/13-12/31	3/20-4/12
1905	2/3-3/5 5/9-5/27	3/6-5/8 5/28-7/7	7/8-8/5	8/6-9/1	9/2-9/26	9/27-10/21	10/22-11/14	11/15-12/8	12/9-12/31				1/1-1/7	1/8-2/2
1906	3/15-4/7	4/8-5/1	5/2-5/26	5/27-6/20	6/21-7/15	7/16-8/10	8/11-9/7	9/8-10/8 12/16-12/25	1/1 10/9-12/15 12/26-12/31	1/2-1/25			1/26-2/18	2/19-3/14

PLACE OF VENUS—1907–1916

	ARIES	TAURUS	GEMINI	CANCER	LEO	VIRGO	LIBRA	SCORPIO	SAGITT.	CAPRI.	AQUAR.	PISCES
1907	4/28-5/22	5/23-6/16	6/17-7/10	7/11-8/3	8/4-8/28	8/29-9/21	9/22-10/15	10/16-11/8	1/1-2/6 11/9-12/2	2/7-3/6 12/3-12/26	3/7-4/1 12/27-12/31	4/2-4/27
1908	2/14-3/9	3/10-4/5	4/6-5/5	5/6-9/8	9/9-10/7	10/8-11/2	11/3-11/27	11/28-12/22	12/23-12/31		1/1-1/20	1/21-2/13
1909	3/29-4/21	4/22-5/16	5/17-6/9	6/10-7/4	7/5-7/28	7/29-8/22	8/23-9/16	9/17-10/11	1/1-1/15 10/12-11/6	1/16-2/8 11/7-12/5	2/9-3/3 12/6-12/31	3/4-3/28
1910	5/7-6/3	6/4-6/29	6/30-7/24	7/25-8/18	8/19-9/12	9/13-10/6	10/7-10/30	10/31-11/23	11/24-12/17	12/18-12/31	1/1-1/15 1/29-4/4	1/16-1/28 4/5-5/6
1911	2/28-3/23	3/24-4/17	4/18-5/12	5/13-6/8	6/9-7/7	7/8-11/8	11/9-12/8	12/9-12/31		1/1-1/10	1/11-2/2	2/3-2/27
1912	4/13-5/6	5/7-5/31	6/1-6/24	6/25-7/18	7/19-8/12	8/13-9/5	9/6-9/30	1/1-1/4 9/31-10/24	1/5-1/29 10/25-11/17	1/30-2/23 11/18-12/12	2/24-3/18 12/13-12/31	3/19-4/12
1913	2/3-3/6 5/2-5/30	3/7-5/1 5/31-7/7	7/8-8/5	8/6-8/31	9/1-9/26	9/27-10/20	10/21-11/13	11/14-12/7	12/8-12/31		1/1-1/6	1/7-2/2
1914	3/14-4/6	4/7-5/1	5/2-5/25	5/26-6/19	6/20-7/15	7/16-8/10	8/11-9/6	9/7-10/9 12/6-12/30	10/10-12/5 12/31	1/1-1/24	1/25-2/17	2/18-3/13
1915	4/27-5/21	5/22-6/15	6/16-7/10	7/11-8/3	8/4-8/28	8/29-9/21	9/22-10/15	10/16-11/8	1/1-2/6 11/9-12/2	2/7-3/6 12/3-12/26	3/7-4/1 12/27-12/31	4/2-4/26
1916	2/14-3/9	3/10-4/5	4/6-5/5	5/6-9/8	9/9-10/7	10/8-11/2	11/3-11/27	11/28-12/21	12/22-12/31		1/1-1/19	1/20-2/13

PLACE OF VENUS—1917–1931

Year												
1917	3/29-4/21	4/22-5/15	5/16-6/9	6/10-7/3	7/4-7/28	7/29-8/21	8/22-9/16	9/17-10/11	1/1-1/14 / 10/12-11/6	1/15-2/7 / 11/7-12/5	2/8-3/4 / 12/6-12/31	3/5-3/28
1918	5/7-6/2	6/3-6/28	6/29-7/24	7/25-8/18	8/19-9/11	9/12-10/5	10/6-10/29	10/30-11/22	11/23-12/16	12/17-12/31	1/1-4/5	4/6-5/6
1919	2/27-3/22	3/23-4/16	4/17-5/12	5/13-6/7	6/8-7/7	7/8-11/8	11/9-12/8	12/9-12/31		1/1-1/9	1/10-2/2	2/3-2/26
1920	4/12-5/6	5/7-5/30	5/31-6/23	6/24-7/18	7/19-8/11	8/12-9/4	9/5-9/30	1/1-1/3 / 9/31-10/23	1/4-1/28 / 10/24-11/17	1/29-2/22 / 11/18-12/11	2/23-3/18 / 12/12-12/31	3/19-4/11
1921	2/3-3/6 / 4/26-6/1	3/7-4/25 / 6/2-7/7	7/8-8/5	8/6-8/31	9/1-9/25	9/26-10/20	10/21-11/13	11/14-12/7	12/8-12/31		1/1-1/6	1/7-2/2
1922	3/13-4/6	4/7-4/30	5/1-5/25	5/26-6/19	6/20-7/14	7/15-8/9	8/10-9/6	9/7-10/10 / 11/29↳	10/11-11/28	1/1-1/24	1/25-2/16	2/17-3/12
1923	4/27-5/21	5/22-6/14	6/15-7/9	7/10-8/3	8/4-8/27	8/28-9/20	9/21-10/14	↳1/1 / 10/15-11/7	1/2-2/6 / 11/8-12/1	2/7-3/5 / 12/2-12/25	3/6-3/31 / 12/26↳	4/1-4/26
1924	2/13-3/8	3/9-4/4	4/5-5/5	5/6-9/8	9/9-10/7	10/8-11/2	11/3-11/26	11/27-12/21	12/22↳		1/1-1/19	1/20-2/12
1925	3/28-4/20	4/21-5/15	5/16-6/8	6/9-7/3	7/4-7/27	7/28-8/21	8/22-9/15	9/16-10/11	↳1/14 / 10/12-11/6	1/15-2/7 / 11/7-12/5	2/8-3/3 / 12/6↳	3/4-3/27
1926	5/7-6/2	6/3-6/28	6/29-7/23	7/24-8/17	8/18-9/11	9/12-10/5	10/6-10/29	10/30-11/22	11/23-12/16	12/17↳	1/8-4/5	4/6-5/6
1927	2/27-3/22	3/23-4/16	4/17-5/11	5/12-6/7	6/8-7/7	7/8-11/9	11/10-12/8	12/9↳		↳1/8	1/9-2/1	2/2-2/26
1928	4/12-5/5	5/6-5/29	5/30-6/23	6/24-7/17	7/18-8/11	8/12-9/4	9/5-9/28	↳1/3 / 9/29-10/23	1/4-1/28 / 10/24-11/16	1/29-2/22 / 11/17-12/11	2/23-3/17 / 12/12↳	3/18-4/11
1929	2/3-3/7 / 4/20-6/2	3/8-4/19 / 6/3-7/7	7/8-8/4	8/5-8/30	8/31-9/25	9/26-10/19	10/20-11/12	11/13-12/6	12/7-12/30	12/31↳	↳1/5	1/6-2/2
1930	3/13-4/5	4/6-4/30	5/1-5/24	5/25-6/18	6/19-7/14	7/15-8/9	8/10-9/6	9/7-10/11 / 11/22↳	10/12-11/21	1/1-1/23	1/24-2/16	2/17-3/12
1931	4/26-5/20	5/21-6/14	6/15-7/9	7/10-8/2	8/3-8/26	8/27-9/20	9/21-10/14	↳1/3 / 10/15-11/7	1/4-2/6 / 11/8-12/1	2/7-3/5 / 12/2-12/25	3/6-3/31 / 12/26↳	4/1-4/25

PLACE OF VENUS—1932-1943

	ARIES	TAURUS	GEMINI	CANCER	LEO	VIRGO	LIBRA	SCORPIO	SAGITT.	CAPRI.	AQUAR.	PISCES
1932	2/13-3/8	3/9-4/4	4/5-5/5 7/13-7/27	5/6-7/12 7/28-9/8	9/9-10/6	10/7-11/1	11/2-11/26	11/27-12/20	12/21›		‹1/18	1/19-2/12
1933	3/28-4/20	4/21-5/14	5/15-6/8	6/9-7/2	7/3-7/27	7/28-8/21	8/22-9/15	9/16-10/10	‹1/13 10/11-11/6	1/14-2/6 11/7-12/5	2/7-3/2 12/6	3/3-3/27
1934	5/6-6/1	6/2-6/27	6/28-7/23	7/24-8/17	8/18-9/10	9/11-10/4	10/5-10/28	10/29-11/21	11/22-12/15	12/16›	4/5	4/6-5/5
1935	2/26-3/21	3/22-4/15	4/16-5/11	5/12-6/7	6/8-7/7	7/8-11/9	11/10-12/8	12/9›		‹1/8	1/9-2/1	2/2-2/25
1936	4/11-5/4	5/5-5/29	5/30-6/22	6/23-7/17	7/18-8/10	8/11-9/3	9/4-9/28	‹1/3 9/29-10/22	1/4-1/28 10/23-11/16	1/29-2/21 11/17-12/11	2/22-3/17 12/12›	3/18-4/10
1937	2/2-3/9 4/14-6/3	3/10-4/13 6/4-7/7	7/8-8/4	8/5-8/30	8/31-9/24	9/25-10/19	10/20-11/12	11/13-12/6	12/7-12/30	12/31›	‹1/5	1/6-2/1
1938	3/12-4/5	4/6-4/29	4/30-5/24	5/25-6/18	6/19-7/13	7/14-8/9	8/10-9/6	9/7-10/13 11/16›	10/14-11/15	‹1/22	1/23-2/15	2/16-3/11
1939	4/26-5/20	5/21-6/13	6/14-7/8	7/9-8/2	8/3-8/26	8/27-9/19	9/20-10/13	‹1/4 10/14-11/6	1/5-2/5 11/7-11/30	2/6-3/5 12/1-12/24	3/6-3/30 12/25›	3/31-4/25
1940	2/12-3/8	3/9-4/4	4/5-5/6 7/6-7/31	5/7-7/5 8/1-9/8	9/9-10/6	10/7-11/1	11/2-11/26	11/27-12/20	12/21›		‹1/18	1/19-2/11
1941	3/27-4/19	4/20-5/14	5/15-6/7	6/8-7/2	7/3-7/26	7/27-8/20	8/21-9/14	9/15-10/10	‹1/13 10/11-11/5	1/14-2/6 11/6-12/5	2/7-3/2 12/6	3/3-3/26
1942	5/6-6/1	6/2-6/27	6/28-7/22	7/23-8/16	8/17-9/10	9/11-10/4	10/5-10/28	10/29-11/21	11/22-12/15	12/16›	‹4/6	4/7-5/5
1943	2/26-3/21	3/22-4/15	4/16-5/10	5/11-6/7	6/8-7/7	7/8-11/9	11/10-12/17	12/8›		‹1/7	1/8-1/31	2/1-2/25

PLACE OF VENUS—1944-1958

Year												
1944	4/11-5/4	5/5-5/28	5/29-6/22	6/23-7/16	7/17-8/10	8/11-9/3	9/4-9/27	1/2 / 9/28-10/22	1/3-1/27 / 10/23-11/15	1/28-2/21 / 11/16-12/9	2/22-3/16 / 12/10	3/17-4/10
1945	2/2-3/10, 4/8-6/4	3/11-4/7, 6/5-7/7	7/8-8/3	8/4-8/30	8/31-9/24	9/25-10/18	10/19-11/11	11/12-12/5	12/6-12/29	12/30	↳1/5	1/6-2/1
1946	3/12-4/4	4/5-4/28	4/29-5/23	5/24-6/17	6/18-7/13	7/14-8/8	8/9-9/6	9/7-10/15, 11/8	10/16-11/7	↳1/22	1/23-2/15	2/16-3/11
1947	4/25-5/18	5/19-6/13	6/14-7/8	7/9-7/31	8/1-8/25	8/26-9/18	9/19-10/13	1/5 / 10/14-11/6	1/6-2/5 / 11/7-11/30	2/6-3/4 / 12/1-12/24	3/5-3/30 / 12/25	3/31-4/24
1948	2/12-3/7	3/8-4/4	4/5-5/6, 6/29-8/2	5/7-6/28, 8/3-9/8	9/9-10/6	10/7-10/31	11/1-11/25	11/26-12/19	12/20	12/20	↳1/17	1/18-2/11
1949	3/26-4/19	4/20-5/13	5/14-6/6	6/7-7/1	7/2-7/26	7/27-8/20	8/21-9/14	9/15-10/9	1/12 / 10/10-11/4	1/13-2/5 / 11/5-12/5	2/6-3/1 / 12/6	3/2-3/25
1950	5/6-6/1	6/2-6/26	6/27-7/22	7/23-8/16	8/17-9/9	9/10-10/3	10/4-10/27	10/28-11/20	11/21-12/14	12/15-12/31	↳4/6	4/7-5/5
1951	2/25-3/21	3/22-4/15	4/16-5/11	5/12-6/7	6/8-7/8	7/9-11/9	11/10-12/7	12/8		1/1-1/7	1/8-1/31	2/1-2/24
1952	4/10-5/4	5/5-5/28	5/29-6/22	6/23-7/16	7/17-8/9	8/10-9/3	9/4-9/27	1/2 / 9/28-10/22	1/3-1/27 / 10/23-11/15	1/28-2/21 / 11/16-12/10	2/22-3/16 / 12/11 ↳	3/17-4/9
1953	2/3-2/14, 4/1-6/5	2/15-3/31, 6/6-7/7	7/8-8/4	8/5-8/30	8/31-9/24	9/25-10/18	10/19-11/11	11/12-12/5	12/6-12/29	12/30	↳1/5	1/6-2/2
1954	3/12-4/4	4/5-4/28	4/29-5/23	5/24-6/17	6/18-7/13	7/14-8/8	8/9-9/6	9/7-10/13, 10/28	10/14-11/6	↳1/22	1/23-2/15	2/16-3/11
1955	4/25-5/19	5/20-6/13	6/14-7/8	7/9-8/1	8/2-8/25	8/26-9/18	9/19-10/12	1/6 / 10/13-11/5	1/7-2/6 / 11/6-11/30	2/7-3/4 / 12/1-12/24	3/5-3/30 / 12/25	3/31-4/24
1956	2/12-3/7	3/8-4/4	4/5-5/8, 6/24-8/4	5/9-6/23, 8/5-9/8	9/9-10/5	10/6-10/31	11/1-11/25	11/26-12/19	12/20	12/20	↳1/17	1/18-2/11
1957	3/26-4/19	4/20-5/13	5/14-6/6	6/7-7/1	7/2-7/26	7/27-8/19	8/20-9/14	9/15-10/9	1/12 / 10/10-11/4	1/13-2/5 / 11/5-12/6	2/6-3/1 / 12/7	3/2-3/25
1958	5/6-6/1	6/2-6/26	6/27-7/22	7/23-8/15	8/16-9/9	9/10-10/3	10/4-10/27	10/28-11/20	11/21-12/14	12/15 ↳	↳4/6	4/7-5/5

PLACE OF VENUS—1959–1969

	ARIES	TAURUS	GEMINI	CANCER	LEO	VIRGO	LIBRA	SCORPIO	SAGITT.	CAPRI.	AQUAR.	PISCES
1959	2/25–3/20	3/21–4/14	4/15–5/10	5/11–6/6	6/7–7/8 9/21–9/24	7/9–9/20 9/25–11/9	11/10–12/7	12/8		1/7	1/8–1/31	2/1–2/24
1960	4/10–5/3	5/4–5/28	5/29–6/21	6/22–7/15	7/16–8/9	8/10–9/2	9/3–9/27	1/2 9/28–10/21	1/3–1/26 10/22–11/15	1/27–2/20 11/16–12/10	2/21–3/5 12/11–12/31	3/16–4/9
1961	2/2–6/4	6/5–7/6	7/7–8/2	8/3–8/28	8/29–9/22	9/23–10/17	10/18–11/10	11/11–12/4	12/5–12/27	12/28	1/1–1/4	1/5–2/1
1962	3/10–4/2	4/3–4/27	4/28–5/22	5/23–6/16	6/17–7/11	7/12–8/7	8/8–9/5	9/6		1/20	1/21–2/13	2/14–3/9
1963	4/24–5/18	5/19–6/11	6/12–7/6	7/7–7/30	7/31–8/24	8/25–9/17	9/18–10/11	1/5 10/12–11/4	1/6–2/4 11/5–11/28	2/5–3/3 11/29–12/22	3/4–3/29 12/23	3/30–4/23
1964	2/10–3/6	3/7–4/3	4/4–5/8 6/17–8/4	5/9–6/16 8/5–9/7	9/8–10/4	10/5–10/30	10/31–11/24	11/25–12/18	12/19		1/16	1/17–2/9
1965	3/25–4/17	4/18–5/11	5/12–6/5	6/6–6/29	6/30–7/24	7/25–8/18	8/19–9/12	9/13–10/8	1/11 10/9–11/4	1/12–2/4 11/5–12/6	2/5–2/28 12/7	3/1–3/24
1966	5/5–5/30	5/31–6/25	6/26–7/20	7/21–8/14	8/15–9/7	9/8–10/2	10/3–10/26	10/27–11/19	11/20–12/12	2/6–2/24 12/13	2/5 2/25–4/5	4/6–5/4
1967	2/23–3/19	3/20–4/13	4/14–5/9	5/10–6/5	6/6–7/7 9/9–9/30	7/8–9/8 10/1–11/8	11/9–12/6	12/7–12/31		1/5	1/6–1/29	1/30–2/22
1968	4/8–5/2	5/3–5/26	5/27–6/20	6/21–7/14	7/15–8/7	8/8–9/1	9/2–9/25	9/26–10/20	1/1–1/25 10/21–11/13	1/26–2/19 11/14–12/8	2/20–3/14 12/9	3/15–4/7
1969	2/2–6/5	6/6–7/5	7/6–8/2	8/3–8/28	8/29–9/22	9/23–10/16	10/17–11/9	11/10–12/3	12/4–12/27	12/28	1/3	1/4–2/1

PLACE OF VENUS—1970–1980

Year												
1970	3/10-4/2	4/3-4/26	4/27-5/21	5/22-6/15	6/16-7/11	7/12-8/7	8/8-9/6	9/7-12/31		→1/20	1/21-2/13	2/14-3/9
1971	4/23-5/17	5/18-6/11	6/12-7/5	7/6-7/31	8/1-8/23	8/24-9/16	9/17-10/10	1/1-1/6 10/11-11/4	1/7-2/4 11/15-11/28	2/5-3/3 11/29-12/22	3/4-3/28 12/23	3/29-4/22
1972	2/10-3/7	3/8-4/2	4/3-5/9 6/11-8/5	5/10-6/10 8/6-9/6	9/7-10/4	10/5-10/29	10/30-11/23	11/24-12/17	12/8→	→1/10	→1/15	1/16-2/9
1973	3/24-4/17	4/18-5/11	5/12-6/4	6/5-6/29	6/30-7/24	7/25-8/18	8/19-9/12	9/13-10/8	→1/10 10/9-11/4	1/11-2/3 11/5-12/16	2/4-2/27 12/7	2/28-3/23
1974	5/4-5/30	5/31-6/24	6/25-7/20	7/21-8/13	8/14-9/7	9/8-10/1	10/2-10/25	10/26-11/18	11/19-12/12	1/29-2/27 12/13	→1/28 2/28-4/5	4/6-5/3
1975	2/23-3/18	3/19-4/12	4/13-5/8	5/9-6/5	6/6-7/8 9/2-10/3	7/9-9/1 10/4-11/8	11/9-12/6	12/7-12/31		→1/5	1/6-1/29	1/30-2/22
1976	4/8-5/1	5/2-5/26	5/27-6/19	6/20-7/13	7/14-8/7	8/8-8/31	9/1-9/25	9/26-10/19	1/11-1/25 10/20-11/13	1/26-2/18 11/14-12/8	2/19-3/14 12/19	3/15-4/7
1977	2/2-6/5	6/6-7/5	7/6-8/1	8/2-8/27	8/28-9/21	9/22-10/16	10/17-11/9	11/10-12/3	12/4-12/26	12/27→	→1/3	1/4-2/1
1978	3/9-4/1	4/2-4/26	4/27-5/21	5/22-6/15	6/16-7/11	7/12-8/7	8/8-9/6	9/7		→1/19	1/20-2/12	2/13-3/8
1979	4/23-5/17	5/18-6/10	6/11-7/5	7/6-7/29	7/30-8/23	8/24-9/16	9/17-10/10	1/6 10/11-11/3	1/7-2/4 11/4-11/27	2/5-3/2 11/28-12/21	3/3-3/28 12/22	3/29-4/22
1980	2/9-3/5	3/6-4/2	4/3-5/11 6/5-8/5	5/12-6/4 8/6-9/6	9/7-10/4	10/5-10/29	10/30-11/23	11/24-12/17	12/18-12/31		→1/15	1/16-2/8

PLACE OF VENUS—1981–1987

	ARIES	TAURUS	GEMINI	CANCER	LEO	VIRGO	LIBRA	SCORPIO	SAGITT.	CAPRI.	AQUAR.	PISCES
1981	3/24–4/16	4/17–5/10	5/11–6/4	6/5–6/28	6/29–7/23	7/24–8/17	8/18–9/11	9/12–10/7	1/1–1/10 10/8–11/4	1/11–2/3 11/5–12/7	2/4–2/27 12/8	2/28–3/23
1982	5/4–5/29	5/30–6/24	6/25–7/19	7/20–8/13	8/14–9/6	9/7–9/30	10/1–10/24	10/25–11/17	11/18–12/11	1/22–3/1 12/12	3/2–4/5 1/21	4/6–5/3
1983	2/22–3/18	3/19–4/12	4/13–5/8	5/9–6/5	6/6–7/9 8/27–10/4	7/10–8/26 10/5–11/8	11/9–12/5	12/6–12/30	12/31	1/4	1/5–1/28	1/29–2/21
1984	4/7–4/30	5/1–5/25	5/26–6/18	6/19–7/13	7/14–8/6	8/7–8/31	9/1–9/24	9/25–10/19	1/24 10/20–11/12	1/25–2/17 11/13–12/7	2/18–3/13 12/8	3/14–4/6
1985	2/2–6/5	6/6–7/5	7/6–8/1	8/2–8/26	8/27–9/20	9/21–10/15	10/16–11/8	11/9–12/2	12/3–12/26	12/27	1/3	1/4–2/1
1986	3/8–4/1	4/2–4/25	4/26–5/20	5/21–6/14	6/15–7/10	7/11–8/6	8/7–9/6	9/7		1/19	1/20–2/11	2/12–3/7
1987	4/22–5/16	5/17–6/10	6/11–7/6	7/5–7/29	7/30–8/22	8/23–9/15	9/16–10/9	4/6 10/10–11/2	1/7–2/3 11/3–11/26	2/4–3/2 11/27–12/21	3/3–3/27 12/22	3/28–4/21

PLACE OF VENUS—1988–2000

Year												
1988	2/9-3/5	3/6-4/2	4/3-5/16 / 5/27-8/5	5/17-5/26 / 8/6-9/6	9/7-10/3	10/4-10/28	10/29-11/22	11/23-12/16	12/17↓	↓1/14	1/15-2/8	
1989	3/23-4/15	4/16-5/10	5/11-6/3	6/4-6/28	6/29-7/22	7/23-8/16	8/17-9/11	9/12-10/7	↓1/9 / 10/8-11/4	1/10-2/2 / 11/5-12/8	2/3-2/26 / 12/9↓	2/27-3/22
1990	5/3-5/29	5/30-6/23	6/24-7/19	7/19-8/12	8/13-9/6	9/7-9/30	10/1-10/24	10/25-11/17	11/18-12/11	1/16-3/2 / 12/12↓	↓1/15 / 3/3-4/5	4/6-5/2
1991	2/22-3/17	3/18-4/11	4/12-5/7	5/8-6/4	6/5-7/10 / 8/21-10/5	7/11-8/20 / 10/6-11/8	11/9-12/5	12/6-12/30	12/31↓	↓1/4	1/5-1/27	1/28-2/21
1992	4/7-4/30	5/1-5/24	5/25-6/18	6/19-7/12	7/13-8/6	8/7-8/30	8/31-9/23	9/24-10/18	↓1/24 / 10/19-11/12	1/25-2/17 / 11/13-12/7	2/18-3/12 / 12/8↓	3/13-4/6
1993	2/2-6/5	6/6-7/4	7/5-7/31	8/1-8/26	8/27-9/20	9/21-10/14	10/15-11/7	11/8-12/1	12/2-12/25	12/26↓	↓1/2	1/3-2/1
1994	3/8-3/31	4/1-4/25	4/26-5/19	5/20-6/14	6/15-7/10	7/11-8/6	8/7-9/6	9/7-10/9	↓1/6 / 10/10-11/2	1/7-2/11 / 11/3-11/26	11/27-12/20 / 12/21↓	2/12-3/7
1995	4/21-5/15	5/16-6/9	5/10-7/4	7/5-7/28	7/29-8/21	8/22-9/15	9/16-10/9	10/10-11/2	1/7-2/3 / 11/3-11/26	2/4-3/1 / 11/27-12/20	3/2-3/27 / 12/21↓	3/28-4/20
1996	2/8-3/4	3/5-4/2	4/3-8/6	8/7-9/6	9/7-9/30	10/1-10/23	10/24-11/16	11/17-12/10	12/11↓	↓1/13	1/14-2/7	
1997	3/23-4/15	4/16-5/9	5/10-6/2	6/3-6/27	6/28-7/22	7/23-8/16	8/17-9/10	9/11-10/7	↓1/9 / 10/8-11/4	1/10-2/1 / 11/5-12/10	2/2-2/25 / 12/11↓	2/26-3/22
1998	5/3-5/28	5/29-6/23	6/24-7/19	7/19-8/12	8/13-9/5	9/6-9/29	9/30-10/23	10/24-11/16	11/17-12/10	1/9-3/3 / 12/11↓	↓1/8 / 3/4-4/5	4/6-5/2
1999	2/21-3/17	3/18-4/11	4/12-5/7	5/8-6/4	6/5-7/11 / 8/15-10/6	7/12-8/14 / 10/7-11/7	11/8-12/4	12/5-12/29	12/30↓	↓1/3	1/4-1/27	1/28-2/20
2000	4/6-4/29	4/30-5/24	5/25-6/17	6/18-7/12	7/13-8/5	8/6-8/29	8/30-9/23	9/24-10/18	↓1/23 / 10/19-11/11	1/24-2/16 / 11/12-12/7	2/17-3/12 / 12/8-12/30	3/13-4/5

YOUR MOST CONSPICUOUS TRAIT: ARIES—Courage; TAURUS—Fortitude; GEMINI—Alertness; CANCER—Loyalty; LEO—Magnanimity; VIRGO—Efficiency; LIBRA—Friendliness; SCORPIO—Determination; SAGITTARIUS—Fidelity; CAPRICORN—Sincerity; AQUARIUS—Cooperation; PISCES—Compassion.

MARS: THE SPARK OF LIFE

Mars is that spark of desire, of passion, the impetus to action that puts us out there in life, doing, acting, being ourselves, putting ourselves forward. It is that first impulse we have—acted upon or not—to connect deeply with another person, to make a move in a situation, or to change a circumstance we are in by taking steps to move out of what is and create what we want things to be.

The placement of Mars in our charts lets us know just how our sexuality is experienced and expressed, the way in which we take action, and what our motivation is in doing what we do. It points to where the life-force is most evident in our lives and where we need to take action to feel alive, vital, and connected with our inner source of being.

Passion and our individual manner of expressing it in our lives—not just sexually but in all that we do—are the domain of Mars. Its symbol is the same as the one for masculine energy, for it represents acting upon, initiating, and overtly expressing our human need to put ourselves forward in ways that let our individuality emerge, come alive, and make an impact on others. Here we are the selves that connect to others in a forceful, overt, physical, assertive, and sometimes leadership way. It is with this energy that we move ahead, make new beginnings, and express that spontaneous inner self that makes for joyful excitement in life and a sense of being separate, unique— a distinct self forging an individual impact on the world and others.

Mars in Aries makes for a dynamic and forceful manner of going after what we want. With the planet in its own sign, action is the place where this individual feels most comfortable. Taking the lead and moving forward in a direct, decisive, and exciting way are part of what attracts others to him or her.

Aries Mars individuals often stimulate others to action as well, inspiring them by example to express whatever their unique individualities may be. Sexually these are passionate and impulsive lovers, likely to move forward aggressively and competently in any situation that involves conflict, competition, or conquest.

Mars in Taurus produces a determined, thorough individual, one who cannot be deterred once forward motion toward a goal has commenced. Satisfaction in completion is one of the themes of this person's life. The identity may also be wrapped up in attachment to material or sensual rewards, desires that can be made manifest in tangible ways.

This person may not seem instantly propelled toward fulfilling a desire but is steadfast and unstoppable in continuing the pursuit until acquisition is assured. Sexually as well, there is a stability and loyalty that come with a Taurus Mars, along with a particularly highly developed sensuality.

Mars in Gemini makes for a variable energy in the individual. This is someone who does innumerable things at once, perhaps not completing any of them but certainly making many connections simultaneously. The desires here are most often expressed verbally, perhaps even to the exclusion of any action at all.

Sexually this is an exciting, entertaining, and charming lover, with a propensity toward ambivalence. Multiple relationships may be looked upon as preferable, or any union may be stimulating only if made up of a great many connections on all levels. This is a Renaissance person, performing a little bit of this and a dash of that, with a marvelous versatility of experiences in a great many fields.

Mars in Cancer impacts upon the emotionality of expression, which makes up a significant part of any action this person takes. Intuitions are particularly strong here, and this is a person who readily senses change in a situation or mood and accordingly alters his or her way of approaching a situation.

Loving is as important as sexual conquest or fulfillment for the Cancer Mars person, whose sexuality is wrapped up with being taken care of and/or nurturing another, marked by a great sensitivity to emotional fluctuations. The sense of self often changes at a moment's notice, as do the emotional whims and reactions of this reactive, passionate, and responsive human being.

Mars in Leo produces a rather overpowering personality, with a glow that sometimes can be blinding but also with a light that can lead the way for others out of the darkness. This indefatigable leader thrives on appreciation and admiration. Action almost doesn't count to this individual unless there's an audience and some form of adulation.

Romance and fun, creativity and excitement are some of the ways in which this person's passion gets expressed. Sex, as part of the Leo Mars person's well-being, is considered of great significance, though overinvolvement with the self sometimes makes passion a one-way affair. With deep creative fulfillment, however, an instinctively loving and generous self emerges.

Mars in Virgo denotes an individual who takes great pains to see that everything is cared for or healed no matter how great the effort it requires. This person takes great pride, too, in figuring out the solutions to all levels and kinds of problems—from those of a practical or medical nature to more complex emotional ones.

The sexuality of this person is subdued and delicate, responsive to subtlety. This individual's great sensuality and emotional sensitivity know no bounds once stimulated, but getting there may be quite some challenge. Mars Virgo's manner of approaching others is likewise an indirect and subtle form of engagement.

Mars in Libra can be quite the flirt, ever alert to the possibility of making new connections with romantic potential. This general sociability could mask an indecisiveness about commitment as well as speak to the truly friendly nature of someone desiring contact and enjoying making others feel good about themselves.

Creating harmony and taking actions that make for peaceful results are how this identity gets expressed. The sexual nature is usually indirect because attracting others is easier for this person than going after whatever or whoever is truly desired. Libra Mars individuals take pleasure in interactions at all levels, especially those with open-minded possibilities.

Mars in Scorpio intensifies the feelings of desire in an individual and simultaneously makes them less easy to be expressed directly. Desire itself is involved with much more here than pure physical responsiveness to beauty or a yearning for connection, fulfillment, or satisfaction. It also connects to deeper, sometimes negative emotional dispositions that speak of the secret, the forbidden, and the unknown in one's psyche and history.

Sexually voracious once repression has lifted, this kind of person may tend to self-destructiveness in relationships. Learning to transform and redirect these tendencies helps the Scorpio Mars personality attain a happier and more fulfilling identity.

Mars in Sagittarius is suggestive of the happy wanderer, an exciting, enthusiastic adventurer whose passionate pursuits inspire some great stories later on. This person finds ease and satisfaction among people, even in completely new social situations, wherever laughter, lightness, and jovial exchanges abound. A desire to expand the horizons leads to emotional, physical, sexual, and spiritual exploration.

Sexually this can be a very generous lover—with an equal likelihood that this generosity is shared by more than one recipient. Having a good time is part of the motto here, though once committed, Sagittarius Mars people live up to their social roles quite nobly.

Mars in Capricorn intensifies the focus on attaining one's object of desire, along with the seriousness and determination with which this is accomplished. There is usually a struggle this person goes through before coming fully to terms with his or her desiring nature. Perhaps a strict or religious upbringing or the absence of one or both parents makes moving optimistically toward what he or she wants a difficult task.

Sexually this is an accomplished lover, though perhaps conventional or formal. Marriage may create a safer environment for Capricorn Mars individuals to explore fully their own depths of sexual and sensual satisfaction.

Mars in Aquarius makes for an unusual energy with surprises and excitement galore. The identity of this individual is complex and unpredictable, with a certain edge of detachment as well. The lack of judgments about or interference with the lives of others makes this person an ideal friend.

Sexually these can be either highly sublimated individuals or people with erratic desire natures that seem to blow hot one day—or year or relationship—and cold the next. But whatever is to be said, they are individuals with flashes of brilliance and intuition that can inspire, shock, excite, and entertain but never bore you.

Mars in Pisces lends a kind of magical undertone to the desire nature, so that sex is often expressed as some unearthly kind of transcendence. It may be difficult for this individual to know just what that real, comfortable inner self wants to pursue. More often, taking life as it comes, the Pisces Mars person bravely confronts and endures whatever befalls.

A free-flowing sensuality is present in all interactions, with private fulfillments remaining much of a mystery to all but the participants. The Pisces Mars person is ever alert to the spiritual and emotional significance of sexual encounters, and his or her mission seems something a bit deeper, farther out than the norm, and more mystical.

How to Find the Place of Mars in Your Chart

Find your birth year in the left-hand column and read across the chart until you find your birth date. The top of that column will tell you where Mars lies in your chart.

PLACE OF MARS—1880–1891

	♈ ARIES	♉ TAURUS	♊ GEMINI	♋ CANCER	♌ LEO	♍ VIRGO	♎ LIBRA	♏ SCORP.	♐ SAGITT.	♑ CAPRI.	♒ AQUAR.	♓ PISCES
1880		2/13	2/14–4/11	4/12–6/1	6/2–7/20	7/21–9/5	9/6–10/21	10/22–12/3	12/4↱			
1881	5/13–6/21	6/22–8/3	8/4–9/23	9/24↱					↳1/13	1/14–2/22	2/23–4/2	4/3–5/12
1882			1/12–2/25	↳1/11 2/26–5/7	5/8–6/30	7/1–8/18	8/19–10/2	10/3–11/14	11/15–12/25	12/26↱		
1883	4/21–5/29	5/30–7/10	7/11–8/23	8/24–10/14	10/15↱					↳2/2	2/3–3/12	3/13–4/20
1884					↳6/4	6/5–7/27	7/28–9/12	9/13–10/25	10/26–12/5	12/6↱		
1885	3/31–5/8	5/9–6/18	6/19–7/31	8/1–9/16	9/17–11/8	11/9↱				↳1/12	1/13–2/19	2/20–3/30
1886						↳7/1	7/2–8/21	8/22–10/5	10/6–11/14	11/15–12/23	12/24↱	
1887	3/11–4/18	4/19–5/29	5/30–7/11	7/12–8/26	8/27–10/13	10/14–12/5	12/6↱				↳1/30	1/31–3/10
1888							↳2/26 3/10–7/21	2/27–3/9 7/22–9/10	9/11–10/22	10/23–12/1	12/2↱	
1889	2/17–3/28	3/29–5/9	5/10–6/22	6/23–8/6	8/7–9/22	9/23–11/10	11/11–12/31				↳1/9	1/10–2/16
1890								1/1–2/28 6/17–7/21	3/1–6/16 7/22–9/23	9/24–11/5	11/6–12/16	12/17↱
1891	1/26–3/7	3/8–4/19	4/20–6/3	6/4–7/19	7/20–9/4	9/5–10/21	10/22–12/7	12/8↱				↳1/25

PLACE OF MARS—1892–1906

Year												
1892	12/28⌐							⌐1/24	1/25–3/13	3/14–5/6	5/7–11/8	11/9–12/27
1893	⌐2/10	2/11–3/28	3/29–5/13	5/14–6/29	6/30–8/15	8/16–10/1	10/2–11/16	11/17–12/31				
1894	6/23–8/18 10/13–12/30	8/19–10/12 12/31⌐						1/1–2/13		2/14–3/27	3/28–5/9	5/10–6/22
1895		⌐3/1					10/30–12/11	12/12⌐				
1896	5/22–7/1	7/2–8/15	8/16–12/31						⌐1/22	1/23–3/2	3/3–4/11	4/12–5/21
1897	1/1–3/21	3/22–5/17	5/18–7/8	7/9–8/25	8/26–10/9	10/10–11/21	11/22⌐					
1898	4/29–6/6	6/7–7/18	7/19–9/2	9/3–10/30	10/31⌐				⌐1/1	1/2–2/10	2/11–3/20	3/21–4/28
1899	1/16–4/14	4/15–6/15	6/16–8/5	8/6–9/20	9/21–11/2	11/3–12/13	12/14⌐					
1900	4/8–5/16	5/17–6/26	6/27–8/9	8/10–9/26	9/27–11/22	11/23⌐			11/24	⌐1/21	1/22–2/28	3/1–4/7
1901		⌐3/1	5/11–7/13	7/14–8/31	9/1–10/14	10/15–11/23	11/24⌐		⌐1/1			
1902	3/19–4/26	4/27–6/6	6/7–7/20	7/21–9/4	9/5–10/23	10/24⌐				⌐1/1	1/2–2/8	2/9–3/18
1903			⌐4/19	4/20–5/30	5/31–8/6	8/7–9/22	9/23–11/2	11/3–12/11	12/12⌐			
1904	2/27–4/6	4/7–5/17	5/18–6/30	7/1–8/14	8/15–10/1	10/2–11/19	11/20⌐					1/20–2/26
1905							⌐1/13	1/14–8/21	8/22–10/7	10/8–11/17	11/18–12/27	12/28⌐
1906	2/5–3/16	3/17–4/28	4/29–6/11	6/12–7/27	7/28–9/12	9/13–10/29	10/30–12/16	12/17⌐				⌐2/4

PLACE OF MARS—1907-1923

	♈ ARIES	♉ TAURUS	♊ GEMINI	♋ CANCER	♌ LEO	♍ VIRGO	♎ LIBRA	♏ SCORP.	♐ SAGITT.	♑ CAPRI.	♒ AQUAR.	♓ PISCES
1907								↳2/4	2/5-4/1	4/2-10/13	10/14-11/28	11/29 ↳1/10
1908	1/11-2/22	2/23-4/6	4/7-5/22	5/23-7/7	7/8-8/23	8/24-10/9	10/10-11/25	11/26 ↳				
1909	7/21-9/26, 11/21 ↳								1/10-2/23	2/24-4/9	4/10-5/25	9/27-11/20, 5/26-7/20
1910	↳1/22	1/23-3/13	3/14-5/1	5/2-6/18	6/19-8/5	8/6-9/21	9/22-11/6	11/7-12/19	12/20 ↳			
1911	6/3-7/15	7/16-9/5, 11/30 ↳	9/6-11/29						↳1/31	2/1-3/13	3/14-4/22	4/23-6/2
1912		↳1/30	1/31-4/4	4/5-5/27	5/28-7/16	7/17-9/2	9/3-10/17	10/18-11/29	11/30 ↳			
1913	5/8-6/16	6/17-7/28	7/29-9/15	9/16 ↳					↳1/10	1/11-2/18	2/19-3/29	3/30-5/7
1914				↳5/1	5/2-6/25	6/26-8/14	8/15-9/28	9/29-11/10	11/11-12/21	12/22 ↳		
1915	4/17-5/25	5/26-7/5	7/6-8/18	8/19-10/7	10/8 ↳					↳1/29	1/30-3/9	3/10-4/16
1916					↳5/28	5/29-7/22	7/23-9/8	9/9-10/21	10/22-12/1	12/2 ↳		
1917	3/27-5/4	5/5-6/14	6/15-7/27	7/28-9/11	9/12-11/1	11/2 ↳				↳1/9	1/10-2/16	2/17-3/26
1918						↳1/10, 2/26-6/23	1/11-2/25, 6/24-8/16	8/17-9/30	10/1-11/10	11/11-12/19	12/20 ↳	
1919	3/7-4/14	4/15-5/25	5/26-7/8	7/9-8/22	8/23-10/9	10/10-11/29	11/30 ↳				↳1/26	1/27-3/6
1920							↳1/31, 4/24-7/10	2/1-4/23, 7/11-9/4	9/5-10/18	10/19-11/27	11/28 ↳	
1921	2/13-3/24	3/25-5/5	5/6-6/18	6/19-8/2	8/3-9/18	9/19-11/6	11/7-12/25	12/26 ↳			↳1/4	1/5-2/12
1922								↳2/18	2/19-9/13	9/14-10/30	10/31-12/11	12/12 ↳
1923	1/21-3/3	3/4-4/15	4/16-5/30	5/31-7/15	7/16-8/31	9/1-10/17	10/18-12/3	12/4-12/31				↳1/20

PLACE OF MARS—1924–1933

	♈ ARIES	♉ TAURUS	♊ GEMINI	♋ CANCER	♌ LEO	♍ VIRGO	♎ LIBRA	♏ SCORP.	♐ SAGITT.	♑ CAPRI.	♒ AQUAR.	♓ PISCES	*♂ Retrograde R	D
1924	12/19↰							1/1-1/19	1/20-3/6	3/7-4/24	4/25-6/24 / 8/25-10/19*	6/25-8/24* / 10/20-12/18	5♓7/24	25♒9/22
1925	↰2/4	2/5-3/23	3/24-5/9	5/10-6/25	6/26-8/12	8/13-9/28	9/29-11/13	11/14-12/27	12/28↰					
1926	6/15-7/31	8/1↰							↰2/8	2/9-3/22	3/23-5/3	5/4-6/14	19♉9/29	4♉12/7
1927		↰2/21	2/22-4/16	4/17-6/5	6/6-7/24	7/25-9/10	9/11-10/25	10/26-12/7	12/8↰					
1928	5/17-6/25	6/26-8/8	8/9-10/2 / 12/20↰	10/3-12/19*					↰1/18	1/19-2/27	2/28-4/7	4/8-5/16	9♋11/12	
1929			↰3/10*	3/11-5/12	5/13-7/3	7/4-8/21	8/22-10/5	10/6-11/18	11/19-12/28	12/29↰				20♊1/27
1930	4/25-6/2	6/3-7/14	7/15-8/27	8/28-10/20	10/21*					↰2/6	2/7-3/16	3/17-4/24	17♌12/19	
1931				2/17-3/29*	↰2/16 / 3/30-6/10	6/11-8/1	8/2-9/16	9/17-10/30	10/31-12/9	12/10↰				27♋3/9
1932	4/3-5/11	5/12-6/21	6/22-8/4	8/5-9/30	10/1-11/13	11/14↰				↰1/17	1/18-2/24	2/25-4/2		
1933						↰7/6	7/7-8/25	8/26-10/8	10/9-11/18	11/19-12/27	12/28↰		20♍1/21	1♍4/13

PLACE OF MARS—1934–1944

	♈ ARIES	♉ TAURUS	♊ GEMINI	♋ CANCER	♌ LEO	♍ VIRGO	♎ LIBRA	♏ SCORP.	♐ SAGITT.	♑ CAPRI.	♒ AQUAR.	♓ PISCES	♂ Retrograde R — D
1934	3/14-4/22	4/23-6/2	6/3-7/15	7/16-8/30	8/31-10/17	10/18-12/10	12/11				↳2/3	2/4-3/13	
1935							↳7/29	7/30-9/16	9/17-10/29	10/30-12/7	12/8		25♎2/28-6♎5/18
1936	2/23-4/2	4/3-5/13	5/14-6/26	6/27-8/10	8/11-9/27	9/28-11/15	11/16				↳1/15	1/16-2/22	
1937							↳1/6	1/7-3/13 5/16-8/9*	3/14-5/15* 8/10-9/30	10/1-11/12	11/13-12/22	12/23	6♐4/15-19♏6/28
1938	2/1-3/13	3/14-4/24	4/25-6/8	6/9-7/23	7/24-9/8	9/9-10/26	10/27-12/12	12/13				↳1/31	
1939								↳1/30	1/31-3/22	3/23-5/25 7/23-9/25*	5/26-7/22* 9/26-11/20	11/21	5♑7/23-23♐8/24
1940	1/5-2/18	2/19-4/2	4/3-5/18	5/19-7/4	7/5-8/20	8/21-10/6	10/7-11/21	11/22				↳1/4	
1941	7/4↳								1/6-2/18	2/19-4/3	4/4-5/17	5/18-7/3	24♈9/7-11♈11/11
1942	↳1/12	1/13-3/8	3/9-4/27	4/28-6/15	6/16-8/2	8/3-9/18	9/19-11/2	11/3-12/16	12/17				
1943	5/29-7/8	7/9-8/24	8/25↳						↳1/27	1/28-3/9	3/10-4/18	4/19-5/28	22♊10/30
1944			↳3/29*	3/30-5/23	5/24-7/13	7/14-8/30	8/31-10/14	10/15-11/26	11/27				5♊1/11

PLACE OF MARS—1945–1960

1945	5/4–6/12	6/13–7/24	7/25–9/8	9/9–11/12 12/28* →	11/13–12/27*				→ 1/6	1/7–2/15	2/16–3/26	3/27–5/3	3♌12/5 →
1946				→ 4/23*	4/24–6/21	6/22–8/10	8/11–9/25	9/26–11/7	11/8–12/18	12/19 →			→ 14♋2/22
1947	4/13–5/22	5/23–7/2	7/3–8/14	8/15–10/2	10/3–12/2	12/3 →				→ 1/26	1/27–3/5	3/6–4/12	
1948					2/14–5/19*	→ 2/13* 5/20–7/18	7/19–9/4	9/5–10/18	10/19–11/27	11/28 →			8♏1/9–18♌3/30
1949	3/23–5/1	5/2–6/11	6/12–7/24	7/25–9/8	9/9–10/28	10/29–12/27	12/28 →			→ 1/5	1/6–2/12	2/13–3/22	
1950						3/30–6/12*	→ 3/29* 6/13–8/11	8/12–9/26	9/27–11/7	11/8–12/16	12/17–12/31		11♎2/13–22♍5/5
1951	3/2–4/10	4/11–5/21	5/22–7/3	7/4–8/18	8/19–10/4	10/5–11/24	11/25 →				1/11–1/22	1/23–3/1	13♎1/2
1952							→ 1/20	1/21–8/27	8/28–10/12	10/13–11/21	11/22–12/30	12/31 →	1♉3/25–1♏6/11
1953	2/9–3/20	3/21–5/1	5/2–6/14	6/15–7/29	7/30–9/14	9/15–11/1	11/2–12/20	12/21 →				→ 2/8	
1954								→ 2/9	2/10–4/12 2/4–8/24*	4/13–7/3* 8/25–10/21	10/22–12/4	12/5 →	8♑5/23–25♐7/30
1955	1/16–2/26	2/27–4/10	4/11–5/26	5/27–7/11	7/12–8/27	8/28–10/13	10/14–11/29	11/30 →				→ 1/15	
1956	12/7 →							→ 1/14	1/15–2/28	2/29–4/14	4/15–6/3	6/4–12/6*	23♊8/11–13♊10/11
1957	→ 1/28	1/29–3/17	3/18–5/4	5/5–6/21	6/22–8/8	8/9–9/24	9/25–11/8	11/9–12/23	12/24 →				
1958	6/8–7/21	7/22–9/21 10/30* →	9/22–10/29*						→ 2/3	2/4–3/17	3/18–4/27	4/28–6/7	2♊10/11–6♉12/21
1959		→ 2/10	2/11–4/10	4/11–6/1	6/2–7/20	7/21–9/5	9/6–10/21	10/22–12/3	12/4 →				
1960	5/12–6/20	6/21–8/2	8/3–9/21	9/22–12/31*					→ 1/14	1/15–2/23	2/24–4/2	4/3–5/11	18♒11/21

PLACE OF MARS—1961–1971

Year	♈ ARIES	♉ TAURUS	♊ GEMINI	♋ CANCER	♌ LEO	♍ VIRGO	♎ LIBRA	♏ SCORP.	♐ SAGITT.	♑ CAPRI.	♒ AQUAR.	♓ PISCES	℞ Retrograde R / D
1961				1/1-5/5*	5/6-6/27	6/28-8/16	8/17-9/30	10/1-11/12	11/13-12/23	12/24			0♋2/7
1962	4/19-5/27	5/28-7/8	7/9-8/21	8/22-10/10	10/11					↳1/31	2/1-3/11	3/12-4/18	24♎12/26
1963					↳6/2*	6/3-7/26	7/27-9/11	9/12-10/24	10/25-12/4	12/5			5♌3/17
1964	3/29-5/6	5/7-6/16	6/17-7/29	7/30-9/14	9/15-11/5	11/6				↳1/12	1/13-2/19	2/20-3/28	
1965						↳6/28*	6/29-8/19	8/20-10/3	10/4-11/13	11/14-12/22	12/23		28♍1/28 / 8♍4/20
1966	3/9-4/16	4/17-5/27	5/28-7/10	7/11-8/24	8/25-10/11	10/12-12/3	12/4				↳1/29	1/30-3/8	
1967							↳2/11	2/12-9/9*	9/10-10/22	10/23-11/30	12/1		3♏3/9 / 15♎5/26
1968	2/17-3/26	3/27-5/7	5/8-6/20	6/21-8/4	8/5-9/20	9/21-11/8	11/9-12/28	12/29			↳1/8	1/9-2/16	16♏4/27 / 1♐7/8
1969								↳2/24	2/25-9/20*	9/21-11/3	11/4-12/14	12/15	
1970	1/24-3/6	3/7-4/17	4/18-6/1	6/2-7/17	7/18-9/2	9/3-10/19	10/20-12/5	12/6-12/31				↳1/23	
1971	12/26							1/1-1/22	1/23-3/11	3/12-5/2	5/3-11/5*	11/6-12/25	21♒7/10℞ / 11♒9/8D

PLACE OF MARS—1972–1980

Year													Right-hand column
1972	↳29	2/10-3/26	3/27-5/11	5/12-6/27	6/28-8/14	8/15-9/29	9/30-11/14	11/15-12/29	12/30	2/12-3/25	3/26-5/7	5/8-6/19	9♈9/19♉ 25♈11/25♊
1973	6/20-8/11 10/29-12/23*	8/12-10/28* ↳12/24	2/27-4/19	4/20-6/8	6/9-7/26	7/27-9/11	9/12-10/27	10/28-12/9	↳2/11				
1974		↳2/26							↳12/10				2♊11/6♋
1975	5/21-6/30	7/1-8/13	8/14-10/16 11/25	10/17-11/24*					↳1/20	1/21-3/2	3/3-4/10	4/11-5/20	
1976		↳3/17*	3/18-5/15	9/1-10/25	10/26 ↳1/25*			11/20-12/31	↳1/20				14♊1/20♋
1977	4/27-6/5	6/6-7/16	7/17-8/31		10/26	8/24-10/7	10/8-11/19			1/1-2/8	2/9-3/19	3/20-4/26	11♋12/12♌
1978			1/26-4/9*		1/25* 4/10-6/13	6/14-8/3	8/4-9/18	9/19-11/1	11/2-12/11	↳1/19 12/12		1/20-2/26	22♌3/1♍
1979	4/7-5/15	5/16-6/25	6/26-8/7	8/8-9/23	9/24-11/18 11/19	7/10-8/28	8/29-10/11	10/12-11/21	11/22-12/29	1/20-2/26	2/27-4/6		
1980				3/11-5/3*	3/10* 5/4-7/9				11/22-12/29 12/30-12/31				15♍/16♎ 25♌4/6♎

*In these periods, Mars (♂) is Retrograde during some or all of the time. See right-hand column.

PLACE OF MARS—1981–1987

	♈ ARIES	♉ TAURUS	♊ GEMINI	♋ CANCER	♌ LEO	♍ VIRGO	♎ LIBRA	♏ SCORP.	♐ SAGITT.	♑ CAPRI.	♒ AQUAR.	♓ PISCES
1981	3/16–4/24	4/25–6/4	6/5–7/17	7/18–8/31	9/1–10/19	10/20–12/14	12/15 ↄ				1/1–2/5	2/6–3/15
1982							ↄ8/2	8/3–9/18	9/19–10/30	10/31–12/9	12/10	
1983	2/24–4/4	4/5–5/15	5/16–6/28	6/29–8/12	8/13–9/28	9/29–11/17	11/18 ↄ				ↄ1/16	1/17–2/23
1984							ↄ1/9	1/10–8/16	8/17–10/4	10/5–11/14	11/15–12/24	12/25 ↄ
1985	2/2–3/14	3/15–4/25	4/26–6/8	6/9–7/23	7/24–9/8	9/9–10/26	10/27–12/13	12/14 ↄ				ↄ2/1
1986							11/23 ↄ	ↄ2/1	2/2–3/26	3/27–10/7	10/8–11/24	11/25 ↄ
1987	1/8–2/19	2/20–4/4	4/5–5/19	5/20–7/5	7/6–8/21	8/22–10/7	10/8–11/22	11/23 ↄ				ↄ1/7

PLACE OF MARS—1988–2000

Year												
1988	7/13-10/22 11/1							↳1/7	1/8-2/21	2/22-4/5	4/6-5/21	5/22-7/12 10/23-10/31
1989	↳1/18	1/19-3/9	3/10-4/27	4/28-6/15	6/16-8/2	8/3-9/18	9/19-11/3	11/4-12/16	12/17 ↓			
1990	5/31-7/11	7/12-8/30 12/14	8/31-12/13						↳1/28	1/29-3/10	3/11-4/19	4/20-5/30
1991		↳1/20	1/21-4/1	4/2-5/25	5/26-7/14	7/15-8/31	9/1-10/15	10/16-11/27	11/28 ↓			
1992	5/5-6/13	6/14-7/25	7/26-9/11	9/12 ↓					↳1/8	1/9-2/16	2/17-3/26	3/27-5/4
1993				↳4/26	4/27-6/22	6/23-8/10	8/11-9/25	9/26-11/7	11/8-12/18	12/19 ↓		
1994	4/14-5/22	5/23-7/2	7/3-8/15	8/16-10/3	10/4-12/11	12/12 ↓				↳1/26	1/27-3/6	3/7-4/13
1995					1/22-5/23	↳1/21 5/24-7/20	7/21-9/6	9/7-10/19	10/20-11/29	11/30 ↓		
1996	3/24-5/1	5/2-6/11	6/12-7/24	7/25-9/8	9/9-10/29	10/30 ↓				↳1/7	1/8-2/14	2/15-3/23
1997					3/8-6/18	1/3-3/7 6/19-8/13	8/14-9/27	9/28-11/8	11/9-12/17	12/18 ↓		
1998	4/12-5/22	5/23-7/5	7/6-8/19	8/20-10/6	10/7-11/26	11/27 ↓				↳1/24	1/25-3/3	3/4-4/11
1999						↳1/25 5/5-7/3	1/26-5/4 7/4-9/1	9/2-10/15	10/16-11/25	11/26 ↓		
2000	3/22-5/2	5/3-6/15	6/16-7/30	7/31-9/15	9/16-11/3	11/4-12/22	12/23-12/31			↳1/2	1/3-2/10	2/11-3/21

YOUR RULING PLANET: ARIES—Mars; TAURUS—Venus; GEMINI—Mercury; CANCER—The Moon; LEO—The Sun; VIRGO—Mercury; LIBRA—Venus; SCORPIO—Mars; SAGITTARIUS—Jupiter; CAPRICORN—Saturn; AQUARIUS—Uranus; PISCES—Neptune.

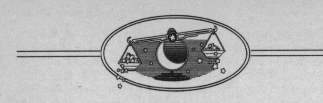

JUPITER: FORTUNE AND BOUNTY

Jupiter represents the potential for your growth and expansion on many levels—physical, mental, and spiritual—as well as the accumulation of such things as material assets, power, and status. Jupiter represents honors, recognition, and personal advancement that come to you. It is also indicative of your father and your father's family and position. It represents higher education—that is, the degrees you obtain or the subjects you pursue on your own after you have reached adulthood. Your religious attitude and training are represented by Jupiter as well as your interest and participation in cultural pursuits. Jupiter represents good fortune in the sense of giving you capacity to enjoy life to the fullest regardless of whether or not you are wealthy.

Jupiter in Aries. The areas in which you experience growth and expansion will have a tendency to get out of control. How inclined or efficient you are at regaining control when it has been lost is indicated by other factors in your natal chart and, of course, is determined by your particular background and the maturity you have developed. For example, you may earn or attract wealth and other assets, but it is likely you also have an equal generosity of spirit when it comes to spending money. If you have not learned efficient methods of handling your income or assets, then you never quite get ahead financially. Another highly possible situation with Jupiter in Aries is your having the good fortune to make a lot of money so fast that you aren't prepared to handle it properly or that you become so busy acquiring money you don't have time to enjoy it. When it comes to expanding your intellectual horizons, Jupiter in Aries is an indication that you may eagerly seek information and education but that in your haste you may easily miss the facts or fail to pay attention to them. You may rush into situations even though you may not have all the knowledge or information required. You want to know everything at once and become impatient with the more plodding, patient approach to learning. You can become passionate concerning the subjects and issues that interest you, and they include religious zeal. Your passion serves as inspiration to others and makes you an effective teacher. You do not pay much attention to limitations, and in your enthusiasm you can easily lose sight of practicality or reality. You are apt to be fond of sports and risk-taking pursuits for both business and pleasure.

Jupiter in Taurus. You are concerned with expanding your physical world, its pleasures and its traditional structures. However, when you gain monetary or other advantages, you may be so worried about hanging on to them that you lose the opportunity to enjoy them or to use them as a step to further progress; much will depend on your individual background and the values you have learned. You are nevertheless comfortable with wealth and status, and it is likely you'll use whatever advantages you gain not only to promote your personal growth and progress but also to improve the quality of life for others. In addition to gaining material wealth, you want your growth in any area to be tangible. In other words, you want physical signs of progress. In the area of education, for example, even if you are a dedicated scholar, you'll want to use your knowledge to earn more money or gain prestige in the community. You have an appreciation for music and art, and if Jupiter is well placed in your natal chart, it can indicate talent in these areas and the opportunity to develop such talent. You may have interest in banking and finance, building and real estate, food and fashion. You may have a green thumb and, if not, certainly an appreciation for plants and flowers even if you don't grow them yourself. Jupiter in Taurus gives the capacity to enjoy physical pleasures and personal comfort. However, when emotionally insecure or upset, you may go to one extreme or the other, either wasting assets you would not normally risk and becoming involved with physical pleasure to the exclusion of more important matters or, on the other hand, becoming very miserly and rejecting personal pleasures and comfort altogether.

Jupiter in Gemini. Jupiter in Gemini indicates that your areas of personal growth and expansion involve your intellect—that is, what you know (or can learn) and your continuing involvement with ideas, information, and communication. It is also an indication that you will broaden your intellectual horizons through marriage or partnership. No matter what you do for a living, your growth as an individual is directly tied to developing a network of connections that continually provides you with information and mental stimulation. Whether this type of personal expansion also happens to make you a wealthy person or advances your standard of living in other ways is coincidental, not an inevitable result. Jupiter in Gemini is also an indication of how well you circulate in your immediate community and of your interest and participation in community activities. While part of your vital learning process is destined to occur in your own neighborhood, travel, whether for business or pleasure, is an important part of your overall education. You will always be able to pick up valuable information and make important connections when you travel. Though Jupiter in Gemini indicates intellectual curiosity that can lead to important discoveries, it unfortunately also includes a tendency for you to become too scattered or overly concerned with trivial matters or gossip. Being able to organize material is just as important as collecting it, and inundating yourself with too much information can be a stumbling block to actually making use of it. Publishing, advertising, engineering, design, teaching, writing, and communications are some particular areas that will attract your interest and participation. Computers, electronic equipment, and transportation are other fields in which you may become involved. You may also have clever mechanical skills and some artistic talent.

Jupiter in Cancer. The strongest area of your personal growth and expansion is connected with your emotional development, which in turn is directly related to the influence of your family background, your family connections and resources, and the state of your domestic environment as a child and as an adult. Whatever you do in life, you need to establish a strong emotional support system for yourself, and perhaps just as important, you must be willing to be part of such a system for others. If your background has unfortunately provided a negative influence, it may be doubly difficult to turn your emotional behavior and attitudes in a positive direction, but the more successfully you manage to do this, the more correspondingly successful you will be as an individual and in many other areas. Another factor is family resources and connections and your ability to make use of them. If you are fortunate enough to have important family connections that help advance your career or you have material wealth through inheritance, there is a lesson to be learned in using them wisely but not automatically depending on them to provide a life-style and advantages without your efforts to do something productively on your own. On the other hand, you have the responsibility of providing and preserving resources and connections for your family. The concept of nurturing is a strong element in this Jupiter sign position, and you are likely to be a talented cook, caterer, psychological counselor, or educator. You may also have a flair for art and design. You may think, learn, and generally do better in an environment near the ocean or other body of water or may receive your higher education in such an environment.

Jupiter in Leo. This sign position indicates that your growth as an individual is directly connected with your spiritual development, expansion of your intellect through higher education or advanced training, and interest and participation in cultural pursuits. Any of these concerns may or may not actually involve your profession or be the means of economic advancement; however, achieving personal growth is often the key to being successful in other areas of life. Your creative instincts are likely to be enhanced with this Jupiter position. Of course, it doesn't guarantee you will have artistic talent, but it does mean that developing the use of whatever creativity and imagination you do possess is an important step in being successful in many other areas. Whatever direction your efforts take, they are liable to be somewhat overdone or exaggerated, as is the usual case with Leo's influence, but that doesn't have to be a negative factor in what you do, unless you lose sight of the fact that things are out of proportion. Generosity as well as maintaining high principles and loyalty are a big part of your growth. The pomp and pageantry of traditional rituals attract your imagination and inspire your enthusiastic participation. Advertising, direct mail, publishing, broadcasting, politics, and foreign trade may be other areas of particular interest for you. In addition to the areas already mentioned, your higher education is apt to involve sociology, philosophy, theology, or anthropology. Working with children or to advance the cause of philanthropic groups is an excellent way to expand your own growth. You are likely to have great interest in sports and risk-taking ventures for both business and pleasure. Long-distance travel is an important stimulating factor in your overall development, and opportunities to travel should not be missed.

Jupiter in Virgo. Jupiter in Virgo signifies important managerial and executive abilities. Even if you yourself don't happen to possess such qualities, you are likely to recognize these talents in others. Part of your personal growth and advancement may be directly connected to your efforts to place qualified people (yourself included) in the positions where they can do the most good. Your efficient organization of material, labor, and other types of systems is another key to success. You want tangible proof of your own growth and progress—that is, some sort of physical evidence or at least irrefutable proof of what your influence and efforts have accomplished. You want to use in some meaningful, even public manner the knowledge and skills that have contributed to your growth as an individual. You want to know that you have made a difference, and unless other factors in your natal chart indicate a more inhibited nature, you want others to be aware of it as well. As suggested above, you are also very often to be found just as seriously involved with the progress, growth, and ultimate effectiveness of others as you are with your own. The idealism associated with Jupiter and the perfection-oriented nature of Virgo can sometimes become a severe limitation for you. When nothing and no one seem good enough or perfect enough, you may tend to use this as an excuse for your own idleness, and on a more personal level, you may give up relationships that might have eventually become valuable emotional contacts if you had managed to overlook certain shortcomings. Your education, religion, and cultural pursuits (including artistic talent) will tend toward your embracing traditional thoughts and expressions. If you are not careful, you can become overly concerned with unimportant details.

Jupiter in Libra. Your personal growth is, to a large extent, likely to be dependent on associations or partnerships you establish with others. Your understanding of (or willingness to understand) human relationships and interactions is somehow going to play an important role in making you a successful person, in your personal relationships as well as in your job or career. Jupiter's influence in Libra indicates an increased capacity to get along with and (if this planet is well placed in your natal chart) to favorably influence others. If you fail to develop this potential, then it is quite possible you will correspondingly fail in other areas of personal growth. Another important part of your growth potential involves developing, increasing, and, above all, using your intellectual abilities. Part of the intellectual understanding you are expected to gain includes being able to equalize Jupiter's tendency for over-abundance and the Libran requirement for balance between excess and austerity. You are likely to encounter many inequitable situations in life, and rather than look around for others to do something about them, it will be up to you to tip the scales to achieve a better equilibrium. Such out-of-balance circumstances will be personal and include your habits or life-style, but they will also include efforts you make in your immediate society because Jupiter in Libra suggests you have an inspired sense of justice. For instance, you may work (professionally or as a volunteer) in such areas as civil rights, housing for the homeless, or improved housing in disadvantaged areas or in the cause of other community issues. Your higher education is likely to be in law, psychology and counseling, or literature. There is also the indication that you have certain aesthetic tastes, an appreciation (and perhaps talent) for art and music.

Jupiter in Scorpio. Jupiter in Scorpio indicates that your intellectual interests are likely to be dictated by intense emotional desires or that your intellectual understanding is accompanied by a good deal of emotional enthusiasm. Your personal growth is connected with emotional development. Destructive emotions like possessiveness, obsessiveness, and jealousy correspondingly limit your growth as an individual. There may also be an unfortunate tendency for manipulation, and you may engage in this practice without fully realizing its destructive potential. If zeal overwhelms reasonableness and moderation, there is danger you may lapse into fanaticism. Your challenge in life is dealing with resources, your own as well as others, material as well as nonmaterial. By making the most of your assets, monetary assets and personal talents and abilities, you will grow as an individual and gain success in other areas as well. This means conservation, as opposed to waste, and careful development and investment. Failing to develop or use resources properly is as bad as wasting them. Other people, their monetary and personal assets, are important human resources. You can become successful through teaching, training, or doing other types of work that help others to be more productive and develop their own potentials. You may be remarkable in your ability to understand nature and its elementary forces and thus may have a flair for science, research, and development. Food is an elementary resource, and in this respect you are apt to be a gourmet as well as gourmand. Conservation means preserving to a certain extent, but it also includes finding ways to turn old and useless items and material into something new. Renovation of buildings and homes, land reclamation, waste recycling all are areas that fall into this category and in which you might be involved.

Jupiter in Sagittarius. Your growth and success as an individual involve developing an effective, dynamic personality. Though others may succeed by other means, a vital factor in your achievements is going to be your ability to influence people and the outcome of circumstances through the force of your physical presence. You must leave others with a strong impression, stamp your efforts with the indelible mark of your personality. This may seem very self-centered, perhaps even shallow, but it doesn't have to be if in addition to developing a forceful, effective personality, you give yourself a depth of knowledge, sincerity, and spiritual awareness. Being known as a seeker of truth, having a real message to give to others, and inspiring others with enthusiasm and energy are the keys to greatness for you. You will benefit greatly from travel. Opportunities to be with and understand people of different cultures should not be missed. Politics, philosophy, languages, and education are particular areas of study or participation. Your work or study may also be in advertising and sales, broadcasting, and theater. You may be interested in banking or finance, and a certain risk-taking spirit may lead you into speculation. There may be a tendency for you to be pompous or overly impressed with wealth and status, or you may have to deal with these traits in other people. If Jupiter is especially well placed in your natal chart, you may experience the type of good fortune that places you in just the right place at the right time. It may not be the kind of luck that enables you to win the lottery (although that possibility can't be ruled out), but it brings you favorable circumstances and more than an average share of advantages in life.

Jupiter in Capricorn. Jupiter in Capricorn signifies that you are not likely to be given the advantages of inspirational factors to guide your thoughts and behavior in life. Trying to achieve personal growth, you will be limited to gaining understanding through experience and maturity rather than being inspired by such things as religion or philosophy. Whether self-taught or formally educated, you will want to turn your knowledge into more earning power or increased status or both. It isn't that you cannot be personally of a more spiritual or esoteric nature or even have a career in one of those areas, for that is indicated by other factors in your natal chart. It is just that most circumstances life presents will come down to matters that require a more worldly approach. You are going to be primarily concerned with the material world since that is where you will be able to achieve the most. In addition, your growth and success will rarely be a matter of whimsy or a lucky break. Luck for you will always be accompanied by responsibility. You either want to or are forced to keep track of where you have been, where you are at present, and where you are going. Jupiter in Capricorn means it will be your responsibility to separate form from substance to get at the heart of matters. There is executive and managerial ability with Jupiter in Capricorn, and you must not only develop your own skills in this area but also help others who have such valuable traits to attain positions of authority and in the process affect your own advancement. Politics, city planning, engineering, design, building, real estate development, law, law enforcement, and education are some particular areas that may interest you.

Jupiter in Aquarius. You will experience your greatest personal growth on an intellectual level. Expanding your intellectual horizons may or may not bring economic success or have anything directly to do with your job or career, but it is likely to have a significant influence on these matters. Success as an individual is one of the surest keys to success in many other areas of life. Jupiter in Aquarius indicates you are likely to have the capacity for operating efficiently with established ideas and institutions while at the same time being receptive to and participating in ideas and activities which appear out of the ordinary, fantastic, or bizarre to other people. The ability to go between the traditional and the nontraditional can make you a valuable member of society. How deeply you are concerned with yourself as an individual is indicated by other factors in your natal chart, but Jupiter in Aquarius signifies that whatever your point of reference, an important part of personal growth involves being an effective member of society. Unless there are negative factors in your natal chart to counteract it, you are likely to have broad-minded social attitudes and can be an effective catalyst within various organizations and groups. Communication is the most important mechanism at your disposal. It won't be enough for you to expand your intellect without your also being able to communicate your knowledge and understanding to others. Nor is it enough for you to develop and use your own skills and methods of communicating; you must also be willing to help others communicate. Jupiter in Aquarius suggests the possibility that you have clever mechanical or artistic skills. You may have interest and may work in the field of computers, engineering, technology, music, finance, or community housing development.

Jupiter in Pisces. Your personal growth is directly connected to emotional development. Understanding your emotions and acquiring the maturity that accompanies personal growth may depend on your ability to make prudent choices that place you in positions of emotional strength. Establishing stable relationships and strong values will help mitigate impediments to proper emotional development. You may have a tendency to take what you consciously or subconsciously perceive as vulnerability and turn it into a risk-taking attitude that can take a wide variety of forms, from foolhardy behavior that others interpret as a death wish to developing the instincts and capabilities of a successful commodities trader. Much will depend on your particular emotional background. The more negative your childhood or circumstances, the more likely you are to develop correspondingly negative risk-taking behavior. Overcoming such a situation may be your biggest struggle, which, of course, will have a significant influence on your success in other areas of life. If Jupiter in your natal chart is particularly well placed, it is an indication that your home and family will prove an encouraging environment for learning. Enhanced emotional capacity demonstrates that you may have artistic talent, psychic abilities, and a particular facility for mathematics and understanding abstract concepts. There can be an unfortunate tendency for a certain emotional dependency, which includes a good deal of overindulgence and even a destructive dependency on addictive substances. Religion, art, and philosophy can supply inspiration that helps you attain growth as an individual, and you should not miss the opportunities to explore these areas. You may find you are more intellectually stimulated and creative near the ocean or other watery environment, and there is the possibility that education or training you receive as an adult will take place in such an environment.

SATURN: THE TEACHER

Saturn, known as the taskmaster of the zodiac, indicates by sign and house placement where an individual needs to take responsibility for his or her own obstacles to satisfaction and success. Connections between Saturn and other planets or luminaries (Sun or Moon) in your own chart note how and which aspects of your personality suffer from a sense of personal limitation. This limitation is often sensed as being the fault of another person or situation that holds you back from getting what you want, expressing what you want to say, or being what you want to be. Looking for clarification to the placement of your Saturn by sign and by house as well (that is, the first-house position of Saturn has certain similarities to the Saturn in Aries reading, etc.) can help you understand just how you feel oppressed, unappreciated, or generally unfulfilled in an area of your life. Along with understanding comes the need for a certain amount of applied discipline toward achieving satisfaction there and in restructuring your thoughts and behavior in such a way that you are able to see yourself overcoming the fear and distrust that impede the joyful reaching of your goals.

As we look directly at the areas in which we find ourselves feeling dissatisfied and perhaps inadequate, we can understand and accept the way we need to take responsibility for a level of strength in decision making that allows us to act to restructure the situation that exists. Once this shift has been made, our perspective is readily translated into a new way of behaving, altering the effect we have on others as well as the kinds of circumstances we create in our lives. Taking responsibility for ourselves is that crucial first step that Saturn focuses upon in order to enable us to reap the rewards in life that we deserve.

Saturn in Aries presents difficulties in spontaneously asserting oneself, along with making it hard for an individual to feel at home with his or her own instincts for leadership and competition. Moving toward success may always be a struggle for this person. Though the talents, resources, and abilities are present, an Aries Saturn tends to undermine his or her best efforts with either a negative attitude or the inner sense of not really deserving the rewards forthcoming.

Becoming aware of how one's own sense of self determines the outcome of a situation is the first step. Once this knowledge and experience of one's own power grow clearer, he or she can then take responsibility for clearing up the mess made of situations that held great promise but were not followed through because of feared inadequacies.

This person tends to doubt the very instincts that can lead to satisfaction, fulfillment, and ultimate success. Instead of moving forward when action is warranted, the Saturn in Aries person needs to overcome the hesitancy that causes him or her to hold back and delay what would have been an instinctively correct move ahead.

Saturn in Taurus indicates difficulties in one's ability to achieve satisfaction and to experience pleasure. A sense of lack—no matter what or how much a person possesses, earns, or owns—or, in extreme cases, the issue of poverty or survival is at the forefront of this person's mind.

Doubting his or her own creative gifts as well, this person may fail to develop what are magnificent talents and end up doing something less than is fulfilling to earn money, forever pursuing the elusive goal of "having enough."

Learning to acknowledge and appreciate the simple gifts and pleasures of life can help the Saturn in Taurus person begin to overcome attitudes that thwart an experience of satisfaction in life. Concentrating on the lack of something tends to perpetuate the sense of poverty, whereas dwelling on the result of efforts one has made successfully can lead directly to greater success.

Saturn in Gemini indicates one who is continually frustrated by a felt inability to express himself or herself. A sense of being either overwhelmed or ignored by others or of never having the right words to say in a given situation can lead to an alienated and isolated state of being.

The Gemini Saturn person is constantly censoring the very thoughts that need to be expressed or so harshly judging any ideas that come to mind that they are never presented, no matter what their actual value. This person may turn out to be his or her own most severe critic, bringing censure in situations where greater acceptance and encouragement are needed.

Habit patterns of this self-censoring attitude are the biggest obstacle and the hardest thing to turn around. The person may be so convinced of the lack of value of his or her own ideas that thinking of them as potentially powerful and transforming could be a concept quite difficult to accept and act upon. In actuality the Saturn in Gemini's thoughtful consideration of all matters leads to exceptionally well-conceived ideas that are evidence of constructive and valuable applications of serious thinking.

Saturn in Cancer could make for difficulty in human relationships because it indicates a way in which a person feels cut off from the deep feeling and nurturing parts of the self. Barriers to knowing what one's most basic emotional needs are make connections of any depth, tenderness, and compassion hard to initiate, let alone to maintain.

Strong defenses are common in people with this planetary setup, for they are often victims of severe emotional deprivation as children, lacking quality parenting as well as examples of good loving. Looking to their personal histories in a truth-seeking, defense-free way (usually with the help of a counselor of some sort) can lead to a clearer understanding of their individual obstacles to creating closeness and cultivating trust with others.

Rather deep-seated defenses need to be confronted to turn around lifelong habits and even to begin to imagine the possibility of letting in the emotionally nourishing relationships too often substituted for by monetary or other obsessions with love substitutes.

Saturn in Leo impedes a sense of fun in life and may also lead to involvement with addictive substances—anything from alcohol or drugs to food—that represent the person's struggle to derive some sensations of pleasure. As the light inside a person dims, a sense of pessimism and even cynicism about life evolves.

Most often this individual has a very dour attitude toward others, distorted expectations about almost every situation that arises, and a less obvious sense of doubt about himself or herself. This negativity about life could produce a person who works extra hard at having fun or totally withdraws from loving connections with others.

Chronic low self-esteem—the sense that he or she hasn't whatever it takes to get to the place most desired or to achieve whatever is most coveted or doesn't deserve to enjoy whatever good comes to pass—plagues the Saturn in Leo person. Once this individual has come to terms with, acknowledged, and released the inner barriers to pleasure and satisfaction, he or she can then joyfully and successfully get involved with what once seemed like a big, bad world out there.

Saturn in Virgo denotes a great strain in an individual's ability to bring joy and ease to everyday life, a sense of serving others, or the enjoyment of good health and well-being. Rigidity about these things could make for the adherence to an unsatisfying routine or getting stuck in an attitude that everything needs to be done in a certain way to be correct but that nothing is ever good enough anyway.

This person may be a chronic complainer or may just feel silently embittered about how everything is so difficult in life. Escape from even the effort of enjoying life could result in one's working so hard to take care of others that the desires and needs of the self are obscured or totally forgotten. Everyday life may be so overscheduled that there is little time for enjoying it.

One of the ways of convincing the Saturn in Virgo person to try to look at life with a renewed sense of satisfaction and constructive purpose is to emphasize how everything gets done so much more easily and successfully with an attitude of joyfulness. This can help turn barriers into bridges toward a positive state of well-being and service.

Saturn in Libra can contribute to a difficulty in giving, sharing, and making the level of connections that foster relationships in our lives. Such challenges relate to a sense of lack in terms of feelings we don't have enough of in our lives: love, affection, loyalty, acknowledgment, and appreciation. We may then tend to withhold those very things from loved ones—especially partners—and thereby perpetuate the situation.

This frustration in connecting with others usually stems from our inability to nurture relationships with a knowledge and assertion of what we ourselves need. In order to improve this situation, we need to become aware of the ways in which we prevent the good feelings from passing between us and others, denying the harmony that we can open up to in relationships.

We also need to face the ways in which we deny ourselves the acceptance we need and instead constantly seek it from others. Once strengthened, our sense of increased self-esteem will allow us to give in relationships what before we expected and demanded that others give to us.

Saturn in Scorpio has a very powerful effect that is usually unconscious and often not readily obvious even to the beholder of such a placement. Scorpio fuels our sense of power and ability to transform the difficult inner workings of our lives into something constructive, enduring, and beautiful. That process is here made doubly difficult because Saturn's presence tends to hold us in a place of negativity so that we either doubt our power or turn it over to others, seeing others as our oppressors, as able to frustrate us from what we desire most, to deny us our deepest fulfillments.

Overcoming the effects of Saturn in Scorpio calls for some in-depth psychological work to overcome the emotional blocks that may have crystallized inside us. It is not unlikely that our sexual sense of self has become frozen into a numbness that needs gentle but continual stimulation on the physical level, as in some kind of bodywork, to reawaken.

The benefit, however, of overcoming these deeply instilled barriers and fears is an awareness of our power to create what we want in our lives, demonstrating it to others as well.

Saturn in Sagittarius tends to foreshorten our perspective, put obstacles in the way of a joyful view of life and the future. We then need to expand our consciousness and work to our full intellectual capacity to improve our lives, to broaden our horizons, overcoming our areas of greatest difficulty.

Facing the fact that we create our own mental limitations—seeing perhaps only our losses and failures to achieve in the material world around us—almost forces us, for the sake of our own well-being, to explore other levels of endeavor and achievement.

Indulging in sports—noncompetitively—or in academic explorations and even involvement with religious pursuits can lead us to the peacefulness that comes from our inner measures of success.

We must allow ourselves to find areas in which we can learn to enjoy the process of what we are doing, letting that be our guide to a life that unfolds from our inner purpose. Joy is our guide here if we will but listen to it and abide.

Saturn in Capricorn signifies a hard worker, but depending upon how that energy is applied in life, it can make either for success and satisfaction or for continual self-denial and frustration. Saturn in its own sign heightens the emphasis on career and a sense of professional purpose in the world. One's public identity becomes the key to challenges to his or her reputation as well as to how his or her works are received.

An overemphasis on public self, however, could lead the individual to cultivating a hollow shell of a self that feels no true inner satisfaction at all. On the other hand, as one learns to look inward for the strength and inner purpose on one's path, great works of value can be achieved, to the benefit of others as well as the self—and to society. The key is to take one's cues from the instinctive sense of what one can do to protect and ensure the safety and success of the lives of those around us and then, surely, successfully, to act from that intuitive knowledge.

Saturn in Aquarius can represent a lack of appreciation and acknowledgment of one's uniqueness and, consequently, a lack of recognition in the world. This may be a person who, always striving to conform to the status quo, may not realize the great worth of living his or her inner values, unique sense of purpose, and individual perspective on the world. In denying the self full expression in this way, he or she is holding back from others the true sharing that makes for a sense of union in relationships as well.

Friendships, too, are hard when one is unable to recognize and share parts of oneself that are difficult to deal with alone. A lack of true companionship can lead to isolation and even a sense of alienation from others.

The Saturn in Aquarius individual first needs to take responsibility for the ways in which the self is not acknowledged and expressed so that others don't become the focus of misdirected anger and frustration. Working to feel and free that self one hides from others—and even from himself or herself—can then liberate an enormous innovative energy with which he or she can make a positive impact on the world.

Saturn in Pisces tends to impede the sense of connection to others in a very basic way. A resulting sense of isolation may then make it hard for us to discover what we want to put forth to others, how to foster deep connections, or even how to relate because we lack the compassion that is necessary for us to connect meaningfully and find satisfaction in our emotional lives. A sense of profound pessimism about the world, stemming from this aloneness, may serve only to reinforce our negativity and keep us bound by our own worst fears.

In order not to drive ourselves to destructive escapism to avoid the world as we see it, we need to turn all that negativity around and with it construct a worldview that acknowledges the great link we all have to one another. This can revitalize our faith in ourselves as well as strengthen our intuitive ways of tapping into the artistic and magical forces that help us bring ourselves out of the darkness and shine light, too, on the paths of others to guide their ways to satisfaction, fulfillment, and joy.

URANUS: THE UNEXPECTED VISITOR

Uranus has to do with the cosmic power of intuitive knowledge, marked by flashes of genius in some, and with the milder forms of intuition that we all possess from time to time to varying degrees in our own unique ways. Heeding our own inner wisdom is the lesson Uranus teaches us all. When we ignore the inner voice that speaks to us of the need for change, accidents may befall us, startling us into paying attention to what we really need to do in order to develop and evolve in consciousness. Uranus is, therefore, also known as the great awakener.

Uranus in Aries (or the first house) produces an uncanny awareness in the individual of what is needed in any situation—one who responds intuitively and quickly as needed. Trust that first reaction, and act on it. This person needs to act out a very individualistic and assertive self.

Uranus in Taurus (or the second house) indicates a certain genius for material affairs. A financial wizard of sorts, this extraordinary innovator is able to create resources needed for survival. Startling revelations help this person attract and dispense material resources for the good of all.

Uranus in Gemini (or the third house) sparks the intellectual acuity of the individual. This person's heightened mental awareness makes for stimulating and inspiring conversation filled with intuitive knowledge and verging on brilliance. Inadvertent truths are revealed in even the most everyday interactions.

Uranus in Cancer (or the fourth house) denotes an emotional depth as well as an impatience with the less conscious members of one's family. The revelation of emotional truths clarifies and enhances others' relationships. If inner needs and feelings aren't fully expressed, erratic emotional outbursts are likely.

Uranus in Leo (or the fifth house) denotes a certain unique playfulness and particular gifts in dealing with children, releasing an awareness of the loving, creative inner child. Creativity needs appreciation as well as expression to blossom into a constructive force here.

Uranus in Virgo (or the sixth house) represents the flair for enhancing the mundane aspects of life with an appreciation of the uniqueness of each moment and every task. This inventor of some efficiency-increasing technique also inspires appreciation of the everyday in others.

Uranus in Libra (or the seventh house) brings to relationships unsettling conditions that are sudden, stimulating, and growth-inducing. This individual brings change into others' lives and forces awareness of a self that would otherwise have remained hidden and unconscious to both parties.

Uranus in Scorpio (or the eighth house) makes for an erratic intensity: first apparent detachment and then sudden eruptions of deep feelings that urgently need expression. A valuable confidant, the individual possesses fantastic objective insights on situations in which there is no personal involvement.

Uranus in Sagittarius (or the ninth house) imparts an unpredictably venturesome nature to one whose greatest source of self-discovery is in academia, on the road, or in exploring higher consciousness. Intellectual genius alternates with apathy; friendships are many, but superficial.

Uranus in Capricorn (or the tenth house) marks the professional pioneer, one whose inventions or innovative works affect the lives of a great many others. This person is, however, definitely a misfit in terms of regular employment, unless his or her uniqueness has been utilized.

Uranus in Aquarius (or the eleventh house) emphasizes the uniqueness of the individual, at home with genius, unpredictability, and sudden change. This person suddenly sparks a friendship of seeming depth and importance and just as suddenly disappears, having enlightened both himself or herself and the other person in some special way.

Uranus in Pisces (or the twelfth house) produces an amazingly intuitive person, sometimes psychic, for whom feelings are mysterious, unpredictable, and uncontrollable. This person needs to channel great energies so that they don't become destructive and can then use that power to great advantage for all.

NEPTUNE: THE DREAMER

Neptune is the outer planet that links us with an inner source of peace, comfort, and unity with all humankind. Where it is placed by sign and house in our charts indicates a place of renewal for us, where we can nurture our souls and find refuge from the wear and tear of our daily lives, the demands or our relationships, and the struggle for survival that our lives may comprise.

Finding that center of inspiration and faith, of replenishment and inner peace enables us to move forward with hope, encouraging others and being assured that we are on the right path for ourselves.

Neptune in Aries (or the first house). Taking action is the way to find a sense of renewal and hope. Trust your instincts; moving ahead with your first impulse helps reinforce your trust in yourself.

Neptune in Taurus (or the second house). Creativity and letting your dreams take tangible form enable you to connect with an inner strength and satisfaction about life. Let your senses guide you, too, to the refreshing respite that nourishes your soul.

Neptune in Gemini (or the third house). Writing, speaking, dialoguing with yourself are all ways of channeling that inner voice that enables you to move forward confidently, at ease with your own decisions. Heed the voice beyond the chatter.

Neptune in Cancer (or the fourth house). Respond affirmatively to the intuitions that guide you in just the right ways to care for yourself emotionally. The compassion emanating from within helps you cultivate an abundance of givingness in dealing with others.

Neptune in Leo (or the fifth house). Total involvement in a hobby, activity, or even free play centers you, bringing back that creative, loving inner self. Dramatizing situations that are difficult for you helps you to generate innovative solutions.

Neptune in Virgo (or the sixth house). Intricate forms of creative involvement—crafts, weaving—help you turn heavily analytical energies into patterns of beauty, easing your burden and bringing inner calm. Create for yourself an oasis of order and perfection.

Neptune in Libra (or the seventh house). Places of great beauty can soothe your soul, as mind and senses glory in their aesthetically pleasing ambience. Moments of sacred communion in relationships also renew your faith in yourself and the kind of life you live.

Neptune in Scorpio (or the eighth house). Stay with difficult feelings, allowing them to expand till they fill you; they then change into something else, yielding the sense of renewal you crave. This is transformation, your path to peace.

Neptune in Sagittarius (or the ninth house). Often an idea or philosophy inspires you to ponder and generate connections and solutions that free you from mental burdens. Meeting others for a sharing of perspectives inspires a sense of hope as well.

Neptune in Capricorn (or the tenth house). Straightening out some mess, solving another's problems, making order out of chaos in a satisfying and visible way help you clear out barriers to an inner sense of strength and purpose. Lists help, too.

Neptune in Aquarius (or the eleventh house). You need to discover your own unique way of renewing hope, to go about your work of inspiring others. Sharing time with a friend also brings you back in touch with the sacred space of your inner being.

Neptune in Pisces (or the twelfth house). You are well acquainted with the source of your own inner refreshment and harmony—in music, poetry, art, the sounds of the ocean, or reciting a childhood prayer. The tools are familiar; sharing them is enhancing.

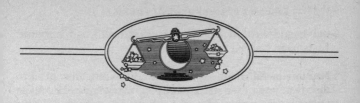

PLUTO: THE POWER PLANET

The farthest of all the planets in our solar system, Pluto symbolically rules that which is deepest within us, most powerful, yet often hardest to grab hold of and focus on in our daily lives. Connected with the concept of transformation, Pluto points in our charts to where conscious change needs to take place. This process involves becoming aware of, acting to own and acknowledge, and then letting go of whatever destructive life patterns we have evolved over time. This is transformation, the most difficult and the most powerful tool we have available to us in changing not only our lives but our inner selves.

Taking negative energy and turning it into a constructive force for good in our personal lives and in our society is a critical, life-preserving task. The work we do—as noted by Pluto's placement in our charts by sign and house position—recreates ourselves and makes our world a healthy place in which we can live and raise future generations.

Pluto in Aries (or the first house). We need to make sure that the impulses we follow are not just our destructive ones. The power we possess must be recognized and directed with consciousness so that its impact on others is positive and inspiring.

Pluto in Taurus (or the second house). Our deep knowledge of pleasure can bring hedonism to the depths of decadence. Instead, we can learn to appreciate and channel our life-force joyfully with whoever we are and in all that we create and enjoy.

Pluto in Gemini (or the third house). The magnificent and magical power of language needs to be recognized so that its destructive potential is not unleashed on the world in our interactions with others. Silence is sacred; it can be a tool for great change.

Pluto in Cancer (or the fourth house). Being faithful to our moods and the shifting tides of our feelings can bring us to a place of truth within ourselves. Knowing when the compassionate, loving emotions are called for comes from this process.

Pluto in Leo (or the fifth house). The place of most challenge and greatest potential is in allowing the inner child to play and be attended. Herein lies the precious gift of abandoning ourselves to joy, too often forgotten on our way to becoming adults.

Pluto in Virgo (or the sixth house). In our illnesses and daily woes comes the stuff of which our healing powers are made. Recognizing our diseases and finding our own cures enable us to extend that gift to others.

Pluto in Libra (or the seventh house). In the disharmony of our relationships are the seeds of answers to what we lack within us. Understanding this brings completeness, the strengthening of ourselves, and our union with others.

Pluto in Scorpio (or the eighth house). Our wishes for self-destruction point the way to which parts of us we need to release in order for our new selves to be born. Letting go of and forgiving who we were pave the way to our own rebirth.

Pluto in Sagittarius (or the ninth house). Beyond competition and intellectual strivings is a power much greater than anything we can aim for or name. Tapping into and channeling it for the good of all require a new understanding and a widened perspective.

Pluto in Capricorn (or the tenth house). Once we have done our best to achieve our goals, it is time to let go. At this point we will realize the truth and power of where we are and be brought to our next best place of success and fulfillment.

Pluto in Aquarius (or the eleventh house). Recognizing the importance of being part of something greater than our individual selves can guide us to taking personal risks that enlarge us at all levels. We then form a new kind of human being, creating an evolved society of humanity.

Pluto in Pisces (or the twelfth house). At one with the suffering of others, we are aware of the deepest, most personal level of being human. Faith then heals all those parts of us and our world—in pain, in lack, or in inability to change.

How to Find the Place of Jupiter, Saturn, Uranus, Neptune, and Pluto in Your Chart

Find your birth year in the left-hand column and read across the chart until you find your birth date. The top of that column will tell you where Jupiter, Saturn, Uranus, Neptune, and Pluto lie in your chart.

Key: ♈ ARIES ♉ TAURUS ♊ GEMINI ♋ CANCER ♌ LEO ♍ VIRGO ♎ LIBRA ♏ SCORPIO ♐ SAGITT. ♑ CAPRI. ♒ AQUAR. ♓ PISCES ℞ Retrograde

PLACE OF JUPITER, SATURN, URANUS, NEPTUNE, AND PLUTO—1880–1885

FIND YOUR BIRTH YEAR HERE	TABLE I-♃ Period including birthday. Your Jupiter is in	Sign	TABLE II-♄ Period including birthday. Your Saturn is in	Sign	TABLE III-♅ Your Uranus is in	Sign	TABLE IV-♆ Your Neptune is in	Sign	TABLE V-♇ Your Pluto is in	Sign
1880	1/1–4/2 4/3–12/31	♓ ♈	All Yr.	♈	All Yr.	♍	All Yr.	♉	All Yr.	♉
1881	1/1–4/11 4/12–12/31	♈ ♉	1/1–4/5 4/6–12/31	♈ ♉	All Yr.	♍	All Yr.	♉	All Yr.	♉
1882	1/1–4/21 4/22–9/19 9/20–11/17 11/18–12/31	♉ ♊ ♋ ♊	All Yr.	♉	All Yr.	♍	All Yr.	♉	All Yr.	♉
1883	1/1–5/4 5/5–9/26 9/27–12/31	♊ ♋ ♌	1/1–5/23 5/24–12/31	♉ ♊	All Yr.	♍	All Yr.	♉	All Yr.	♉
1884	1/1–1/16 1/17–5/21 5/22–10/17 10/18–12/31	♌ ♋ ♌ ♍	All Yr.	♊	1/1–10/13 10/14–12/31	♍ ♍ ♎	All Yr.	♉	All Yr.	♉
1885	1/1–2/25 2/26–6/14 6/15–11/15 11/16–12/31	♍ ♌ ♍ ♎	1/1–7/5 7/6–12/31	♊ ♋	1/1–4/11 4/12–7/28 7/29–12/31	♍ ♍ ♎ ♎	All Yr.	♉	All Yr.	♊

PLACE OF JUPITER, SATURN, URANUS, NEPTUNE, AND PLUTO—1886–1893

Year	Jupiter	Saturn	Uranus	Neptune	Pluto
1886	1/1–3/29 ♎ 3/30–7/15 ♍ 7/16–12/16 ♎ 12/17–12/31 ♏	All Yr. ♋	All Yr. ♎	All Yr. ♉	All Yr. ♊
1887	1/1–4/28 ♏ 4/29–8/15 ♎ 8/16–12/31 ♏	1/1–8/18 ♋ 8/19–12/31 ♌	All Yr. ♎	1/1–8/15 ♉ 8/16–9/21 ♊ 9/22–12/31 ♉	All Yr. ♊
1888	1/1–1/14 ♏ 1/15–6/2 ♐ 6/3–9/10 ♏ 9/11–12/31 ♐	1/1–3/9 ♌ 3/10–4/20 ♋ 4/21–12/31 ♌	All Yr. ♎	1/1–5/25 ♉ 5/26–12/31 ♊	All Yr. ♊
1889	1/1–2/5 ♐ 2/6–7/23 ♑ 7/24–9/25 ♐ 9/26–12/31 ♑	1/1–10/6 ♌ 10/7–12/31 ♍	All Yr. ♎	1/1–3/20 ♉ 3/21–12/31 ♊	All Yr. ♊
1890	1/1–2/22 ♑ 2/23–12/31 ♒	1/1–2/24 ♍ 2/25–6/27 ♌ 6/28–12/31 ♍	1/1–12/9 ♎ 12/10–12/31 ♏	All Yr. ♊	All Yr. ♊
1891	1/1–3/7 ♒ 3/8–12/31 ♓	1/1–12/26 ♍ 12/27–12/31 ♎	1/1–4/4 ♏ 4/5–9/25 ♎ 9/26–12/31 ♏	All Yr. ♊	All Yr. ♊
1892	1/1–3/16 ♓ 3/17–12/31 ♈	1/1–1/22 ♎ 1/23–8/29 ♍ 8/30–12/31 ♎	All Yr. ♏	All Yr. ♊	All Yr. ♊
1893	1/1–2/24 ♈ 2/25–8/20 ♉ 8/21–10/19 ♊ 10/20–12/31 ♉	All Yr. ♎	All Yr. ♏	All Yr. ♊	All Yr. ♊

PLACE OF JUPITER, SATURN, URANUS, NEPTUNE, AND PLUTO—1894–1900

FIND YOUR BIRTH YEAR HERE	TABLE I-♃-Find Period including birthday. Your Jupiter is in	Sign	TABLE II-♄-Find Period including birthday. Your Saturn is in	Sign	TABLE III-♅-Your Uranus is in	Sign	TABLE IV-Ψ-Your Neptune is in	Sign	TABLE V-♇-Your Pluto is in	Sign
1894	1/1-4/1 4/2-8/13 8/14-12/31	♉ ♊ ♋	1/1-11/6 11/7-12/31	♎ ♏	All Yr.	♏	All Yr.	♊	All Yr.	♊
1895	1/1-4/10 4/11-9/4 9/5-12/31	♊ ♋ ♌	All Yr.	♏	All Yr.	♏	All Yr.	♊	All Yr.	♊
1896	1/1-2/29 3/1-4/17 4/18-9/27 9/28-12/31	♌ ♋ ♌ ♍	All Yr.	♏	All Yr.	♏	All Yr.	♊	All Yr.	♊
1897	1/1-10/27 10/28-12/31	♍ ♎	1/1-2/16 2/7-4/9 4/10-10/26 10/27-12/31	♏ ♏ ♐ ♏ ♐ ♐	1/1-12/1 12/2-12/31	♏ ♐	All Yr.	♊	All Yr.	♊
1898	1/1-11/26 11/27-12/31	♎ ♏	All Yr.	♐	1/1-7/3 7/4-9/10 9/11-12/31	♐ ♏ ♐	All Yr.	♊	All Yr.	♊
1899	1/1-12/25 12/26-12/31	♏ ♐	All Yr.	♐	All Yr.	♐	All Yr.	♊	All Yr.	♊
1900	All Yr.	♐	1/1-1/20 1/21-7/18 7/19-10/16 10/17-12/31	♐ ♑ ♐ ♑	All Yr.	♐	All Yr.	♊	All Yr.	♊

PLACE OF JUPITER, SATURN, URANUS, NEPTUNE, AND PLUTO—1901–1911

Year	Jupiter	Saturn	Uranus	Neptune	Pluto
1901	1/1-1/18 ♐; 1/19-12/31 ♑	All Yr. ♑	All Yr. ♐	1/1-7/19 ♊; 7/20-12/25 ♋; 12/26-12/31 ♊	All Yr. ♊
1902	1/1-2/6 ♑; 2/7-12/31 ♒	All Yr. ♑	All Yr. ♐	1/1-5/20 ♊; 5/21-12/31 ♋	All Yr. ♊
1903	1/1-2/19 ♒; 2/20-12/31 ♓	1/1-1/19 ♑; 1/20-12/31 ♒	All Yr. ♐	All Yr. ♋	All Yr. ♊
1904	1/1-2/29 ♓; 3/1-8/6 ♈; 8/9-8/31 ♓; 9/1-12/31 ♈	All Yr. ♒	1/1-12/19 ♐; 12/20-12/31 ♑	All Yr. ♋	All Yr. ♊
1905	1/1-3/7 ♈; 3/8-7/20 ♉; 7/21-12/4 ♊; 12/5-12/31 ♉	1/1-4/12 ♒; 4/13-8/16 ♓; 8/17-12/31 ♒	All Yr. ♑	All Yr. ♋	All Yr. ♊
1906	1/1-3/9 ♉; 3/10-7/30 ♊; 7/31-12/31 ♋	1/1-1/7 ♒; 1/8-12/31 ♓	All Yr. ♑	All Yr. ♋	All Yr. ♊
1907	1/1-8/18 ♋; 8/19-12/31 ♌	All Yr. ♓	All Yr. ♑	All Yr. ♋	All Yr. ♊
1908	1/1-9/11 ♌; 9/12-12/31 ♍	1/1-3/18 ♓; 8/19-12/31 ♈	All Yr. ♑	All Yr. ♋	All Yr. ♊
1909	1/1-10/11 ♍; 10/12-12/31 ♎	All Yr. ♈	All Yr. ♑	All Yr. ♋	All Yr. ♊
1910	1/1-11/11 ♎; 11/12-12/31 ♏	1/1-5/16 ♈; 5/17-12/14 ♉; 12/15-12/31 ♈	All Yr. ♑	All Yr. ♋	All Yr. ♊
1911	1/1-12/9 ♏; 12/10-12/31 ♐	1/1-1/19 ♈; 1/20-12/31 ♉	All Yr. ♑	All Yr. ♋	All Yr. ♊

PLACE OF JUPITER, SATURN, URANUS, NEPTUNE, AND PLUTO—1912–1920

FIND YOUR BIRTH YEAR HERE	TABLE I-♃-Find Period including birthday. Your Jupiter is in	Sign	TABLE II-♄-Find Period including birthday. Your Saturn is in	Sign	TABLE III-♅ Your Uranus is in	Sign	TABLE IV-♆ Your Neptune is in	Sign	TABLE V-♇ Your Pluto is in	Sign
1912	All Yr.	♐	1/1–7/6 7/17–11/30 12/1–12/31	♉ ♊ ♉	1/1–1/30 1/31–9/4 9/5–11/11 11/12–12/31	♑ ♒ ♑ ♒	All Yr.	♋	All Yr.	♊
1913	1/1+2 1/3–12/31	♐ ♑	1/1–3/25 3/26–12/31	♉ ♊	All Yr.	♒	All Yr.	♋	All Yr.	♊
1914	1/1–1/21 1/22–12/31	♑ ♒	1/1–8/24 8/25–12/6 12/7–12/31	♊ ♋ ♊	All Yr.	♒	1/1–9/22 9/22–12/14 12/15–12/31	♋ ♌ ♋		♊ ♋
1915	1/1–2/3 2/4–12/31	♒ ♓	1/1–5/11 5/12–12/31	♊ ♋	All Yr.	♒	1/1–7/18 7/19–12/31	♋ ♌	All Yr.	♋
1916	1/1–2/11 2/12–6/25 6/26–10/26 10/27–12/31	♓ ♈ ♉ ♈	1/1–10/16 10/17–12/7 12/8–12/31	♋ ♌ ♋	All Yr.	♒	1/1–3/19 3/20–5/1 5/2–12/31	♌ ♋ ♌	All Yr.	♋
1917	1/1–2/12 2/13–6/29 6/30–12/31	♈ ♉ ♊	1/1–7/23 7/24–12/31	♋ ♌	All Yr.	♒	All Yr.	♌	All Yr.	♋
1918	1/1–6/12 6/13–12/31	♊ ♋	All Yr.	♌	All Yr.	♒	All Yr.	♌	All Yr.	♋
1919	1/1–8/1 8/2–12/31	♋ ♌	1/1–8/11 8/12–12/31	♌ ♍	1/1–3/31 4/1–8/16 8/17–12/31	♒ ♓ ♒	All Yr.	♌	All Yr.	♋
1920	1/1–8/26 8/27–12/31	♌ ♍	All Yr.	♍	1/1–1/21 1/22–12/31	♒ ♓	All Yr.	♌	All Yr.	♋

PLACE OF JUPITER, SATURN, URANUS, NEPTUNE, AND PLUTO—1921–1931

Year	Jupiter	Saturn	Uranus	Neptune	Pluto
1921	1/1-9/25 ♍ 9/26-12/31 ♎	1/1-10/7 ♍ 10/8-12/31 ♎	All Yr. ♓	All Yr. ♌	♋
1922	1/1-10/26 ♎ 10/27-12/31 ♏	All Yr. ♎	All Yr. ♓	All Yr. ♌	♋
1923	1/1-11/24 ♏ 11/25-12/31 ♐	1/1-12/19 ♎ 12/20-12/31 ♏	All Yr. ♓	All Yr. ♌	♋
1924	1/1-12/17 ♐ 12/18-12/31 ♑	1/1-4/5 ♏ 4/6-9/13 ♎ 9/14-12/31 ♏	All Yr. ♓	All Yr. ♌	♋
1925	All Yr. ♑	All Yr. ♏	All Yr. ♓	All Yr. ♌	♋
1926	1/1-1/5 ♑ 1/6-12/31 ♒	1/1-12/2 ♏ 12/3-12/31 ♐	All Yr. ♓	All Yr. ♌	♋
1927	1/1-1/17 ♒ 1/18-6/5 ♓ 6/6-9/10 ♈ 9/11-12/31 ♓	All Yr. ♐	1/1-3/30 ♓ 3/31-11/4 ♈ 11/5-12/31 ♓	All Yr. ♌	♋
1928	1/1-1/22 ♓ 1/23-6/3 ♈ 6/4-12/31 ♉	All Yr. ♐	1/1-1/12 ♓ 1/13-12/31 ♈	1/1-9/20 ♌ 9/21-12/31 ♍	♋
1929	1/1-6/11 ♉ 6/12-12/31 ♊	1/1-3/14 ♐ 3/15-5/4 ♑ 5/5-11/29 ♐ 11/30-12/31 ♑	All Yr. ♈	1/1-2/19 ♍ 2/20-7/23 ♌ 7/24-12/31 ♍	♋
1930	1/1-6/26 ♊ 6/27-12/31 ♋	All Yr. ♑	All Yr. ♈	All Yr. ♍	♋
1931	1/1-7/17 ♋ 7/18-12/31 ♌	All Yr. ♑	All Yr. ♈	All Yr. ♍	♋

PLACE OF JUPITER, SATURN, URANUS, NEPTUNE, AND PLUTO—1932–1939

FIND YOUR BIRTH YEAR HERE	TABLE I-♃-Find Period including birthday. Your Jupiter is in	Sign	TABLE II-♄-Find Period including birthday. Your Saturn is in	Sign	TABLE III-♅ Your Uranus is in	Sign	TABLE IV-♆ Your Neptune is in	Sign	TABLE V-♇ Your Pluto is in	Sign
1932	1/1–8/11 8/12–12/31	♌ ♍	1/1–2/23 2/24–8/13 8/14–11/19 11/20–12/31	♑ ♒ ♑ ♒	All Yr.	♈	All Yr.	♍	All Yr.	♋
1933	1/1–9/10 9/11–12/31	♍ ♎	All Yr.	♒	All Yr.	♈	All Yr.	♍	All Yr.	♋
1934	1/1–10/11 10/12–12/31	♎ ♏	All Yr.	♒	1/1–6/6 6/7–10/10 10/11–12/31	♈ ♉ ♈	All Yr.	♍	All Yr.	♋
1935	1/1–11/9 11/10–12/31	♏ ♐	1/1–2/14 2/15–12/31	♒ ♓	1/1–3/28 3/29–12/31	♈ ♉	All Yr.	♍	All Yr.	♋
1936	1/1–12/2 12/3–12/31	♐ ♑	All Yr.	♓	All Yr.	♉	All Yr.	♍	All Yr.	♋
1937	1/1–12/20 12/21–12/31	♑ ♒	1/1–4/25 4/26–10/18 10/19–12/31	♓ ♈ ♓	All Yr.	♉	All Yr.	♍	10/7–11/26 11/27–12/31	♋ ♌
1938	1/1–5/14 5/15–7/30 7/31–12/29 12/30–12/31	♒ ♓ ♒ ♓	1/1–1/14 1/15–12/31	♓ ♈	All Yr.	♉	All Yr.	♍	1/1–8/3 8/4–12/31	♋ ♌
1939	1/1–5/11 5/12–10/30 10/31–12/20 12/21–12/31	♓ ♈ ♓ ♈	All Yr.	♈	All Yr.	♉	All Yr.	♍	1/1–2/7 2/8–6/13 6/14–12/31	♌ ♋ ♌

PLACE OF JUPITER, SATURN, URANUS, NEPTUNE, AND PLUTO—1940–1949

1940	1/1–5/16 5/17–12/31	♈ ♉	1/1–3/20 3/21–12/31	♈ ♉	All Yr.	♉	All Yr.	♍	All Yr.	♌
1941	1/1–5/26 5/27–12/31	♉ ♊	All Yr.	♉	1/1–8/7 8/8–10/5 10/6–12/31	♉ ♊ ♉	All Yr.	♍	All Yr.	♌
1942	1/1–6/10 6/11–12/31	♊ ♋	1/1–5/8 5/9–12/31	♉ ♊	1/1–5/14 5/15–12/31	♉ ♊	1/1–10/3 10/4–12/31	♍ ♎	All Yr.	♌
1943	1/1–6/30 7/1–12/31	♋ ♌	All Yr.	♊	All Yr.	♊	1/1–4/18 4/19–8/2 8/3–12/31	♎ ♍ ♎	All Yr.	♌
1944	1/1–7/26 7/27–12/31	♌ ♍	1/1–6/20 6/21–12/31	♊ ♋	All Yr.	♊	All Yr.	♎	All Yr.	♌
1945	1/1–8/25 8/26–12/31	♍ ♎	All Yr.	♋	All Yr.	♊	All Yr.	♎	All Yr.	♌
1946	1/1–9/25 9/26–12/31	♎ ♏	1/1–8/2 8/3–12/31	♋ ♌	All Yr.	♊	All Yr.	♎	All Yr.	♌
1947	1/1–10/24 10/25–12/31	♏ ♐	All Yr.	♌	All Yr.	♊	All Yr.	♎	All Yr.	♌
1948	1/1–11/15 11/16–12/31	♐ ♑	1/1–9/19 9/20–12/31	♌ ♍	1/1–8/30 8/31–11/12 11/13–12/31	♊ ♋ ♊	All Yr.	♎	All Yr.	♌
1949	1/1–4/12 4/13–6/27 6/28–11/30 12/1–12/31	♑ ♒ ♑ ♒	1/1–4/3 4/4–5/29 5/30–12/31	♍ ♌ ♍	1/1–6/10 6/11–12/31	♊ ♋	All Yr.	♎	All Yr.	♌

PLACE OF JUPITER, SATURN, URANUS, NEPTUNE, AND PLUTO—1950–1957

FIND YOUR BIRTH YEAR HERE	TABLE I-♃-Find Period including birthday. Your Jupiter is in	Sign	TABLE II-♄-Find Period including birthday. Your Saturn is in	Sign	TABLE III-♅ Your Uranus is in	Sign	TABLE IV-♆ Your Neptune is in	Sign	TABLE V-♇ Your Pluto is in	Sign
1950	1/1–4/14 4/15–9/13 9/14–11/30 12/1–12/31	♒ ♓ ♒ ♓	1/1–11/20 11/21–12/31	♍ ♎	All Yr.	♋	All Yr.	♎	All Yr.	♌
1951	1/1–4/21 4/22–12/31	♓ ♈	1/1–3/7 3/8–8/13 8/14–12/31	♎ ♍ ♎	All Yr.	♋	All Yr.	♎	All Yr.	♌
1952	1/1–4/28 4/29–12/31	♈ ♉	All Yr.	♎	All Yr.	♋	All Yr.	♎	All Yr.	♌
1953	1/1–5/9 5/10–12/31	♉ ♊	1/1–10/22 10/23–12/31	♎ ♏	All Yr.	♋	All Yr.	♎	All Yr.	♌
1954	1/1–5/24 5/25–12/31	♊ ♋	All Yr.	♏	All Yr.	♋	All Yr.	♎	All Yr.	♌
1955	1/1–6/12 6/13–11/17 11/18–12/31	♋ ♌ ♍	All Yr.	♏	1/1–8/24 8/25–12/31	♋ ♌	1/1–12/23 12/24–12/31	♎ ♏	1/1–10/19	♌
1956	1/1–1/18 1/19–7/7 7/8–12/12 12/13–12/31	♍ ♌ ♍ ♎	1/1–1/12 1/13–5/14 5/15–10/10 10/11–12/31	♏ ♐ ♏ ♐	1/1–1/28 1/29–6/9 6/10–12/31	♌ ♋ ♌	1/1–3/11 3/12–10/13 10/19–12/31	♏ ♎ ♏	10/20–12/31	♍
1957	1/1–2/19 2/20–8/6 8/7–12/31	♎ ♏ ♎	All Yr.	♐	All Yr.	♌	1/1–6/16 6/17–8/4 8/5–12/31	♏ ♎ ♏	1/1–1/15 1/16–8/18 8/19–12/31	♍ ♌ ♍

PLACE OF JUPITER, SATURN, URANUS, NEPTUNE, AND PLUTO—1958-1965

	Jupiter	Saturn	Uranus	Neptune	Pluto
1958	1/1–1/13 ♎ 1/14–3/20 ♏ 3/21–9/7 ♎ 9/8–12/31 ♏	All Yr. ♐	All Yr. ♌	All Yr. ♏	1/1–4/12 ♍ 4/13–6/10 ♌ 6/11–12/31 ♍
1959	1/2–2/10 ♏ 2/11–4/24 ♐ 4/25–10/5 ♏ 10/6–12/31 ♐	1/1–1/5 ♐ 1/6–12/31 ♑	All Yr. ♌	All Yr. ♏	All Yr. ♍
1960	1/1–3/1 ♐ 3/2–6/10 ♑ 6/11–10/25 ♐ 10/26–12/31 ♑	All Yr. ♑	All Yr. ♌	All Yr. ♏	All Yr. ♍
1961	1/1–3/14 ♑ 3/15–8/11 ♒ 8/12–11/3 ♑ 11/4–12/31 ♒	All Yr. ♑	1/1–10/31 ♌ 11/1–12/31 ♍	All Yr. ♏	All Yr. ♍
1962	1/1–3/24 ♒ 3/25–12/31 ♓	1/1–1/2 ♑ 1/3–12/31 ♒	1/1–1/9 ♍ 1/10–8/8 ♌ 8/9–12/31 ♍	All Yr. ♏	All Yr. ♍
1963	1/1–4/3 ♓ 4/4–12/31 ♈	All Yr. ♒	All Yr. ♍	All Yr. ♏	All Yr. ♍
1964	1/1–4/11 ♈ 4/12–12/31 ♉	1/1–3/23 ♒ 3/24–9/16 ♓ 9/17–12/15 ♒ 12/16–12/31 ♓	All Yr. ♍	All Yr. ♏	All Yr. ♍
1965	1/1–4/21 ♉ 4/22–9/20 ♊ 9/21–11/16 ♋ 11/17–12/31 ♊	All Yr. ♓	All Yr. ♍	All Yr. ♏	All Yr. ♍

PLACE OF JUPITER, SATURN, URANUS, NEPTUNE, AND PLUTO—1966–1971

FIND YOUR BIRTH YEAR HERE	TABLE I-♃-Find Period including birthday. Your Jupiter is in	Sign	TABLE II-♄-Find Period including birthday. Your Saturn is in	Sign	TABLE III-♅ Your Uranus is in	Sign	TABLE IV-♆ Your Neptune is in	Sign	TABLE V-♇ Your Pluto is in	Sign
1966	1/1-5/4 5/5-9/26 9/27-12/31	♊ ♋ ♌	All Yr.	♓	All Yr.	♍	All Yr.	♏	All Yr.	♍
1967	1/1-1/15 1/16-5/22 5/23-10/18 10/19-10/31	♌ ♋ ♌ ♍	1/1-3/2 3/3-12/31	♓ ♈	All Yr.	♍	All Yr.	♏	All Yr.	♍
1968	1/1-2/26 2/27-6/14 6/15-11/14 11/15-12/31	♍ ♌ ♍ ♎	All Yr.	♈	1/1-9/27 9/28-12/31	♍ ♎	All Yr.	♏	All Yr.	♍
1969	1/1-3/29 3/30-7/14 7/15-12/15 12/16-12/31	♎ ♍ ♎ ♏	1/1-4/28 4/29-12/31	♈ ♉	1/1-5/20 5/21-6/23 6/24-12/31	♎ ♍ ♎	All Yr.	♏	All Yr.	♍
1970	1/1-4/30 5/1-8/14 8/15-12/31	♏ ♎ ♏	All Yr.	♉	All Yr.	♎	1/1-1/3 1/4-5/2 5/3-11/5 11/6-12/31	♏ ♐ ♏ ♐	1/1-12/31	♍
1971	1/1-1/13 1/14-6/4 6/5-9/10 9/11-12/31	♏ ♐ ♏ ♐	1/16-6/17 6/18-12/31	♉ ♊	All Yr.	♎	All Yr.	♐	1/1-10/5 10/6-12/31	♍ ♎

PLACE OF JUPITER, SATURN, URANUS, NEPTUNE, AND PLUTO—1972–1980

Year	Jupiter	Saturn	Uranus	Neptune	Pluto
1972	1/1-2/5 ♐ 2/6-7/23 ♑ 7/24-9/24 ♐ 9/25-12/31 ♑	1/1-1/9 ♊ 1/10-2/20 ♉ 2/21-12/31 ♊	All Yr. ♎	All Yr. ♐	1/1-4/17 ♎ 4/18-6/30 ♍ 7/1-12/31 ♎
1973	1/1-2/22 ♑ 2/23-12/31 ♒	1/1-7/31 ♊ 8/1-12/31 ♋	All Yr. ♎	All Yr. ♐	All Yr. ♎
1974	1/1-3/7 ♒ 3/8-12/31 ♓	1/1-1/6 ♋ 1/7-4/17 ♊ 4/18-12/31 ♋	1/1-11/20 ♎ 11/21-12/31 ♏	All Yr. ♐	All Yr. ♎
1975	1/1-3/17 ♓ 3/18-12/31 ♈	1/1-9/16 ♋ 9/17-12/31 ♌	1/1-4/30 ♏ 5/1-9/7 ♎ 9/8-12/31 ♏	All Yr. ♐	All Yr. ♎
1976	1/1-3/25 ♈ 3/26-8/22 ♉ 8/23-10/15 ♊ 10/16-12/31 ♉	1/1-1/13 ♌ 1/14-6/4 ♋ 6/5-12/31 ♌	All Yr. ♏	All Yr. ♐	All Yr. ♎
1977	1/1-4/2 ♉ 4/3-8/19 ♊ 8/20-12/31 ♋	1/1-11/15 ♌ 11/16-12/31 ♍	All Yr. ♏	All Yr. ♐	All Yr. ♎
1978	1/1-4/10 ♋ 4/11-9/4 ♌ 9/5-12/31 ♋	1/1-1/4 ♍ 1/5-7/25 ♌ 7/26-12/31 ♍	All Yr. ♏	All Yr. ♐	All Yr. ♎
1979	1/1-2/28 ♋ 3/1-4/19 ♌ 4/20-9/28 ♋ 9/29-12/31 ♌	All Yr. ♍	All Yr. ♏	All Yr. ♐	All Yr. ♎
1980	1/1-10/26 ♌ 10/27-12/31 ♍	1/1-9/20 ♍ 9/21-12/31 ♎	All Yr. ♏	All Yr. ♐	All Yr. ♎

PLACE OF JUPITER, SATURN, URANUS, NEPTUNE, AND PLUTO—1981–1989

FIND YOUR BIRTH YEAR HERE	TABLE I-♃—Find Period including birthday. Your Jupiter is in		TABLE II-♄—Find Period including birthday. Your Saturn is in		TABLE III-♅ Your Uranus is in		TABLE IV-♆ Your Neptune is in		TABLE V-♇ Your Pluto is in	
	Period	Sign	Period	Sign	Period	Sign	Period	Sign	Period	Sign
1981	1/1–11/25 11/26–12/31	♎ ♏	All Yr.	♎	1/1–2/16 2/17–3/19 3/20–11/15 11/16–12/31	♏ ♐ ♏ ♐	All Yr.	♐	All Yr.	♎
1982	1/1–12/24 12/25–12/31	♏ ♐	1/1–11/28 11/29–12/31	♎ ♏	All Yr.	♐	All Yr.	♐	All Yr.	♎
1983	All Yr.	♐	1/1–5/5 5/6–8/23 8/24–12/31	♏ ♎ ♏	All Yr.	♐	All Yr.	♐	1/1–11/5 11/6–12/31	♎ ♏
1984	1/1–1/18 1/19–12/31	♐ ♑	All Yr.	♏	All Yr.	♐	1/1–1/17 1/18–6/21 6/22–11/20 11/21–12/31	♐ ♑ ♐ ♑	1/1–5/19 5/20–8/27 8/28–12/31	♏ ♎ ♏
1985	1/1–2/5 2/6–12/31	♑ ♒	1/1–11/15 11/16–12/31	♏ ♐	All Yr.	♐	All Yr.	♑	All Yr.	♏
1986	1/1–2/19 2/20–12/31	♒ ♓	All Yr.	♐	All Yr.	♐	All Yr.	♑	All Yr.	♏
1987	1/1–3/1 3/2–12/31	♓ ♈	All Yr.	♐	All Yr.	♐	All Yr.	♑	All Yr.	♏
1988	1/1–3/7 3/8–7/20 7/21–11/29 11/30–12/31	♈ ♉ ♊ ♉	1/1–2/12 2/13–6/9 6/10–11/11 11/12–12/31	♐ ♑ ♐ ♑	1/1–2/13 2/14–5/25 5/26–12/2 12/2–12/31	♐ ♑ ♐ ♑	All Yr.	♑	All Yr.	♏
1989	1/1–3/9 3/10–7/29 7/30–12/31	♉ ♊ ♋	All Yr.	♑	All Yr.	♑	All Yr.	♑	All Yr.	♏

PLACE OF JUPITER, SATURN, URANUS, NEPTUNE, AND PLUTO—1990–2000

Year	Jupiter	Saturn	Uranus	Neptune	Pluto
1990	1/1–8/17 ♋ 8/18–12/31 ♌	All Yr. ♑	All Yr. ♑	All Yr. ♑	All Yr. ♏
1991	1/1–9/11 ♌ 9/12–12/31 ♍	1/1–2/5 ♑ 2/6–12/31 ♒	All Yr. ♑	All Yr. ♑	All Yr. ♏
1992	1/1–10/9 ♍ 10/10–12/31 ♎	All Yr. ♒	All Yr. ♑	All Yr. ♑	All Yr. ♏
1993	1/1–11/9 ♎ 11/10–12/31 ♏	1/1–5/20 ♒ 5/21–6/29 ♓ 6/30–12/31 ♒	All Yr. ♑	All Yr. ♑	All Yr. ♏
1994	1/1–12/8 ♏ 12/9–12/31 ♐	1/1–1/27 ♒ 1/28–12/31 ♓	All Yr. ♑	All Yr. ♑	1/1–12/31 ♏
1995	1/1–12/31 ♐	All Yr. ♓	1/1–3/31 ♑ 4/1–6/7 ♒ 6/8–12/31 ♑	All Yr. ♑	1/1–1/16 ♏ 1/17–4/21 ♐ 4/22–11/8 ♏ 11/9–12/31 ♐
1996	1/1–1/2 ♐ 1/3–12/31 ♑	1/1–4/6 ♓ 4/7–12/31 ♈	1/1–1/11 ♑ 1/12–12/31 ♒	All Yr. ♑	All Yr. ♐
1997	1/1–1/20 ♑ 1/21–12/31 ♒	All Yr. ♈	All Yr. ♒	All Yr. ♑	All Yr. ♐
1998	1/1–2/3 ♒ 2/4–12/31 ♓	1/1–6/8 ♈ 6/9–10/24 ♉ 10/25–12/31 ♈	All Yr. ♒	1/1–1/27 ♑ 1/28–8/21 ♒ 8/22–11/26 ♑ 11/27–12/31 ♒	All Yr. ♐
1999	1/1–2/11 ♓ 2/12–6/27 ♈ 6/28–10/22 ♉ 10/23–12/31 ♈	1/1–2/27 ♈ 2/28–12/31 ♉	All Yr. ♒	All Yr. ♒	All Yr. ♐
2000	1/1–2/13 ♈ 2/14–6/29 ♉ 6/30–12/31 ♊	1/1–8/8 ♉ 8/9–10/14 ♊ 10/15–12/31 ♉	All Yr. ♒	All Yr. ♒	All Yr. ♐

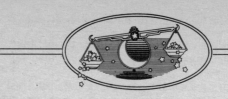

SUCCESSFUL PLANNING WITH THE MOON SIGN GUIDE

"Where is the Moon?" is a question enlightened thinkers of all ages, irrespective of Sun Sign, have asked before coming to a decision or beginning a venture. You, too, should have the benefit of using the wisdom of ancient lunar science. The paragraphs that follow reveal the activities that can be pursued when the Moon occupies a certain sign and is favorably aspected.

Moon in Aries (♈): Begin new enterprises or ventures; make job applications; hire employees; bargain; pioneer some new idea or article; purchase objects made of metal; participate in sports; inspire others with your enthusiasm.

Moon in Taurus (♉): Begin things you desire to be permanent or want to last a long time; buy durable clothing; boost personal income; add to possessions; deal with bankers; open accounts.

Moon in Gemini (♊): Take short journeys; write letters; prepare articles for publication; advertise; give public speeches; make changes that are not apt to be permanent; interview employees; make contacts.

Moon in Cancer (♋): Deal with family matters or women in business or in the home, especially in connection with commodities, food, furniture; plan ocean trips; take care of domestic and property needs; purchase antiques.

Moon in Leo (♌): Contact persons in authority; ask for favors; buy and sell, especially jewelry, gold ornaments, quality clothes and articles; pursue love, social life, entertainment; attend the theater; display executive ability.

Moon in Virgo (♍): Pursue studies that will enhance your skills; seek employment; find improvements in health, hygiene; study statistics; stress the quality of services rendered to others; tend to the needs of pets or dependents.

Moon in Libra (♎): Strengthen marital ties; pursue partnership and cooperative affairs; purchase perfumes, jewelry, home decorations, beauty items, art objects; attend cultural events.

Moon in Scorpio (♏): Take care of tax and estate matters; boost joint resources; exploit hidden talents; make decisions, especially when shrewdness is required; rejuvenate valuable possessions; pursue confidential transactions.

Moon in Sagittarius (♐): Engage in outdoor activities, such as horse racing, hiking, sports, exercise in general; make realistic plans for the future; deal with lawyers, physicians, religious leaders, professional people; plan long journeys or academic goals.

Moon in Capricorn (♑): Be attentive to duties and responsibilities; engage in business related to management or organization, government interests, parental concerns; see influential people; undertake business and career pursuits.

Moon in Aquarius (♒): Pursue hopes and wishes, friendships, social contacts; enjoy clubs or fraternal societies, or seek membership in them; boost revenues from business, occupation; stress humanitarianism; engage in politics.

Moon in Pisces (✕): Overcome limitations and problems; express charitable and sympathetic leanings; pursue peaceful and spiritual interests; boost self-confidence; find the causes for fears, worries, doubts; take care of confidential matters; visit those who are ill, convalescing, or confined.

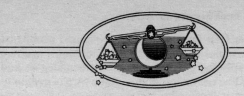

DAILY PREDICTIONS

(All times listed in the following section are E.S.T.)

October 1990

Monday, October 1 (Moon in Aquarius to Pisces 8:43 A.M.). With your high energy level and your eagerness to get moving on special projects, today can be a real winner in terms of achievement and recognition. The good fortune of having an influential friend in a key position won't hurt your cause, either.

Tuesday, October 2 (Moon in Pisces). You may be immersed in a challenging assignment today, and because your motivation is soaring, you'll sail through it triumphantly. There may be, however, a few sharp words between you and a co-worker, but this can quickly simmer down. A former colleague may surface tonight.

Wednesday, October 3 (Moon in Pisces to Aries 12:43 P.M.). Misinformation could be misleading in the A.M., so check all vital matters thoroughly. A partnership endeavor that may have started off brilliantly may now be encountering squalls; whether related to business or romance, the P.M. is no time to force issues.

Thursday, October 4 (FULL MOON in Aries). Don't look for either cooperation or approval from your mate or partner today. In fact, take extra precautions against confrontation and bringing up old grievances. You may, however, see a problem more clearly or innovate ways of handling a sensitive domestic matter.

Friday, October 5 (Moon in Aries to Taurus 2:07 P.M.). Stellar patterns now focused in your sign impel you to feel extra confident and optimistic. These qualities can help you to overcome obstacles and charm colleagues. But today may require you to downplay your assertiveness for best results in the P.M.

Saturday, October 6 (Moon in Taurus). Although you and a partner are not likely to see eye to eye on everything, today's rapport can result in mutually beneficial monetary activity. (Your personal finances are something else, but we won't go into that!) Today also favors academic interests and travel plans.

Sunday, October 7 (Moon in Taurus to Gemini 2:48 P.M.). Family or friends at a distance may be in touch today, or perhaps you are planning to visit someone in another region in the near future. During this month, you should be getting your act together, as planetary patterns support your efforts and expanding interests.

Monday, October 8 (Moon in Gemini). Get an early start on whatever you want to accomplish today. You'll have the momentum and the bold new ideas. Some of you can gain through contracts and legal maneuvers now, while others will find that love is the most important of interests. Watch what you say in the evening hours.

Tuesday, October 9 (Moon in Gemini to Cancer 4:30 P.M.). Late in the day, an unexpected chance to aim for very high stakes at work can find you ready, willing, and able to move ahead. A neighborhood project might also call on your time and talents. A social situation may require delicate handling tonight.

Wednesday, October 10 (Moon in Cancer). Whether you're out of step with everyone else or they are out of step with you, today could be one of those near misses, in terms of achievement and good rapport with others. Evening may bring confusion or a disappointment in romance, so don't rely too much on a loved one.

Thursday, October 11 (Moon in Cancer to Leo 8:17 P.M.). Postmidnight hours may accentuate a conflict with someone close to you, but it looks as though this will be favorably resolved; the rest of the day becomes more positive. Evening hours will be enlivened by a social event or an impending invitation to one.

Friday, October 12 (Moon in Leo). Early in the day you had better come to an agreement with an associate concerning weekend plans; compromise could be the answer. With this cleared away, look for social and ultra-romantic pleasures in the P.M., along with enjoyable conviviality and stimulating conversation.

Saturday, October 13 (Moon in Leo). Stay away from speculation in early-morning hours, but enjoy the day's activities—which seem to be right in tune with your mood and desires at this time. You will be especially articulate and persuasive today, and can influence those around you to go along with your agenda.

Sunday, October 14 (Moon in Leo to Virgo 2:21 A.M.). A creative solution to a long-standing personal dilemma might be at your fingertips today. Take advantage of an expert's advice, and don't hesitate to build innovative changes into a standard procedure. Ways in which to improve a domestic problem will emerge.

Monday, October 15 (Moon in Virgo). A surprise or a secret may make today exciting, especially in the area of finances. There may even be a "mystery person" somewhere in the wings. Although matters concerning travel or litigation might be disturbing in the early hours, later developments compensate.

Tuesday, October 16 (Moon in Virgo to Libra 10:27 A.M.). Undercurrents may flow to your advantage this morning, but today's problems could stem from stress in your home environment or a personality clash with your mate or lover. These could be delicate situations and a temper flare-up or impulsive break can backfire.

Wednesday, October 17 (Moon in Libra). Today's mixed trends support travel, dealings with people at a distance, social pleasures, romance, and an academic project. Not on the favored list are property dealings, family confrontation, and trying to escape a soundly established responsibility (you can't do it!).

Thursday, October 18 (NEW MOON in Libra to Scorpio 8:25 P.M.). New ways of generating income and of promoting your favorite objectives should be explored today. You could also find yourself to be the center of attention at a gathering, with your views or opinions much in demand. A legal triumph is due soon.

Friday, October 19 (Moon in Scorpio). You can make good progress in a business matter today, provided you call on that noted Libran balance and poise and refrain from going overboard in your expectations. Curb extravagant spending, too, as well as overromanticism, and/or overindulgence! Easy does it in the P.M.

Saturday, October 20 (Moon in Scorpio). Unless you are spending weekend time in profitable financial activity, you are more likely to devote your energies to a competitive sport—or a romantic challenge. In any case, it looks as though you can emerge a clear winner, whether the stakes are high or low.

Sunday, October 21 (Moon in Scorpio to Sagittarius 8:10 A.M.). A grand plan may be forming in your mind, involving love and an exotic travel adventure. Whether all of this is attainable is in question, but you are currently optimistic and confident of your capabilities—so, who knows? A late-P.M. call is exciting.

Monday, October 22 (Moon in Sagittarius). You have abundant mental and physical energy at your disposal today and can excel in various directions, including study, competitive endeavors, money-making activity, and getting a high rating in romance. Not so favored is dealing with lawyers and family affairs.

Tuesday, October 23 (Moon in Sagittarius to Capricorn 9:04 P.M.). An intriguing opportunity today can place success within your grasp, whether in the tangible area of money or the intangible realm of romance. Evening hours may find you entertaining business-social cohorts in your home, with upbeat results.

Wednesday, October 24 (Moon in Capricorn). Being creative, money-smart, and knowing just when to take decisive action and just when to be passive, will come easily to you today and can help you to make significant business-career strides. Evening brings its own rewards as your personal life glows.

Thursday, October 25 (Moon in Capricorn). You can make economic strides today if you keep your eyes open for an innovative way to turn a trend into a financial landslide—in your direction! Seeking the advice or counsel of an expert will be helpful in implementing a home project, such as interior decorating.

Friday, October 26 (Moon in Capricorn to Aquarius 9:15 A.M.). Today is not the day for investments or other speculative activity, no matter how strongly you are tempted. You can, however, take the germ of a creative idea and build it up into a real showstopper. This can have financial rewards as well.

Saturday, October 27 (Moon in Aquarius). If you can afford to overspend on today's pleasures, which might include a glamorous trip, a romantic rendezvous, or a social splash, by all means do so; the personal rewards can be great, though your cash reserves will be decidedly slimmer. (Money isn't everything!)

Sunday, October 28 (Moon in Aquarius to Pisces 6:23 P.M.). An affair of the heart could be at the top of your agenda today and you'll be honing your charms in every way. Evening may produce a personal responsibility, however—one that you cannot fail to fulfill for the sake of your own peace of mind.

Monday, October 29 (Moon in Pisces). Time spent with a co-worker could be surprisingly valuable today. At the same time, an extra push on your part may be necessary to complete a current project. Creative thinking will enhance your presentation. Late P.M. may produce an exciting financial surprise.

Tuesday, October 30 (Moon in Pisces to Aries 11:15 P.M.). An on-the-job rivalry may spur you on to an even greater performance than you'd been planning. You are exceptionally quick-witted in money matters today and can be a subtly competitive winner. In the P.M., teamwork will be to your advantage.

Wednesday, October 31 (Moon in Aries). Whether you are improving an important relationship or breaking ground for a new project, your success potential will be in proportion to your quick thinking and your diplomacy. Evening hours are more relaxing and favor social interests, joint ventures, and travel plans.

November 1990

Thursday, November 1 (Moon in Aries). After a considerable amount of early-morning anxiety, you'll find that a financial transaction turns exactly as you had hoped. Later in the day, you may call upon a close associate to fill in the missing gaps in your knowledge or information. Observe others' actions, too.

Friday, November 2 (Moon in Aries to Taurus 12:32 A.M. FULL MOON in Taurus). The partnership theme accelerates and takes a decidedly practical turn as you and your mate or partner review major plans for financial growth. But in the P.M., try to avoid clashing, if diverse views on joint funds arise abruptly.

Saturday, November 3 (Moon in Taurus). Early-morning hours show a spillover from yesterday's money problems with someone close to you. However, a solid accord will be reached, and the balance of the day supports domestic and family pleasures. Late P.M. may bring an upbeat contact from a good friend at a distance.

Sunday, November 4 (Moon in Taurus to Gemini 12:07 A.M.). Your main goal seems to be more clearly defined than ever now. It may be an important commitment, a legal triumph, an academic blue ribbon, or an increase in earning power. Though early-A.M. expectations may be slightly overblown, later hunches are more accurate.

Monday, November 5 (Moon in Gemini). Postmidnight hours suggest caution is the key word in financial or speculative activity. A business-oriented trip may be in the works, or a family matter may require a get-together. Someone from a distance who really cares for you may be responsible for a new opportunity.

Tuesday, November 6 (Moon in Gemini to Cancer 12:08 A.M.). As confident and astute as you may be, a career move you make today might receive a slightly hostile reception. It could be a case of some basic flaw in your premise, or perhaps an associate is not ready for your brand of creative thinking right now.

Wednesday, November 7 (Moon in Cancer). Today is much more promising for business-career aims and—if you can get past a delaying tactic someone presents early in the A.M., all should be well. Your own motivation is also increasing, and becoming more focused on priorities. Evening supports study, research, consultation.

Thursday, November 8 (Moon in Cancer to Leo 12:52 A.M.). A well-earned financial break may be yours now, and there is also a hint of some social or community recognition coming due for you around now. An admirer may invite you to a prestigious event in the near future. Your P.M. restlessness finds an outlet in communicating.

Friday, November 9 (Moon in Leo). A delightful postmidnight call or visit could be related to a proposed travel itinerary or exciting family news. Today's business or job agenda may be disappointing, however, as a financial snafu or a setback in proposed negotiations creates a deadlock. Tonight is happily social.

Saturday, November 10 (Moon in Leo to Virgo 7:49 A.M.). A confidential matter you work on today shows good chances for success. You might also be the recipient of support from a key person in your current career game plan. In a different context, travel, sports participation, or working out give you a mighty lift.

Sunday, November 11 (Moon in Virgo). Offstage negotiations can be more profitable for you than a direct approach. But detour any arrangement that might leave you open to criticism from a VIP. Mixing and mingling with socially active people this evening can produce interesting information, and perhaps a vital fact or two.

Monday, November 12 (Moon in Virgo to Libra 4:09 P.M.). A rewarding development in a secret romance during postmidnight hours could brighten your outlook for the entire day. This evening, your charisma blossoms, and you will be able to promote successfully one of your favorite plans to just the right person.

Tuesday, November 13 (Moon in Libra). Mixed trends support personal interests, opportunities to increase your mobility, and a budding romance. On the downside, a domestic issue or a career challenge might need to be dealt with—without ruffling any feathers or upsetting any apple-carts! News from a distant friend is due now.

Wednesday, November 14 (Moon in Libra). Despite your efforts to mollify a touchy person in the A.M., you proba-bly won't be able to maintain total harmony, so don't worry about it. Later, things proceed more to your liking; your attempts to resolve a small crisis at work via diplo-matic mediation ought to work nicely.

Thursday, November 15 (Moon in Libra to Scorpio 2:40 A.M.). Unexpected financial gains may flow in after a carefully outlined strategy appeared to be getting nowhere. Also on tap now may be a promising investment program you have had exhaustively analyzed. Domestic plans may include a new look for an area of your home.

Friday, November 16 (Moon in Scorpio). Financial affairs may be unpredictable, and monetary news somewhat un-reliable today. However, you could pick up some impor-tant facts through a talk with a knowledgeable cohort. Be wary in joint matters, and although conservative invest-ment activity may appeal to you, use restraint.

Saturday, November 17 (NEW MOON in Scorpio to Sag-ittarius 2:40 P.M.). If you are thinking about a wage increase and see good omens on the job, you are probably on the right track now. In fact, a recently started upswing in your personal finances may be a strong clue to future benefits. Late-day news is encouraging.

Sunday, November 18 (Moon in Sagittarius). Plans for a dinner or a shopping spree may have to be rescheduled due to an unexpected development (perhaps in transporta-tion). You will know just the right words to use in persuad-ing a colleague to support your grand scheme (which could include both travel and romance).

Monday, November 19 (Moon in Sagittarius). An early start on a trip will benefit you, especially if a business transaction is your incentive. News or information you receive today can include golden morsels of truth—which you can indeed turn to your own advantage. Contact with a distant person is fulfilling.

Tuesday, November 20 (Moon in Sagittarius to Capricorn 3:32 A.M.). Your initiative in presenting new ideas or marketing tools will pay off, as a higher-up could be in a very receptive mood. The evening can be enjoyably social, with a surprise visit from someone you deeply admire adding to the festivities.

Wednesday, November 21 (Moon in Capricorn). Domestic interests flourish, and though you may be planning an elaborate redecorating program, you also feel pretty secure about your plans for obtaining money for such work. In any case, it looks as though you and your mate or assorted family members are in accord now.

Thursday, November 22 (Moon in Capricorn to Aquarius 4:08 P.M.). A trip to a nearby locale will be on the agenda for many of you today, perhaps to visit family or close friends for a convivial gathering. Also on the happy agenda could be an intriguing romantic attraction that, for some, may be the start of something big.

Friday, November 23 (Moon in Aquarius). Today has the potential for delightful relaxation with congenial companions; but the truth of the matter is that your emotions may get the better of you in an off-key love duet or in clashing with a friend. Try to stay on an even keel. Avoid financial risk in the P.M. as well.

Saturday, November 24 (Moon in Aquarius). Except for an inexplicable change in plans early in the day (possibly tied in with a friend's cost-consciousness), today can be favorable for creative work, children's interests, recreational pleasures, and your love life. Or, you may decide to enjoy out-of-town delights.

Sunday, November 25 (Moon in Aquarius to Pisces 2:33 A.M.). Today, you may ponder a recent development in your particular workplace, taking all factors into consideration. Try to be realistic in your assessments and don't consider any promises binding. You'll gain through discussing this matter with an expert.

Monday, November 26 (Moon in Pisces). You'll have a sense of achievement as you resolve problems and initiate action that brings firm results, especially at work or in connection with health matters. Those around you can be helpful, but late P.M. may bring a misunderstanding; don't force a difficult issue now.

Tuesday, November 27 (Moon in Pisces to Aries 9:07 A.M.). If you let your mate or favorite companion set the pace, especially in communications, you may find you are each running in a different direction! Consolidation is the key word (along with cooperation) for best results. Avoid a clash of personalities in the P.M.

Wednesday, November 28 (Moon in Aries). Today's mixed trends strongly support love and romance, social excitement, travel, a court case, creativity, and speculation; on the downside, however, are domestic issues, family relationships, and property matters. An authority figure may make demands in the late evening.

Thursday, November 29 (Moon in Aries to Taurus 11:38 A.M.). Postmidnight hours can be rewardingly happy—perhaps lucky, too, as planetary trends are decidedly upbeat, most especially in the realms of romance and money. A partnership seems to be very much supported now, and you can persuade someone to play it your way.

Friday, November 30 (Moon in Taurus). You may feel a bit reckless and in the mood to take a risk with some portion of joint funds—but be aware that if you do (with loss as a result), retribution will be swift and sure from your alert mate or partner! On the other hand, shared decisions today will help wheels to turn smoothly.

December 1990

Saturday, December 1 (Moon in Taurus to Gemini 11:23 A.M.). Your imagination and originality are flowing today. Try to promote your inspirations to the right people, or gear your game plan for the immediate future. Tonight is socially stimulating and may bring communication with a key person on your current agenda.

Sunday, December 2 (FULL MOON in Gemini). Welcome news from a distance may prompt you to restructure your plans to include a business-motivated trip. But on a personal note, your current reluctance to make totally firm plans, or a commitment, might be the subject of some lively discussion with your favorite companion.

Monday, December 3 (Moon in Gemini to Cancer 10:28 A.M.). Your timing could be off today as you seek a key person to whom you wish to confide your latest career plans. Perhaps additional work on your project could also make a difference. In any case, clean up any loose ends, and spend today doing constructive repairs.

Tuesday, December 4 (Moon in Cancer). You'll probably work extra hard to attain a career goal today, only to discover that a basic misunderstanding has clouded part of your presentation to a VIP. However, this can be quickly corrected and late afternoon should bring upbeat financial developments. Domestic pressures ease up in the P.M.

Wednesday, December 5 (Moon in Cancer to Leo 11:01 A.M.). This should be a totally satisfying day, particularly in the realms of romance and social excitement. You might also be in line for an honor or award of some kind, related to community or academic efforts. Contact with a dynamic distant friend also stimulates good feelings.

Thursday, December 6 (Moon in Leo). You could be really getting into the holiday spirit early this month, with numerous contacts with cohorts planning a lively seasonal agenda. Someone may raise the subject of overspending, however, which might act as a damper to further innovative (and costly) ideas—at least for the moment.

Friday, December 7 (Moon in Leo to Virgo 2:40 P.M.). A dynamic luncheon today may help to put the frosting on the cake in a subtle business transaction. Later, you may be considering a confidential alliance, but do be careful about disclosing your plans to others; strict secrecy might be a better approach than shared secrets!

Saturday, December 8 (Moon in Virgo). Still on the theme of confidentiality, quiet discussions today will require most explicit information and detailed instructions. Don't assume that someone knows the facts; verify it. Guard your health against carelessness or overindulgence in the P.M., and drive carefully.

Sunday, December 9 (Moon in Virgo to Libra 10:01 P.M.). You might want to get some extra rest this morning before you sally forth into a quietly rewarding social gathering. A slight cloud seems to be hovering over a romantic situation, though, as your reticence to make a commitment becomes a point of dispute.

Monday, December 10 (Moon in Libra). Today could be filled with excitement as well as contradictions, as a change in domestic or family plans will mean a whole new agenda for social-romantic-travel dates. Be flexible, and make the most of an opportunity to promote one of your personal goals in the late-evening hours.

Tuesday, December 11 (Moon in Libra). A chance to shine in your career environment or in connection with a neighborhood project brings you flattering attention. But in the evening, someone in your home surroundings may make life a bit difficult, through either criticism or reproach. Try to remain aloof from the fray.

Wednesday, December 12 (Moon in Libra to Scorpio 8:28 A.M.). A kinder and gentler note can be heard in your household today, as you seem to be given credit for your efforts in someone's behalf. Another upscale development could relate to your personal finances, which may begin to zig upward instead of zagging downward.

Thursday, December 13 (Moon in Scorpio). Business and money interests predominate on this mixed-trend day, when monetary risks (such as in speculation) should be avoided, and matters concerning property, rentals, leases can be successful. A late-P.M. business call can be very informative if you listen between the lines.

Friday, December 14 (Moon in Scorpio to Sagittarius 8:45 P.M.). Lots of activity in a joint financial venture—or it may be that a marital or business partnership is producing more income—will dominate the day until late afternoon. After that, a slowdown may stir up anxieties, as some money activities diminish.

Saturday, December 15 (Moon in Sagittarius). You will enjoy a surge of energy, plenty of action plans fill your calendar in the foreseeable future. A short trip could be a near-future event, and tonight's social delights can include late-hour conviviality. Unattached Librans could be extra romance-prone now.

Sunday, December 16 (NEW MOON in Sagittarius). Getting an early start on a trip will be helpful today, landing you at your destination ahead of the swarms. On the other hand, travel may be the catalyst that starts you off on a dynamic new romance. Your intuition and creativity soar now and can be personally rewarding.

Monday, December 17 (Moon in Sagittarius to Capricorn 9:36 A.M.). Whether you stay close to home and its demands, or are out and about in your pursuit of career-financial success, practical considerations will be uppermost in your mind. As a Libran, you are sometimes known to choose glamour over pragmatic concerns, but not today.

Tuesday, December 18 (Moon in Capricorn). Today can be totally supportive for property and domestic interests as well as for the promotion of a well-prepared business project. You are especially keen-minded now and can spot opportunity and potential money schemes a mile away. This evening favors talk of love and marriage.

Wednesday, December 19 (Moon in Capricorn to Aquarius 10:00 P.M.). You might have to get up early to take advantage of a surprise opportunity, which could be related to property or an innovative career venture. Substantial support from a VIP follows, while P.M. hours continue this dynamic trend romantically.

Thursday, December 20 (Moon in Aquarius). Promoting a creative idea that's buzzing around your brain this morning can increase job potential. Children's interests are also favored, along with arrangements for convivial holiday activities. Late P.M. could see expenses mounting or a social bash overextending itself.

Friday, December 21 (Moon in Aquarius). A business problem arising around noon will take a bit of maneuvering in your own subtle way. Weekend plans may be getting crowded, or you could learn that you'll have more guests than you expected at a festive gathering. Domestic-family obligations can be adroitly juggled.

Saturday, December 22 (Moon in Aquarius to Pisces 8:49 A.M.). Joint finances may be a subject of slightly heated discussion this morning, possibly due to a speculative move made by one of you. Chores related to a festive event will keep you busy, but there are special rewards in this project and you feel elated.

Sunday, December 23 (Moon in Pisces). Postmidnight hours can be glamorously romantic, but this entire day will be tailor-made for convivial pleasures, entertaining, or visiting favorite friends. Evening hours continue the theme of harmony and shared pleasures. Good health news is welcomed about someone close to you.

Monday, December 24 (Moon in Pisces to Aries 4:46 P.M.). Those around you contribute cooperatively to the day's agenda. Welcome business-financial news could make your day. Later, tension with your spouse or a partner may cloud the evening's activities, but try to keep this from becoming a major brouhaha.

Tuesday, December 25 (Moon in Aries). Frankly, today will be more pleasurable for you outside your home than in it. Those around you may be overtired or inclined to overreact at the slightest excuse. Try to spend some time with someone who meshes with your temperament more harmoniously. Tonight may generate peace.

Wednesday, December 26 (Moon in Aries to Taurus 9:10 P.M.). An authority figure may not be receptive to your carefully thought out approach, so put your agenda aside until a more auspicious occasion (which might be tomorrow). Contact with someone at a distance can lift your spirits, especially if a meeting is planned.

Thursday, December 27 (Moon in Taurus). Although you may be tempted to splurge on a social event today, you can probably afford to do so and feel in a festive mood anyway. Among favored interests now are romance, personal finances, as well as joint funds, creativity, and matters concerning family members and property.

Friday, December 28 (Moon in Taurus to Gemini 10:27 P.M.). Aside from a business-financial dispute this morning, the day proceeds smoothly enough, and can launch you into a generally rewarding weekend. Social invitations continue to fill your calendar and a trip is almost sure to be in the planning stages now.

Saturday, December 29 (Moon in Gemini). Someone close to you adds just the right touch of both humor and glamour and, in a social setting, can balance your own personality traits enjoyably. It's possible you are involved in a legal matter these days and may be spending a few late-night hours researching it.

Sunday, December 30 (Moon in Gemini to Cancer 10:03 P.M.). Try to avoid bickering with a relative or neighbor this afternoon, as nothing much would be settled anyway. Use a different tactic later, if it's that important. Evening hours find you working on strategies for 1991, especially in the business-career arena.

Monday, December 31 (FULL MOON in Cancer). Be flexible and ready with alternate plans today, as surprising turns of events may mean rescheduling a few appointments. Someone in your business environment may overreact to a minor incident, or someone at home could be difficult. Usher in the New Year with discretion and restraint.

January 1991

Tuesday, January 1 (Moon in Cancer to Leo 9:55 P.M.). Don't be surprised if you meet with resistance to one of your major career schemes; the opposition may come from a family member or close friend and might not be diplomatically expressed. Evening social plans may be promising, but might not live up to expectations.

Wednesday, January 2 (Moon in Leo). Your friends may seem to be like family today, as their strongly nurturing influence makes you feel invincible. Early evening could bring a fortunate encounter, or a special person will build up the force of your self-esteem.

Thursday, January 3 (Moon in Leo to Virgo 11:58 P.M.). If you have been holding off making a decision concerning a relative or a domestic project, today you will see the whole picture more clearly. However, there may be a financial cloud in the sky, particularly in the realm of joint funds; avoid secret maneuvers.

Friday, January 4 (Moon in Virgo). Inspiration can flood your mind today; write down your impressions and unusual new ideas. You may be called upon to make a sacrifice of some sort for a family member or in connection with a domestic or property matter. Intuitive promptings will help you to resolve a puzzle.

Saturday, January 5 (Moon in Virgo). The romance theme is heard loud and clear today and may be the subject of your carefully concealed plots and plans. A financial angle is on the brink of working out exactly as you've intended. Check travel directions or social instructions carefully in the evening hours.

Sunday, January 6 (Moon in Virgo to Libra 5:34 A.M.). Postmidnight hours support financial negotiations concerning a joint endeavor. Early in the day, you'll confirm that romantic and/or social plans for later are proceeding just as hoped. You may, however, be in a reckless mood as midnight approaches, so beware!

Monday, January 7 (Moon in Libra). Don't bypass an interesting social or investment opportunity in the wee small hours of this morning simply because you are in a rebellious mood. Later in the day, discord at home or in your career environment may be based on a simple misunderstanding; do not act in haste.

Tuesday, January 8 (Moon in Libra to Scorpio 3:00 P.M.). The inspired words you intend to say to a higher-up this morning might not come out in just the way you intended; be ready to smooth things over if necessary. The financial trend that begins this afternoon may develop its ups and downs, so be prepared to cope.

Wednesday, January 9 (Moon in Scorpio). This is not the day to engage in speculation or to take other financial risks; opt for the tried-and-true methods. In the evening, you may learn from an expert or receive valuable information concerning property or the future trends in your own particular career field.

Thursday, January 10 (Moon in Scorpio). Today you will probably feel like being bold and imaginative in financial matters and you can put this urge to good use in the morning hours. Later, and particularly just prior to midnight, joint funds may be the subject of friction as you and a partner clash over diverse views.

Friday, January 11 (Moon in Scorpio to Sagittarius 3:07 A.M.). The spotlight shifts to personal interests, especially romantic ones, as well as social plans for the weekend and perhaps the development of a new and potentially helpful friendship. An informal gathering in the P.M. could prove to be rewarding.

Saturday, January 12 (Moon in Sagittarius). Postmidnight hours will be either exceptionally enjoyable in a social setting or immensely profitable in terms of a new business-financial opportunity coming your way. Later, the day is favorable for taking care of local errands, correspondence, calling distant friends.

Sunday, January 13 (Moon in Sagittarius to Capricorn 4:01 P.M.). Mixed trends today could produce a bit of welcome news in the afternoon, but there's a daylong warning in effect against speculation, endangering a treasured romance, and/or risking health, money, or other resources through being overly daring and confident.

Monday, January 14 (Moon in Capricorn). There may be a home or family problem that needs to be resolved at this time. Possibly a sudden development or a misunderstanding will bring the entire matter to a head. This could be when you'll put your flair for diplomatic management to good use, as you direct the action.

Tuesday, January 15 (Moon in Capricorn—NEW MOON Solar Eclipse 6:51 P.M.). A domestic or property matter may require your attention quite insistently today and you should take extra care not to be bedazzled by a charismatic person's sales pitch (whatever may be promoted). A late-night decision may challenge you.

Wednesday, January 16 (Moon in Capricorn to Aquarius 4:05 A.M.). Today's emphasis on social-romantic interests—as well as on creative thinking and planning—opens up a brighter picture for you to contemplate. If you are unattached, a new attraction may develop in a business-financial environment; be alert to this!

Thursday, January 17 (Moon in Aquarius). Postmidnight hours bring another one of those occasions when reckless behavior or decisions can lead you down a totally unproductive garden path (whether we are talking love or money—or both). A more dependable romance could be linked with a morning phone call or encounter.

Friday, January 18 (Moon in Aquarius to Pisces 2:24 P.M.). For some of you, this could be the day when you have to face the music, as prior actions now present their "rewards." Don't look for harmony on the home front, or in connection with marital or partnership funds. P.M. favors exercise, self-improvement, rest.

Saturday, January 19 (Moon in Pisces). There should be plenty of openings today for mending domestic relations that may have been damaged lately. Today is also a fortunate time to arrange for home repairs and/or enhancement. Don't be afraid to utilize a new method or develop new plans for home beautification.

Sunday, January 20 (Moon in Pisces to Aries 10:28 P.M.). Today you may feel as though all the world is yours and all the doors are opening to you—and you could be at least partly right. New stellar trends involve your Libra Sun-Sign in wonderfully promising romance, travel, academic, and partnership opportunities.

Monday, January 21 (Moon in Aries). Postmidnight hours may find you prone to making wrong choices and following flawed ideas. Get back on track, in order to take advantage of a personal or career opportunity in late afternoon. In the P.M., resist any urge to break ties, issue an ultimatum, or make a move.

Tuesday, January 22 (Moon in Aries). Family concerns are still prominent on your agenda, but if you are tempted to involve yourself in a postmidnight showdown—don't!

Nothing but misunderstandings and missed signals will result. Midafternoon presents a more harmonious time for "talking things over."

Wednesday, January 23 (Moon in Aries to Taurus 4:02 A.M.). Today you might give the impression of someone walking—*very* carefully—through a mine field. Especially if the subject is money, avoid confrontation or even conversation on the subject with your mate, partner, or other associate. Better safe than sorry.

Thursday, January 24 (Moon in Taurus). Although things quiet down with a reasonable amount of harmony in your environment, midafternoon may produce another financial conflict or dilemma, so be prepared to cope with sensitive feelings as well as recriminations. Speculation is a no-no in the P.M.; so are love spats.

Friday, January 25 (Moon in Taurus to Gemini 7:07 A.M.). Your level head and practical judgment will be a financial asset this morning. Later, lovely developments at a distance may lead to travel, a partnership opportunity (or marital offer), and general good fortune. Legal and family interests prosper.

Saturday, January 26 (Moon in Gemini). Today's emphasis on both travel and education could mean you're preparing for a trip to another country by studying another language, or perhaps getting ready to pursue an academic course in another locale. In any case, your mind is brimming with new ideas and creative plans.

Sunday, January 27 (Moon in Gemini to Cancer 8:24 A.M.). You could be guided by a single idea or concept today—one that has excellent business-financial potential. Step carefully through a few hazards on the course and make sure to talk to the right person about it, or wait until you can see this individual.

Monday, January 28 (Moon in Cancer). Unfortunately, today's key word is "opposition," and that is what you are apt to encounter no matter which way you turn. So try to develop an agenda that works around this situation and avoids confrontations. Late afternoon does have a good money aspect, but take no risks in the P.M.

Tuesday, January 29 (Moon in Cancer to Leo 9:04 A.M.). A smart move for you today (especially after an early-A.M. conflict or disappointment at work) will be to utilize an influential connection in order to support a special aim rather than trying to do it all on your own. Late P.M. can be a great time to meet a VIP.

Wednesday, January 30 (Moon in Leo—FULL MOON Lunar Eclipse 1:11 A.M.). Follow your own early-A.M. hunch concerning a business-financial course of action instead of relying on another's line of thought. In the P.M., listen politely as a friend gives you business advice, but such advice could be off target.

Thursday, January 31 (Moon in Leo to Virgo 10:45 A.M.). Don't expect too much from love and romance today, as you and your loved one may be on totally different modes. Look into the past for a clue as to what could have gone wrong (temporarily) and then find a way to mend the fences without making a big to-do about it.

February 1991

Friday, February 1 (Moon in Virgo). Working quietly and efficiently behind the scenes today will gain you more advantages than unmistakable self-promotion is apt to do. Sound practical advice from a relative may help you to advance a property or money-making project. Or, remembering prior training or an old lesson will do it.

Saturday, February 2 (Moon in Virgo to Libra 3:03 P.M.). Creative inspiration can add to your basic program in a business-career endeavor. Earned rewards could materialize in the afternoon. P.M. could be glamorous, romantic, and may produce a dynamic type of person, with whom you develop an instant rapport.

Sunday, February 3 (Moon in Libra). Don't expect support from your nearest and dearest (especially family members) today. Fortunately, your own self-esteem and assurance are high, so this lack of support will not hinder you. A newcomer on the social-romantic scene can make this evening a most productive one.

Monday, February 4 (Moon in Libra to Scorpio 11:02 P.M.). Business and/or domestic chores make this a so-so day, while evening hours might produce a replay of some family or property-related challenge. This might have its basis in a clash of wills between you and another person; look for a compromise.

Tuesday, February 5 (Moon in Scorpio). Don't miss an early-afternoon business opportunity by taking too long a lunch hour! A long-term agreement can be reached later in the day which might not be everything you want but is worth accepting. P.M. features romance, perhaps a pleasant social occasion.

Wednesday, February 6 (Moon in Scorpio). A longtime domestic or family responsibility may be about to fade, but don't allow your newfound freedom to go to your head; extravagance and/or speculation could bring dim results sooner than you think. On the other hand, this new trend may signify a family addition!

Thursday, February 7 (Moon in Scorpio to Sagittarius 10:24 A.M.). If you have creative ability, newly developing stellar patterns can impel you to get serious about nurturing such gifts. A job advantage may also be yours at this time. Be cautious in P.M. travel and transportation and avoid verbal friction.

Friday, February 8 (Moon in Sagittarius). Postmidnight luck could arrive in the form of good news, opportunity at a distance, or a brilliant money-making idea. Later, avoid bickering with a co-worker or getting your signals crossed concerning a luncheon date. Talk from a position of strength to a personal adversary.

Saturday, February 9 (Moon in Sagittarius to Capricorn 11:17 P.M.). Some overall misunderstanding concerning a financial matter (such as allocating expense obligations or how to split profits from a joint venture) can lead to a big brouhaha early in the day if you're not careful. Opt for peace by noon.

Sunday, February 10 (Moon in Capricorn). Think carefully before sharing your ideas and plans with friends or family members; you may want to revise a few issues before revealing all. This will be a good day to review your health regimen and exercise program. Romance and a surprise may make P.M. interesting.

Monday, February 11 (Moon in Capricorn). Smooth sailing in career matters today can reflect your creative planning and use of information available to you. A financial advantage in the afternoon may stem from a family contact or a longtime supporter. Upbeat report regarding someone's health provides a lift.

Tuesday, February 12 (Moon in Capricorn to Aquarius 11:17 A.M.). Postmidnight hours may bring exciting news from a distance or a travel or academic opportunity may help to fulfill a dream. If you are unattached, a serious romance may be brewing, with clues becoming rather obvious starting today.

Wednesday, February 13 (Moon in Aquarius). Postmidnight hours may find you with mixed emotions, as a friend could be antagonistic to one of your romance prospects—at the same time that opportunity for an expanded lifestyle seems available to you. Listening to your own heart could be the very best solution.

Thursday, February 14 (Moon in Aquarius—NEW MOON at 12:33 P.M.—to Pisces 9:00 P.M.). Morning hours bring an excellent financial opportunity, business connection, or favor from a VIP. You may derive a new slant on an emotional situation from careful self-analysis. Evening favors arranging for a rigorous exercise agenda.

Friday, February 15 (Moon in Pisces). Colleagues and co-workers tend to be sensitive and super touchy this morning; choose your words carefully and don't rock the boat (it might be wise to have your lunch with a personal friend, or alone). You may be surprised at the ease with which a domestic dilemma is solved in the P.M.

Saturday, February 16 (Moon in Pisces). A wage increase may be in the offing, as your job performance has been noted. You may find that sports, exercise, or dancing makes you feel in tip-top shape this afternoon, so find a favorite companion and share the exhilaration. P.M. may bring romance or a rewarding friendship.

Sunday, February 17 (Moon in Pisces to Aries 4:12 A.M.). Your mate or partner may spot the creative solution to an ongoing dilemma even before you do. Social pleasures brighten the evening hours, and word fram afar could concern multiple advantages, relating to a family member, a proposed trip, an academic goal.

Monday, February 18 (Moon in Aries). This day doesn't start off very well, as a domestic problem may darken the early hours, followed by a garbled or disappointing financial message at work. However, by dint of your thoughtful efforts, by the end of the workday, there do seem to be answers to most problems.

Tuesday, February 19 (Moon in Aries to Taurus 9:25 A.M.). The focus is on joint funds and/or any other arrangements for shared income, expenses, investments, and so on. Unfortunately, the storm clouds seem to be gathering and someone apparently has a score to settle or a few demands to make. Be diplomatic.

Wednesday, February 20 (Moon in Taurus). A domestic or property problem could have a surprise solution this morning—perhaps via some line of action you had not thought of. By midevening, storm clouds have again gathered around the subject of money, with your views clashing with those of your mate or partner.

Thursday, February 21 (Moon in Taurus to Gemini 1:11 P.M.). Usually on target, your early-A.M. intuition seems to be askew; rethink the problem involved. A pleasant long-range plan is beginning to take shape; at this particular point, the only cloud on the horizon could be related to a key person's health.

Friday, February 22 (Moon in Gemini). Unattached Librans should take advantage of a delightful cycle of marital opportunity, beginning today and lasting until mid-March. For starters, a planned trip could have intriguing potential for a new encounter of the happily-ever-after sort. A research project may be involved.

Saturday, February 23 (Moon in Gemini to Cancer 3:57 P.M.). News or a rumor concerning your business-career environment could prompt you to get the authentic facts (which can be very much to your advantage). An early-A.M. date could have worthwhile potential on a personal level, but later a conflict may arise.

Sunday, February 24 (Moon in Cancer). Postmidnight hours could find you receiving pleasant attention in connection with a social or community project. However, afternoon hours may be tense because of a family or domestic conflict, as your views and aims seem to trigger off opposition from another.

Monday, February 25 (Moon in Cancer to Leo 6:13 P.M.). Being an early bird can work wonders in a business-career endeavor today. In the evening, a social or group project might wind up with everyone in a tizzy as egos clash and original objectives get lost in the shuffle. Try to remain uninvolved and serene.

Tuesday, February 26 (Moon in Leo). This can be a super day in your love life, with marriage potential for unattached Librans. Also on the upswing are business alli-

ances, legal triumphs, travel plans, and dealings with relatives and distant friends. Making travel and other future
plans now is a wise move.

**Wednesday, February 27 (Moon in Leo to Virgo 8:51
P.M.).** You may awaken with a financial worry in the
forefront of your mind. Though there seems to be no
imminent money problem, make a note to forgo extravagance and speculation, just to be on the safe side. Quiet
introspection may appeal to you tonight.

**Thursday, February 28 (Moon in Virgo—FULL MOON at
1:26 P.M.).** Avoid a squabble with a colleague or co-worker
in the late-morning hours; no one can win an argument in
such an emotionally charged atmosphere. Take extra precautions in transportation and travel in the P.M. Concentrate on creative work tonight.

March 1991

Friday, March 1 (Moon in Virgo). You may feel more
introspective than outgoing today, perhaps in the mood for
reflective analysis of recent events or for a few hours of
quiet time dedicated to creative efforts. In any case, a late-
P.M. communication could shed some light on a work-
related question or decision.

Saturday, March 2 (Moon in Virgo to Libra 1:04 A.M.).
Overnight, your mood changes and today you'll be more
than ready for extroverted activities—social gatherings,
romance momentum, participating in a community project.
There may be a slight problem with your mate, partner, or
special friend in midevening; tact required.

Sunday, March 3 (Moon in Libra). The conflict that arises
in or concerning your home environment may include a
family problem as well. Actually, despite the stress in-

volved, the one sure way to resolve this dilemma will involve service to others, rendered by you, freely and lovingly. This will be clear in the P.M.

Monday, March 4 (Moon in Libra to Scorpio 8:09 A.M.). Postmidnight hours bring a warning against verbal warfare with an associate, and overdoing in some way on the health circuit. Later in the day, bypass money-related arguments (especially on the home front) and don't risk a valuable relationship through a whim.

Tuesday, March 5 (Moon in Scorpio). You could be in the mood to share the wealth today, via a shopping spree, dining in splendid elegance, or otherwise passing the money from your hands to another's! On a more practical note, this could be a fortunate day for business transactions and gains through partnership interests.

Wednesday, March 6 (Moon in Scorpio to Sagittarius 6:36 P.M.). The extra effort you put into a financial project will pay off today. Evening hours feature rewarding communications, including the plans made by you and a colleague to take a short trip for business or pleasure motives (most probably for both).

Thursday, March 7 (Moon in Sagittarius). Your crowded social calendar gets even more jam-packed today, as some festive events seem to be in the offing. But be alert to a possible problem concerning your spouse or a partner, perhaps due to a basic misunderstanding of each other's motivation and/or emotional reactions.

Friday, March 8 (Moon in Sagittarius). Mixed trends are almost sure to add a note of confusion to an already stressed situation at work or at home. There may also be a concern involving health. Don't put too much faith in news or rumors you hear now, as it is quite possible that someone is exaggerating.

Saturday, March 9 (Moon in Sagittarius to Capricorn 7:15 P.M.). Torn between personal issues and work demands, you may not be in top form on the decision-making angle. In fact, you might feel that a certain judgment recently made has much room for improvement. Domestic-family interests dominate in P.M.

Sunday, March 10 (Moon in Capricorn). If you've scheduled entertainment at home today, your gathering is sure to be a big success. A chance encounter might be the link to resolving a domestic or family problem, or a late-night phone call could provide you with just the ammunition you need to wage a winning campaign.

Monday, March 11 (Moon in Capricorn to Aquarius 7:32 P.M.). A household disturbance may upset your emotional balance in the A.M., but by early-evening hours delightful social or romantic developments make you know that all is well. Cultural interests are stimulating, too, and tend to arouse your own creativity.

Tuesday, March 12 (Moon in Aquarius). After doing a bit of tossing and turning and perhaps a few sleepless hours concerning a current weighty problem, you'll realize that any extreme action is not going to resolve the matter. Being a wise Libran, you will adopt a wait-and-see attitude and avoid forcing issues.

Wednesday, March 13 (Moon in Aquarius). Smart thinking will lead you to resist an A.M. urge to speculate or take other financial risks. Later, a decision concerning a child, an artistic or cultural project, or the future of an important relationship can be right on target. A partnership flourishes in the P.M.

Thursday, March 14 (Moon in Aquarius to Pisces 5:12 A.M.). This may be a lazy, quiet sort of day, when any dynamic plans are due to take a backseat or become bogged down in delays. You may spend some time on a health, diet, or exercise program, or perhaps catch up on relatively unimportant leftover chores.

Friday, March 15 (Moon in Pisces). A well-planned work agenda can find you getting a lot done on the job or in connection with a special project for which you are responsible. Later, your leisure activities may be curtailed for reasons beyond your control; a communications snafu, or a feud between friends.

Saturday, March 16 (Moon in Pisces—NEW MOON at 3:11 A.M.—to Aries 11:39 A.M.). An innovative job procedure can help you to cut work time in half this morning. Later, marital and partnership goals are favorably accented. Unattached Librans could meet promising new romance prospects in the P.M. hours.

Sunday, March 17 (Moon in Aries). Mixed trends support open discussion between you and your spouse or partner concerning a current problem. On the other hand, domestic, household, and property interests are not too well aspected and you should probably postpone a firm commitment or forcing a showdown.

Monday, March 18 (Moon in Aries to Taurus 3:41 P.M.). The day begins with great promise and you could finalize a business or personal agreement in the A.M. After that, it's all downhill, and by late evening hours a love relationship or a domestic problem (or both) will need your most diplomatic Libran finesse.

Tuesday, March 19 (Moon in Taurus). The answer to one of your financial questions could lie in utilizing a partnership or other joint arrangement you have recently entered into. Think carefully around all the angles of your special circumstances and the potential backing you have at your disposal. Think creatively.

Wednesday, March 20 (Moon in Taurus to Gemini 6:38 P.M.). During postmidnight hours guard your possessions and your cash. Later in the day, communications with distant contacts can be filled with good news and optimistic reports. A new trend beginning in the late P.M. accentuates marital interests or opportunity.

Thursday, March 21 (Moon in Gemini). Your creative fires are burning brightly and you may wake up with an excellent (and practical) money-making inspiration. During evening hours, however, be very wary about commiting yourself to someone's monetary suggestions, especially as there is a strong element of risk in them.

Friday, March 22 (Moon in Gemini to Cancer 9:28 P.M.). Morning hours might bring anxiety concerning a youngster, or news that an investment is sagging—or perhaps a creative assignment finds you without even the germ of an idea! You'll get through this somehow. Late P.M. could bring a dynamic career communication.

Saturday, March 23 (Moon in Cancer). You and your mate or partner may be at odds concerning a joint (or individual) career move. Early-A.M. financial news should be encouraging, but a P.M. clash of wills at work or at home might result in a lively discussion and probably inflammatory statements from both sides.

Sunday, March 24 (Moon in Cancer). Postmidnight hours continue the brouhaha, with misunderstandings all around adding to the confusion. It could be afternoon before the sun shines on an important relationship—but it's well worth the wait (and the stormy prelude) since a wonderful new rapport is building between you.

Monday, March 25 (Moon in Cancer to Leo 12:44 A.M.). A friend can be helpful in terms of providing you with an important contact of vital business information. On the other hand, don't be too quick to follow the well-meant (but possibly flawed) advice of a cohort. Social plans for the evening proceed smoothly.

Tuesday, March 26 (Moon in Leo). Disappointing news just before noon could concern a monetary favor or advantage you've been seeking. If you think carefully, you'll realize there are other sources available. Evening hours find a strong rapport you have with a very special someone deepening and glowing brightly.

Wednesday, March 27 (Moon in Leo to Virgo 4:42 A.M.). Relying on your inner strengths today will enable you to dispel negative thinking and discover ways to cope successfully with tough situations. This is not the day on which to push for results or promote an important personal or business objective.

Thursday, March 28 (Moon in Virgo). Within your mind or in the fastness of your own office or hideaway, you could suddenly come upon the answer to a stubborn puzzle that's been giving you an occasional sleepless night. This may concern a romance, an obligation, or an old dream. The way is now clear and brightly lit.

Friday, March 29 (Moon in Virgo to Libra 9:50 A.M.). Avoid traffic hazards in case you are out in the wee small hours (or on a predawn assignment). Later in the day, all signals seem to be slanted in your direction in a most positive manner; both material and emotional developments are rewarding in the P.M.

Saturday, March 30 (Moon in Libra—FULL MOON at 2:18 A.M.). Postmidnight may bring a pleasant romantic surprise, perhaps a call or a visit from a special loved one. But later in the day, especially at home, you'll probably notice that tempers are high, sensitives are super touchy, and you can't win!

Sunday, March 31 (Moon in Libra to Scorpio 5:02 P.M.). You and a close associate may find yourselves talking at cross purposes today; spell out important ideas and reactions in order to avoid misunderstandings. Travel plans can be stimulating in the afternoon, but be wary in financial transactions in the late P.M.

April 1991

Monday, April 1 (Moon in Scorpio). Postmidnight influences are not to be trusted, particularly in areas concerning love and money. However, early afternoon could find you dredging up a truly creative idea with strongly practical overtones; this may concern property. Evening entertainment may have business overtones.

Tuesday, April 2 (Moon in Scorpio). There's more than a hint of friction in today's prospects, particularly if you are involved in a partnership or shared monetary arrangement. Also on the horizon is a dynamic new influence in your career environment, which may reflect advantageously on your own aims if you are receptive.

Wednesday, April 3 (Moon in Scorpio to Sagittarius 3:00 A.M.). Be alert to the opportunity inherent in a midmorning development in your job or business environment. In fact, it's a promising day for career progress. But be on guard against a sudden or unexpected strain on a close alliance; avoid a break.

Thursday, April 4 (Moon in Sagittarius). Early-A.M. stress could stem from a financial battle being waged between you and a close associate. Early afternoon brings likelihood of delays and slowdowns in matters pertaining to travel and communications; try to arrange your affairs so that there is room for maneuvering.

Friday, April 5 (Moon in Sagittarius to Capricorn 3:20 P.M.). You should be able to handle domestic affairs with ease once you get past an A.M. argument, which could very well concern career demands that interfere with a smooth-running household schedule. Use your noted tact and finesse to subjugate storm clouds.

Saturday, April 6 (Moon in Capricorn). This can be a so-so day until the P.M., when—unfortunately—some old grievance that just won't fade away once more rises to haunt you as your spouse or partner again runs through a catalog of complaints! Whether silence or a lively self-defense is the best response is a key question.

Sunday, April 7 (Moon in Capricorn). Domestic or real-estate matters could require extra care today, and perhaps a touch of flattery or pampering as well, in order to keep the peace in the early afternoon. Later, romance and/or a pleasant entertainment program can do wonders for your psyche as well as your self-esteem.

Monday, April 8 (Moon in Capricorn to Aquarius 4:01 A.M.). Someone you talk with today is probably going to bend the truth beyond all recognition. This might not matter unless the subject is money, in which case listen very carefully and don't be too quick to part with your hard-earned cash. P.M. accents obligations.

Tuesday, April 9 (Moon in Aquarius). This would be the day for you to boost a loved one's ego and to keep off the subjects of shortcomings and financial errors. Your own best behavior can result in your hopes and wishes coming closer to fruition. Shared viewpoints will make communication with your loved one rewarding.

Wednesday, April 10 (Moon in Aquarius to Pisces 2:19 P.M.). It's possible you are making too much of a disappointment or misunderstanding with a romantic companion. Look at the incident calmly and impartially. Immerse yourself in a job assignment; there could be intriguing developments if you do your very best work.

Thursday, April 11 (Moon in Pisces). Today you can enjoy the satisfaction that comes when your plan or procedure operates successfully; a VIP will also appreciate your efforts. Your renewed interests in physical fitness will keep you on your feet tonight and moving around energetically, whether via aerobics or dancing.

Friday, April 12 (Moon in Pisces to Aries 8:50 P.M.). An encouraging financial development makes you feel appreciated (and probably a bit extravagant as well!). The P.M. brings an intensified interest in travel plans, which almost certainly are linked to a romantic attraction. A late-P.M. communication inspires you.

Saturday, April 13 (Moon in Aries). Mental rapport with a partner may be under much strain today, as this person seeks to dominate your thinking and perhaps pressure you to agree on controversial issues. You'll be better off to delay any decisions than to go along with the pressure simply to preserve the peace.

Sunday, April 14 (Moon in Aries—NEW MOON at 2:39 P.M.). Postmidnight hours may bring a disappointment concerning a partner's attitude or reactions to one of your favorite plans. Late afternoon favors conferences with close associates, perhaps putting heads together in connection with a new business project or creative program.

Monday, April 15 (Moon in Aries to Taurus 12:06 A.M.). Let your intuition run free in the afternoon; this could lead to the solution of a financial problem or set the stage for a new joint venture. P.M. may produce helpful feedback on a business or investment plan from your spouse, partner, or interested bystander.

Tuesday, April 16 (Moon in Taurus). Today's theme is firmly set in the early A.M. and sounds a happy note of financial and/or romantic progress. A trip may be shaping up, with at least a double motivation of business and pleasure (with perhaps a little family contact on the side). Joint funds present a small challenge.

Wednesday, April 17 (Moon in Taurus to Gemini 1:42 A.M.). Travel plans still prevail, although some of you will also be taking advantage of a fortunate turn of events in a legal matter. Any delay in confirming your agenda and itinerary can be used in a positive way in order to check certain angles meticulously.

Thursday, April 18 (Moon in Gemini). Share your philosophical views with a loved one and benefit from the input. Your mind may reach out beyond limited horizons at this time as your creative plans take shape. Don't be in a rush to promote sparkling new concepts, as these will mellow rewardingly as time goes on.

Friday, April 19 (Moon in Gemini to Cancer 3:18 A.M.). Your enthusiasm can be a determining factor in the success of a career project today. Someone is admiring your belief in your dreams and your confidence in yourself (proving that others often take us at our own valuation!). P.M. finds you sharing joy with a loved one.

Saturday, April 20 (Moon in Cancer). The climate is right today for putting across one of your creative ideas for a community program or organizational activity. However, you will still have to convince a close associate or a family member that the time you spend on this matter is really necessary!

Sunday, April 21 (Moon in Cancer to Leo 6:05 A.M.). Mixed trends today favor social pleasures (and perhaps your receiving a special honor or award). But there's a strong note of caution against overspending and/or indulging in any form of speculation. An evening date might need to be rescheduled.

Monday, April 22 (Moon in Leo). You might gain a new friend today, or perhaps find that an old one is more valuable than you'd realized. Membership in a business or professional organization might also pay off now, as good contacts can help to pave your way on the road to success. Your creativity may sag a bit in the P.M.

Tuesday, April 23 (Moon in Leo to Virgo 10:30 A.M.). A covert operation can be beneficial for you at this time; in other words, don't be too confiding of your plans, especially to blabbermouths. Instead, work quietly behind the scenes, possibly with the help of an expert. You may make a fresh start in a private matter.

Wednesday, April 24 (Moon in Virgo). It's possible that communications with someone at a distance will produce an obstacle (or at least a question) concerning an academic or travel plan. However, this can be quickly, even surprisingly, straightened out. Late P.M. features a welcome financial development.

Thursday, April 25 (Moon in Virgo to Libra 4:37 A.M.). Postmidnight hours carry a warning signal in flashing strobes! Do not take speculative risks with your money. It will also be a good idea not to risk a love relationship either, perhaps through an excess of optimism, confidence, or adventurousness. P.M. hours find you more realistic.

Friday, April 26 (Moon in Libra). You may feel torn every which way today, as trends alternately spark your wisdom and practicality and arouse your yen to be a daring do-or-die personality. Try to stay on a middle road (with those Libra scales reasonably balanced!). A P.M. talk with a loved one can help you to stay afloat.

Saturday, April 27 (Moon in Libra). Postmidnight hours might produce a serious rift between you and your partner; aside from being in a different thought pattern, you may differ on personal issues and perhaps over monetary plans, as well. Avoid making decisions, judgments, and joint plans at this particular time.

Sunday, April 28 (Moon in Libra to Scorpio 12:35 A.M.—FULL MOON at 3:59 P.M.). If you are out during postmidnight hours, avoid travel/transportation mishaps; if you are at home, bypass a family quarrel. Stay away from the subject of money in all conversations and try not to force any issues at all!

Monday, April 29 (Moon in Scorpio). Today brings the sunshine after the storm (at least figuratively). Personal and career matters proceed nicely and midafternoon could bring good financial news or business advancement. Money moves are favored today, and with an eye to the future you'll make wise ones.

Tuesday, April 30 (Moon in Scorpio to Sagittarius 10:43 A.M.). You could find a market for your ideas today if you look around carefully. Information or a communiqué can bring helpful facts for you to use. Evening can find you savoring the glamour of a social event, and some unattached Librans might fall in love.

May 1991

Wednesday, May 1 (Moon in Sagittarius). If you are prepared for a trip, this might be when you'll welcome the chance to leave. This may pertain to an educational project or a family interest. Late P.M. finds you and your spouse or partner thinking as one on an issue important to both. A legal matter could be winding up.

Thursday, May 2 (Moon in Sagittarius to Capricorn 10:55 P.M.). Weigh carefully what you ask for this morning because you could get it sooner than you expect (consider whether you're wasting a beneficial contact for a mere trifle). Evening hours may be spent perusing travel brochures or disposing of nonessentials.

Friday, May 3 (Moon in Capricorn). For some time now you may have been experiencing a conflict between your business-career aims and your domestic or family responsibilities. From time to time the conflict becomes quite challenging; this could be one of those days, with the added pressure of misunderstanding at home base.

Saturday, May 4 (Moon in Capricorn). Although there may still be vestiges of yesterday's tensions, especially in dealing with a business colleague or family member, this can be a more productive and upbeat day. Creative work is particularly favored, and if it is part of a collaborative effort, so much the better.

Sunday, May 5 (Moon in Capricorn to Aquarius 11:52 A.M.). Household interests keep you busy until early afternoon, when a social or romantic trend is delightfully ushered in, perhaps via a glamorous invitation. Late P.M. may find you in too adventurous a mood, however—which, when combined with poor judgment, needs restraint.

Monday, May 6 (Moon in Aquarius). You begin the week in an industrious and ambitious mood and can achieve excellent financial-business results if you remain steady-on-the-course and super practical. Evening may find you a bit tax in terms of guarding your material assets; some may need a reminder to guard emotions, too.

Tuesday, May 7 (Moon in Aquarius to Pisces 11:05 P.M.). Postmidnight hours are not conducive to gains through speculation. Later, the financial picture brightens considerably, with extra emphasis on a partnership venture, a real-estate transaction, and possible gains through litigation. P.M. may find you health-conscious.

Wednesday, May 8 (Moon in Pisces). There could be extra work to be done today and you can make a good impression by volunteering to do it. This might even lead to a job break that can spell advancement. You may want to take advantage of a chance to get extra rest tonight, thereby rebuilding your vitality.

Thursday, May 9 (Moon in Pisces). Maybe a good night's sleep is what you needed! You are full of vim, vigor, and enthusiasm today and can pretty much write your own ticket in business and personal matters. But in the late P.M., be careful not to outshine or overpower someone whose support or cooperation you need.

Friday, May 10 (Moon in Pisces to Aries 6:36 A.M.). An anticipated favor from a VIP might not materialize today, but don't be discouraged; it's bound to come along sooner or later. An agreement can be reached in a partnership this evening that can reward you on a personal level as well as in a monetary way.

Saturday, May 11 (Moon in Aries). Controversy with your spouse or partner seems almost inevitable today. On the other hand, a confrontation could have its bright side by resulting in a breakthrough of understanding between you. Remember that achieving a mutual goal is more important than a difference of opinion.

Sunday, May 12 (Moon in Aries to Taurus 10:08 A.M.). Postmidnight hours can be memorable because of a decision you make concerning another person (a marriage proposal could be answered in the affirmative!). Evening hours signal a red flag against speculation, financial arguments, and extravagant spending.

Monday, May 13 (Moon in Taurus—NEW MOON at 11:37 P.M.). The week begins on an auspicious money note, as your blend of imagination and practicality can work wonders in a business or investment matter. Evening hours might bring a brief conflict with an associate concerning joint funds, but this is easily resolved.

Tuesday, May 14 (Moon in Taurus to Gemini 11:03 A.M.). Listen and learn today, for someone's remarks or a news items told you in confidence could be worth a small fortune to you in some way or other. You may be planning to set forth on an adventure in the near future, via actual travel or a mental excursion.

Wednesday, May 15 (Moon in Gemini). An educational topic may be on today's agenda. Perhaps your employer will suggest you take a job-related class—or perhaps studying another language will fit in with your future travel plans. This can be a good day on which to build foundations under your creative dreams.

Thursday, May 16 (Moon in Gemini to Cancer 11:15 A.M.). Good news from a cohort brightens the A.M., while the balance of the workday is focused on career aims and how best to attain them. A conflict in the P.M. could relate to a friendship or romance, which may be temporarily under siege due to opposing viewpoints.

Friday, May 17 (Moon in Cancer). Mixed trends today support a career boost and positive financial progress, but present you once more with that long-lasting either-or situation regarding home obligations versus business-career ambitions. By day's end you will have handled the problem with the finesse gained from long experience.

Saturday, May 18 (Moon in Cancer to Leo 12:31 P.M.). Getting an early start on the day's activities will put you one step ahead of the competition, whether you are deeply into a community project, an exercise or sports program—or involved in a social-romantic contest. You may decide to curtail some expenses.

Sunday, May 19 (Moon in Leo). Postmidnight hours may produce the opening strains of a romantic quarrel, but fortunately that is nipped in the bud and all continues to be serene in your love life. Impromptu entertainment will be enjoyable, but keep the conversation off of a sensitive topic for some—the money theme.

Monday, May 20 (Moon in Leo to Virgo 4:01 P.M.). Knowledge you've recently acquired can be helpful to a friend today, but don't allow yourself to be drawn too deeply into a no-win situation. You may be tempted to play the role of private eye this evening, but be careful not to stir up added problems at home.

Tuesday, May 21 (Moon in Virgo). A lighthearted approach can help to keep a touchy topic from zooming up into a federal case. You won't mind being alone when paying attention to a task, project, or creative work that absorbs you totally. Word from a distance confirms your positive feelings about a proposed trip.

Wednesday, May 22 (Moon in Virgo to Libra 10:09 P.M.). Throughout the day (starting in the wee small hours of the morning) red flags of warning accompany the financial theme. Be guided accordingly and stay away from speculation, overspending, overextending credit, and making bad loans. Late P.M. brings more stable conditions.

Thursday, May 23 (Moon in Libra). Early hours are favorable for career advancement, sound investments, and promoting your ideas to key people. Your charisma is heightened now—but even that probably won't help you in a family or domestic conflict that arises in the evening. Don't waste time trying to sway opinions.

Friday, May 24 (Moon in Libra). Early morning can continue the brouhaha and/or misunderstanding that seems to permeate your domestic environment. You might not get too much help or support from your spouse or partner, either. If you follow your instincts and take the lead in a relationship, expect a few fireworks.

Saturday, May 25 (Moon in Libra to Scorpio 6:42 A.M.). Today's single bright spot is liberally laced with dollar signs, as a fortunate development in one of your money-making projects really pays off. But don't look for any rejoicing or congratulations from your nearest and dearest, who are wrapped up in negativity.

Sunday, May 26 (Moon in Scorpio). Adroitly sidestep a money quarrel with a partner in the A.M. Then you can devote the day to the pleasantly emerging social-romantic ambience scheduled to include you in its agenda. Somewhere along the way, you could meet a person who will prove to be helpful in a business way.

Monday, May 27 (Moon in Scorpio to Sagittarius 5:22 P.M.). Money figures again in today's scheme of things; perhaps you can wrap up a business negotiation early in the day, and then get on with your plans for a pleasantly social P.M. Someone you meet could contribute a really bright idea to one of your plans.

Tuesday, May 28 (Moon in Sagittarius—FULL MOON at 6:38 A.M.). Errands or a short trip may be important in today's schedule, and though some people you encounter may be tense and tend to overreact, you'll sail along unscathed. You seem to be mentally and physically coordinated to achieve success at this time.

Wednesday, May 29 (Moon in Sagittarius). Feel free to express your opinions, even though your views may meet with a stony silence (at best) or a verbal onslaught (at worst) from an associate. You'll feel better for having spoken out. In the meantime, plan quietly for the promotion of a financial project.

Thursday, May 30 (Moon in Sagittarius to Capricorn 5:41 A.M.). Your promising crop of new ideas may include a real winner; this could be related to travel, an academic achievement, or a humanitarian project with rewarding publicity overtones. Domestic issues seem to have quieted down and all looks peaceful.

Friday, May 31 (Moon in Capricorn). Your words can influence a household situation favorably today and you may win unexpected and heartful praise from a least likely source. Impromptu entertaining in the evening can be both successful and rewarding. You and your partner agree on a question of values.

June 1991

Saturday, June 1 (Moon in Capricorn to Aquarius 6:43 P.M.). Your powers of persuasion can easily defuse a touchy domestic situation this morning. Later, you and your loved one will have such a good rapport that words will not be necessary. Your lively personality can enhance a social event in the evening.

Sunday, June 2 (Moon in Aquarius). Mixed trends today may result in a romantic triangle or a friend-versus-a-lover situation. But you know where your loyalties lie and can deal with such goings-on quite smoothly. Avoid overspending on a pleasure spree this afternoon. Evening could bring word from a distant loved one.

Monday, June 3 (Moon in Aquarius). Don't risk your money or possessions in the early A.M. Later, a career boost seems likely—if not now then soon—and an unexpected opportunity could play right into your hands concerning a sound investment or getting to know someone you have admired from a distance.

Tuesday, June 4 (Moon in Aquarius to Pisces 6:37 A.M.). A co-worker may need a pep talk today, or you may be asked to instruct someone in a business procedure.

Physical fitness exerts a strong appeal this evening. You may become involved in a contest or a sport and find you have a real aptitude for it.

Wednesday, June 5 (Moon in Pisces). An assignment in which you are immersed today could call on all your talents and efforts, but this could be a case of working hard and winning the prize, so keep at it! Evening hours take on a glamorously social-romantic overtone and you could have several "irons in the fire"!

Thursday, June 6 (Moon in Pisces to Aries 3:26 P.M.). Finishing up a difficult task or assignment this morning might not be easy but it will be worth the effort. This evening accentuates partnership—personal, creative, or business-related. Make the most of a very auspicious stellar trend and make a partnership work.

Friday, June 7 (Moon in Aries). Although a domestic problem may raise its familiar head once more, don't allow this to interfere with your day's agenda—which could easily include a romantic commitment, a weekend trek to a nearby spa, a festive social gathering, and/or a fascinating new acquaintance.

Saturday, June 8 (Moon in Aries to Taurus 8:14 P.M.). You can learn from a partner or associate today. Do not hesitate to ask questions and get to the roots of the matter. A social gathering in the P.M. could produce a valuable new contact that may be more business-related than social or romantic.

Sunday, June 9 (Moon in Taurus). Face it—this can be a difficult day, primarily because of the discordant financial theme (that plays over and over and over again!). Either you are doing something that meets with family or marital disapproval, or you are neglecting to do something they wish you would do!

Monday, June 10 (Moon in Taurus to Gemini 9:37 P.M.). Postmidnight hours could bring you a brilliant solution to your monetary woes—or, at least, a brilliant solution to your being nagged about them! This just might have a connection with a sound investment, a legal transaction, or a distant friend.

Tuesday, June 11 (Moon in Gemini). It's clear skies and smooth sailing today, whether you are immersed in travel or vacation itineraries, a lively social agenda, a romantic escapade, or a legal maneuver. Someone you talk with this evening, possibly from a distance, can provide fascinating facts you need to know.

Wednesday, June 12 (Moon in Gemini—NEW MOON at 7:07 A.M.—to Cancer 9:17 P.M.). A worry or feelings of uneasiness, perhaps concerning a youngster or other loved one, may make you tense in early-morning hours. If possible, make a call or visit to reassure yourself that all is well. Set no limits on your dreams today; reach for the stars!

Thursday, June 13 (Moon in Cancer). This could be one of those busy-busy days when you never stop working yet nothing much is accomplished! In fact, P.M. may bring another round of frustrating domestic or family discords. Nevertheless, concentrate on ways and means to achieve a favorite career-financial goal.

Friday, June 14 (Moon in Cancer to Leo 9:11 P.M.). An early-A.M. inspiration could send you off to your job with a positive financial attitude and a promising money-making scheme. It's possible that a late-morning development will offer you a dynamic route to your main goals. Be on the alert for opportunity.

Saturday, June 15 (Moon in Leo). An early-A.M. spat with a loved one will be quickly over. Later, a whole array of planets lights up your social life (with intriguing romantic fringe benefits). A commitment to a group project might also be in the works for you and could prove to be advantageous in several ways.

Sunday, June 16 (Moon in Leo to Virgo 11:04 P.M.).
You can sparkle brilliantly in group situations today, and
colleagues will appreciate your efforts in behalf of a community project. Or, it may be simply an impromptu gathering of friends at which you will make a good impression.
Late P.M. brings interesting news.

Monday, June 17 (Moon in Virgo). Take time to relax and
to recharge your energy batteries today. Work quietly
toward favorite goals, but refrain from pushing too hard,
too soon, or toward the wrong people. Creative thinking
and finding original solutions to personal problems are
supported at this time.

Tuesday, June 18 (Moon in Virgo). Today's luck and
opportunity can be powerful, perhaps concerning your
love life, a social or group project, the welfare or advancement of a child, or a sound investment program. In any
case, take advantage (but don't overdo in the P.M.) and
don't miss the boat by gazing too long at the stars.

**Wednesday, June 19 (Moon in Virgo to Libra 4:02
A.M.).** This is when you could feel confident and secure
enough to really promote yourself and your skills to a key
person as you seek advancement in your work or profession. The curtain may be rising on a new scene in your
quest for fame and fortune!

Thursday, June 20 (Moon in Libra). Today you will feel
more like a front-runner than a follower, well able to shape
your own destiny. This can be an accurate scenario of the
day's events, but when it comes to P.M. hours in your
domestic circle, the outlook gets a bit cloudy with misunderstandings.

Friday, June 21 (Moon in Libra to Scorpio 12:19 P.M.).
A special award or honor could come your way early in
the day—after which a most positive emphasis on your
career-financial blend can provide you with much to hope

for. But don't expect miracles in the late P.M., when a money risk could backfire.

Saturday, June 22 (Moon in Scorpio). Mixed trends reveal very clearly that matters connected with social splurging, speculation, and other monetary risks are not due to prosper today. Stick with the tried and true methods, the conservative approach to business and financial dealings, and you can emerge unscathed.

Sunday, June 23 (Moon in Scorpio to Sagittarius 11:17 P.M.). Of primary importance today to many an unattached Libran will be a midafternoon trend that helps to intensify romantic desires. More practical considerations include a mildly favorable trend toward balancing your own personal budget—at least slightly!

Monday, June 24 (Moon in Sagittarius). An expected message may not arrive today, or perhaps a job assignment is overdue. In any case, though you begin the day with high hopes, by evening you may feel that you've been rushing through white waters without an oar. Do the best you can and try to get some rest.

Tuesday, June 25 (Moon in Sagittarius). How you look and what you say can influence the decisions of others— even though a special financial project might not proceed as hoped. Make a note, too, to stay away from speculation. A short trip in the evening hours may be linked with romance, a family matter, or a creative venture.

Wednesday, June 26 (Moon in Sagittarius to Capricorn 11:50 A.M.—FULL MOON Lunar Eclipse at 9:50 P.M.). A garbled message (or perhaps no message at all) in the A.M. can influence your day's agenda. Don't look for comfort or understanding in your domestic circle tonight, and don't discuss any sensitive subjects.

Thursday, June 27 (Moon in Capricorn). For a change, an unexpected reversal of mood—plus a welcome financial advancement—makes conditions in your home much pleasanter than in recent weeks. A long-standing problem might be resolved, or a flash of insight and intuition might lead to better rapport and understanding.

Friday, June 28 (Moon in Capricorn). You may entertain friends this evening and be contentedly rushing about during the day making the preparations. Or, it may be a home-refurbishment program that has you in an upbeat mood. Word from a good friend or a loved one in the early evening adds to the day's pleasures.

Saturday, June 29 (Moon in Capricorn to Aquarius 12:48 A.M.). Stellar patterns indicate that a serious love commitment is likely today for unattached Librans; or, for others it may be a commitment concerning a child, or a creative project. In any case, both personal satisfaction and responsibility are involved.

Sunday, June 30 (Moon in Aquarius). Murphy's law is said to be in effect when anything that can possibly go wrong, does so. Today Murphy's law is in effect for you! Especially in matters concerning love, romance, social or group plans, creative expression, speculation, and financial transactions. Be patient!

July 1991

Monday, July 1 (Moon in Aquarius to Pisces 12:52 P.M.). It may not be as easy to put theories into practice in a work procedure as you first imagined. An associate could be less helpful than you anticipate, but you'll struggle along because you believe in your idea. P.M. may find you in need of relaxation.

Tuesday, July 2 (Moon in Pisces). Information you glean today may help you in a job project or perhaps in a financial decision. Tonight, you may find it easier than you expected to make a firm agreement in a property transaction or purchase of household items. Late P.M. brings interesting money news.

Wednesday, July 3 (Moon in Pisces to Aries 10:24 P.M.). Today could have a quiet sort of eve-of-holiday tempo at work. However, you may be extra busy with little things that have to be taken care of prior to your departure on a trip, preparations for an entertainment plan, or simply because you want to catch up.

Thursday, July 4 (Moon in Aries). Be extra cautious during postmidnight hours of this holiday, especially in transportation, travel, and close relationships that might be on the brink of disruption. Things calm down a bit later in the day, but P.M. hours again bring potential for tensions, pressures, and strain.

Friday, July 5 (Moon in Aries). If you can avoid inadvertently bruising a partner's ego today, good rapport will contribute to relaxing enjoyment. Harmony prevails for most of the day, and social plans, impromptu and otherwise, remain high on this week's agenda. A new friendship could be developing now.

Saturday, July 6 (Moon in Aries to Taurus 4:53 A.M.). It looks as though you may be torn between a valued friendship and a volatile romance. Trying to attain even a bit of that Libra balance will not be easy, inasmuch as your mental and emotional natures are at war with each other. Discuss but try not to argue.

Sunday, July 7 (Moon in Taurus). Mixed trends today spotlight morning hours as best to begin a new venture or get started on a pleasure plan. As the day wears on, problems involving conflict in social plans and financial pressures and plain misunderstandings with relatives, cohorts, or a loved one build up relentlessly.

Monday, July 8 (Moon in Taurus to Gemini 7:43 A.M.). Postmidnight hours do not support speculation or other risks with money (or emotions). But the picture brightens by afternoon hours, when reason, logic, and your own philosophical attitudes come to the rescue of a relationship or a personal project. You're in control.

Tuesday, July 9 (Moon in Gemini). Good news concerning a loved one (a youngster away at camp? a traveling lover? a favorite relative?) starts the day off on a happy note. You could be working on larger issues than immediate plans, such as academic plans, a long-distance pilgrimage at a later date, an expanding spiritual awareness.

Wednesday, July 10 (Moon in Gemini to Cancer 8:04 A.M.). Your prior work and plans could pay off today, as a career-financial boost appears to be in the offing. Also on the upswing is a romantic interest, which could be growing and glowing rewardingly. Domestic issues can be handled with greater ease these days.

Thursday, July 11 (Moon in Cancer—NEW MOON Solar Eclipse at 2:07 P.M.). A career move may be under consideration today, but do nothing on impulse and try to avoid forcing an issue with a colleague. A new romantic trend at this time hints at a "secret love affair" that could be developing behind the scenes.

Friday, July 12 (Moon in Cancer to Leo 7:36 A.M.). You may be in the mood for convivial company and outgoing friendships, but today could be a disappointment in that regard. Friends tend to be moody or preoccupied, and a social plan might have to be delayed or postponed. Rely on your own inner resources.

Saturday, July 13 (Moon in Leo). Aside from the possibility that financial considerations may interfere with your full involvement in a pleasure project, you will find today a more relaxed and enjoyable time for meeting with friends. Happy news or a romantic phone call in midmorning sounds the day's theme.

Sunday, July 14 (Moon in Leo to Virgo 8:12 A.M.). You'll enjoy being the center of attention in a group setting (or in the eyes of a loved one) but you may also find that you have the urge to review your special plans and dreams in seclusion. Outlining a business game plan will also require undivided attention.

Monday, July 15 (Moon in Virgo). Postmidnight communication will almost surely have colorfully romantic overtones. Avoid verbal clashes about money with an associate in the morning—but take advantage of a financial opportunity later in the day. A confidential matter is turning out better than you had hoped.

Tuesday, July 16 (Moon in Virgo to Libra 11:35 A.M.). Your personal magnetism intensifies today, along with your self-assurance and desire to move onward and upward in business-career activity. However, early evening could find you with seriously flawed judgment in financial matters, so postpone investment decisions.

Wednesday, July 17 (Moon in Libra). You'll have to skip with nimble steps through a veritable mine field of potential problems this morning, especially in matters concerning home and family members (and perhaps career activity as well). All's well that ends well, though, and P.M. brings the right solutions.

Thursday, July 18 (Moon in Libra to Scorpio 6:42 P.M.). If you analyze a situation carefully, you could amaze people (and maybe yourself, too) with your ability to use creative solutions in practical ways. A monetary tip or advice from an expert in the P.M. will enable you to make the most of a financial opportunity.

Friday, July 19 (Moon in Scorpio). Management of money and possessions should go well today, especially as you may have reason to recall a rather bitter lesson you recently learned in connection with spending patterns. You may entertain an unusually gifted and creative person tonight or meet him/her at a social soirée.

Saturday, July 20 (Moon in Scorpio). Your basic instincts concerning resources and future security are sound today; don't allow yourself to swerve over into the grasshopper column when you are doing so well by following the wise example of the industrious ant. If someone promotes an investment, just say no!

Sunday, July 21 (Moon in Scorpio to Sagittarius 5:17 A.M.). Health may be an issue today, whether your own or the health of someone close to you. Burning the candle at both ends is a noted Libran habit—or, at least, pleasure-prone Librans tend in that direction. Make sure you get enough rest and the proper nutrition.

Monday, July 22 (Moon in Sagittarius). Travel is favored for you today, whether business or personal. Your companion could be a bright colleague or a favorite romantic cohort. You may be searching for the answer to a puzzle, or a missing part of a monetary tangle. In any case, P.M. hours may produce the answer.

Tuesday, July 23 (Moon in Sagittarius to Capricorn 5:56 P.M.). Communications or private study can be key factors in today's potential. In the P.M. you are reminded that it's time to focus on people and activities close to home, where someone in your domestic surroundings could really use your caring attention.

Wednesday, July 24 (Moon in Capricorn). Household duties may demand your presence and expertise. But you won't mind, as you see your environment improve and become more glamorous. Somewhere along the line your love life will prosper and late P.M. shows the likelihood that love will take total command.

Thursday, July 25 (Moon in Capricorn). Today you may take a long, hard look at one of your main goals in life, with an eye to polishing up your technique and perhaps to make your expectations a bit more realistic. In this connection, you may be checking out methods to improve your work performance or creative output.

Friday, July 26 (Moon in Capricorn to Aquarius 6:50 A.M.—FULL MOON Lunar Eclipse at 1:25 P.M.). Postmidnight hours can be intensely romantic; in fact, as the way wears on, your love life becomes increasingly the motivation for your plans. Unfortunately, evening brings the potential for a major clash of wills.

Saturday, July 27 (Moon in Aquarius). If you find yourself becoming too serious or downhearted, try to lighten up; you have a better chance of patching up problem areas with a light touch than with a dreary approach. Financial confusion in the P.M. can work itself out if you refrain from taking drastic action.

Sunday, July 28 (Moon in Aquarius to Pisces 6:36 P.M.). Devote as much time as you can today to a creative project; it could have the potential to be an impressive piece of work. P.M. may find you restless and tense or perhaps disturbed by an incomplete bit of news or gossip. Opt for a relaxing routine and early to bed.

Monday, July 29 (Moon in Pisces). A secret romance or other behind-the-scenes activities may not go so well today. Or, some prior responsibility or ailment may resurface. Whatever the cause, you may be seeking an antidote and the best one is to be found through the advice of an expert. By P.M. hours, all is well.

Tuesday, July 30 (Moon in Pisces). What really picks up your spirits today is a job break that could spell advancement. Follow your intuition and exercise your creativity. A colleague's invitation may be another upbeat development, as it promises to be both interesting and potentially helpful via new contacts.

Wednesday, July 31 (Moon in Pisces to Aries 4:21 A.M.). Mental rapport with a loved one gives you feelings of security. Give your wholehearted attention to your mate or partner; unattached Librans could find they are in demand for wedding plans. Share your feelings with that special someone and watch what happens.

August 1991

Thursday, August 1 (Moon in Aries). If you are enjoying a good, productive discussion with your spouse or partner, don't dwell on domestic issues; explore possibilities for dreams-come-true activities instead. Agreement on a matter concerning a child, investment, or recreational plan could be reached in the P.M.

Friday, August 2 (Moon in Aries to Taurus 11:33 A.M.). Another person's input may bring fewer benefits to a financial venture than was expected. This is not the day to dabble in speculation or other risks. But evening hours could produce an advantageous agreement (confidential) with an influential type.

Saturday, August 3 (Moon in Taurus). A clandestine romance may seem thrilling in the postmidnight hours, but later in the day you may think twice about continuing it! Although this is not the greatest day for monetary interests (especially joint resources) matters linked with property and domesticity prosper.

Sunday, August 4 (Moon in Taurus to Gemini 3:55 P.M.). Postmidnight hours could find you overextending your resources—whether financial or physical—and regretting it later. Dealings with people in a distant locale brighten the evening hours; it looks as though a long-hoped-for arrangement is in the making.

Monday, August 5 (Moon in Gemini). It's possible that one of your closely guarded secrets may be on the brink of discourse. If the ball has started rolling, you probably can't stop it; so, instead, be prepared to handle the consequences and divert unpleasantness. In the meantime, the news from out-of-town is good.

Tuesday, August 6 (Moon in Gemini to Cancer 5:48 P.M.). Vacation or other travel plans are supported today, as well as legal transactions, dealings with publishers, academic types, and the clergy. You may be contemplating a study course that can have a direct bearing on your career potential (or future career).

Wednesday, August 7 (Moon in Cancer). Although you may have to cope with a temperamental cohort today, you will still be able to make solid career strides—especially since an authority figure is firmly behind your work. Evening hours may bring an unusual but practical solution to a domestic-family dilemma.

Thursday, August 8 (Moon in Cancer to Leo 6:10 P.M.). Don't look for speed or accuracy in communications at this time, as the general tempo has temporarily slowed down. If you are involved in planning or co-hosting a near-future social event, you'll probably find your cohorts in disarray this evening.

Friday, August 9 (Moon in Leo—NEW MOON at 9:29 P.M.). Accept the slower pace now prevailing and you can still get a number of personal chores done today. An elegant gathering this evening could usher in a new project or achievement, in which you may play a prominent role. It should be added, though, that expenses are involved!

Saturday, August 10 (Moon in Leo to Virgo 6:36 P.M.). Business and pleasure combine today and that matches your morning mood of optimism and confidence. Even the fact that one or more of your social-romantic plans is bound to be quite costly doesn't dampen your upbeat outlook or your high expectations.

Sunday, August 11 (Moon in Virgo). In a quiet, off-stage sort of way, this can be a rewarding day, when important personal interests (such as a love relationship, a child's progress, or finding the best way to handle an obligation) proceed smoothly. Even usually problem-filled matters seem to be less challenging.

Monday, August 12 (Moon in Virgo to Libra 8:53 P.M.). Secret maneuvers today may make it possible for you to finesse your way through a sensitive situation. Evening hours support assertive action in a personal matter. You could also spend time to good advantage by rearranging certain plans to match current trends.

Tuesday, August 13 (Moon in Libra). Postmidnight hours could produce a welcome contact with someone who means a great deal to you, perhaps a "voice from the past" or one who has special expertise. Later, a clash of wills between you and a domestic companion (or an authority figure) is apt to drag on, inconclusively.

Wednesday, August 14 (Moon in Libra). Your personal powers are in top form today. If there is anyone you should see, in order to obtain a favor or other special attention, this will be a promising day on which to talk with such a person. A significant task may hinge upon your initiative now, so give it some thought.

Thursday, August 15 (Moon in Libra to Scorpio 2:34 A.M.). Sidestep a high-risk financial situation in the A.M. Later, a confidential agreement could be to your monetary advantage—or a little detective work on your part might unearth a few unknown facts that will be a useful addition to your money-making arsenal.

Friday, August 16 (Moon in Scorpio). If you allow your intuition to soar in the A.M., it could lead you to just the right next step in a financial predicament. Later, discussion with an expert will help to shed some light on a tangled business negotiation. Weekend plans may be up in the air, so get a restful night.

Saturday, August 17 (Moon in Scorpio to Sagittarius 12:12 P.M.). Postmidnight hours will be disappointing if you are anticipating romantic bliss or financial gains. Midday brings a new trend, which might be hampered by some private problem or responsibility. However, evening hours find love triumphing over all.

Sunday, August 18 (Moon in Sagittarius). A lighthearted manner will make communication with a sensitive friend easier than if you were to be overly serious. You will welcome helpful advice about a travel itinerary you are working on. However, unexpected changes may call for extra flexibility; be prepared with alternate plans.

Monday, August 19 (Moon in Sagittarius). An irritated colleague may make life briefly miserable for you this morning, but if you maintain your Libran serenity, you will appreciate the changed circumstances by midafternoon. Plans for the months ahead include a few still-uncertain social dates, under discussion now.

Tuesday, August 20 (Moon in Sagittarius to Capricorn 12:35 A.M.). You may discover that the more of yourself you invest in home-related activities, the more you will gain in intangible ways—including a happier ambience on the domestic scene. Tonight, a surprise guest or message can give a new slant to a friendship.

Wednesday, August 21 (Moon in Capricorn). Household demands may compete for your time against a really busy business-career schedule. Try to do justice to both sets of interests. This afternoon, a love message, a brilliant flash of creativity, or good news concerning an investment could make your heart sing.

Thursday, August 22 (Moon in Capricorn to Aquarius 1:28 P.M.). You could receive sound advice from a family member concerning a purchase you're considering. Early afternoon starts a super-romantic trend when both the glamour and the seriousness of a commitment blend in a very favorable love trend.

Friday, August 23 (Moon in Aquarius). An investment opportunity may enable you to revise your financial plans and put some money to work for you. Your regular work may be irksome today, but if you follow through with your best efforts anyway, the payoff could be well worth the amount of time spent.

Saturday, August 24 (Moon in Aquarius). Letting your heart rule your head could bring you more regrets than rewards today. Although happy news arrives in the A.M., it might not be enough on which to pin all your romantic hopes and dreams. You might even be expecting too much from this alliance too soon.

Sunday, August 25 (Moon in Aquarius to Pisces 12:52 A.M.—FULL MOON at 4:08 A.M.). It's possible that your energies and vitality are at a low ebb, what with job demands, domestic responsibilities, and your natural pre-dilection for squeezing in as much social-romantic activity as possible! Opt for an early night.

Monday, August 26 (Moon in Pisces to Aries 10:02 P.M.). Speedy action on the job today can help you to complete a tiresome assignment and get on to something more interesting. Late P.M. brings a current relationship into focus; this is when you may decide whether or not to continue the alliance as is, or change it.

Tuesday, August 27 (Moon in Aries). Postmidnight hours can be super romantic; you may be with someone who recently entered your life—or perhaps this will usher in the revival of a former flame. In either case, the day reflects your happy attitude, and by midday there's a chance that new plans will include amour.

Wednesday, August 28 (Moon in Aries). A partner's antagonism is merely superficial, so don't attach too much importance to it. Teamwork in your job surroundings may be hard to achieve today, but if you can go your own way without making too much of the lacks of others, it will be better for you in the long run.

Thursday, August 29 (Moon in Aries to Taurus 5:01 P.M.). An about-face in attitudes bring your mate or other colleagues into the fold today as cooperation flows freely and advantages can be gained by all concerned. In the evening, your social plans may include a rather expensive entertainment, but you're in the mood for it!

Friday, August 30 (Moon in Taurus). You could have the Midas touch today, though it must be admitted that your spouse or partner could have a role in the financial accumulation. P.M. hours can be creatively rewarding, especially in connection with home-related beautification or experiments with form and color.

Saturday, August 31 (Moon in Taurus to Gemini 10:03 P.M.). Even the fact that previously delayed projects and communications resume their normal pace today does not help much to dispel the general negativity. Mostly linked with financial worries or arguments, the clouds don't roll by until early P.M.

September 1991

Sunday, September 1 (Moon in Gemini). An upsurge of both energy and charisma can make you practically unstoppable today—even though there might be a brief flurry of complaints by an associate in the early afternoon (this could be travel-related). Distant interests beckon and family affairs need order.

Monday, September 2 (Moon in Gemini). Some of you will be en route to another locale today, for business, family, or academic reasons. Excellent trends can help make your trip and various contacts successful. Late-day developments may bring an expert into your immediate circle, whose advice can be valuable.

Tuesday, September 3 (Moon in Gemini to Cancer 1:20 A.M.). Mixed trends may impel you to be overly aggressive with a higher-up or suddenly unpredictable with a longtime cohort—neither attitude being an asset for attaining your present goals. Evening hours support confidential talks and agreements.

Wednesday, September 4 (Moon in Cancer). Be willing to listen to good advice about how to win out over the competition in a career project; sometimes it's an advantage to get all sorts of viewpoints in order to cover all the bases. A financial upswing could be in the works as well. P.M. supports domestic interests.

Thursday, September 5 (Moon in Cancer to Leo 3:14 A.M.). Though you may give the impression that you are totally immersed in your job today, underneath the surface you are building up to a joyful social-romantic fling. A celebration may be in order (someone's anniversary or birthday, perhaps).

Friday, September 6 (Moon in Leo). A small but disturbing monetary development in the early A.M. may prompt you to take precautionary measures with your personal finances. But late afternoon and P.M. hours find you pretty much dedicated to the pleasures of friendship and the excitement of romantic allures.

Saturday, September 7 (Moon in Leo to Virgo 4:36 A.M.). Postmidnight hours continue the party theme and there is also a chance that you will encounter a new personality who can have a positive effect on your career or a creative talent. Later, you may feel like taking advantage of a lazy Saturday's relaxations.

Sunday, September 8 (Moon in Virgo—NEW MOON at 6:02 A.M.). Inspiration burns brightly today and can be evident in anything from devising new ways to complete ordinary chores in record time, to a game plan involving a big romance and your secret dreams. You may also perform a humanitarian deed today.

Monday, September 9 (Moon in Virgo to Libra 6:52 A.M.). The first order of business today may be your decision to participate in a financial-security program—after which you will probably devote your considerable energy and expertise toward locking in a partnership venture. Avoid domestic strife in the P.M.

Tuesday, September 10 (Moon in Libra). Consult with a knowledgeable friend if you feel the need for another's viewpoint on a personal matter. Pay extra attention to confusing details of a work assignment and enjoy a P.M. impromptu dinner date with a longtime cohort who always brings out your higher motives.

Wednesday, September 11 (Moon in Libra to Scorpio 11:43 A.M.). Others might not have your degree of dedication today—but they may be quicker to leave the starting gate; be alert to right timing. A business or financial problem in the afternoon needs extra careful study and perhaps a quiet helping hand.

Thursday, September 12 (Moon in Scorpio). This can be a splendid day for advancement and self-realization. Your inner resources are intensifying, and you may also find you have a special friend who is in an excellent background position to support your efforts now and then. A business triumph is due in the P.M.

Friday, September 13 (Moon in Scorpio to Sagittarius 8:15 P.M.). Resist the urge to overspend or speculate this morning, no matter how promising the outlook. A news item or bit of gossip you hear this evening should not be accepted as gospel truth; considerable embellishment has probably been added for effect.

Saturday, September 14 (Moon in Sagittarius). Mixed trends suggest you still exercise caution about believing everything you hear, especially if it is presented as a secret. Your powers of communication are stimulated rewardingly today; you ought to be able to persuade others to follow your line of thinking.

Sunday, September 15 (Moon in Sagittarius). A local trip today could be linked with a joyful social event or happy gathering. Somewhere along the way you may be urged to participate in a behind-the-scenes plan that you should think about very carefully before accepting. All the cards may not be on the table.

Monday, September 16 (Moon in Sagittarius to Capricorn 8:05 A.M.). If you are out in the wee small hours of the morning, do be careful and avoid mishaps in travel or transportation or otherwise. There may also be some domestic friction in the air today. Later, and in the P.M., the picture brightens and the news is good.

Tuesday, September 17 (Moon in Capricorn). Don't be too quick to snap at a cohort or colleague this morning; patience will win you more benefits than a critical attitude. The personal satisfaction (and financial gains) stemming from your creative thinking provide you with a real lift as this day dwindles down.

Wednesday, September 18 (Moon in Capricorn to Aquarius 8:59 P.M.). Completing a long drawn-out work assignment today brings you a sense of accomplishment (also of relief at having it over and done with!). You may be strongly focused on a romantic commitment in the P.M., or it could be an investment decision.

Thursday, September 19 (Moon in Aquarius). With luck, love, intuition, and creative flair going for you today, you shouldn't have any problems promoting your favorite plans and dreams. Although sometimes you tend to be hesitant in asserting yourself in pursuit of special goals, today you have no such scruples.

Friday, September 20 (Moon in Aquarius). Today is not one of those winning days. In fact, both money and love are subjects you'd do well to leave alone, inasmuch as their downsides seem to prevail over any bright promise. What you could do is review some of your recent actions and sift the wise from the foolish.

Saturday, September 21 (Moon in Aquarius to Pisces 8:21 A.M.). Don't take anything for granted at work or in your leisure life today, as things may not be as glowing as they seem at first glance. Opt for logic and practical realities rather than pie-in-the-sky hopes. On the other hand, P.M. brings pleasant news.

Sunday, September 22 (Moon in Pisces). Outdoor exercise, sports, or games could do you a world of good today (weather permitting, of course). Or, a day's outing with congenial friends in a different and stimulating locale could be beneficial. Try to avoid a domestic misunderstanding in the afternoon.

Monday, September 23 (Moon in Pisces to Aries 4:57 P.M.—FULL MOON at 5:41 P.M.). Your new birthday cycle begins today, as the Sun makes its annual return to Libra. Added stability in your life-style is indicated, as well as a probable important decision concerning a close relationship. Inner poise is essential.

Tuesday, September 24 (Moon in Aries). You may encounter a situation in which your self-discipline and balanced judgment (neither of which will be easy to maintain) could spell the difference between the success or failure of an alliance (business or personal). Keep in mind what stakes are involved.

Wednesday, September 25 (Moon in Aries to Taurus 11:00 P.M.). By midday you will probably know whether or not a special amour is here to stay or about to take off for distant horizons. Whatever the outcome, you should opt for a clear, logical mind in the late evening when a financial showdown may occur.

Thursday, September 26 (Moon in Taurus). Today's good news is that your monetary interests (especially marital or partnership finances) appear to be in good shape. If you are seeking advice in money matters, you are likely to find just the right expert to help you advance in the right direction for security.

Friday, September 27 (Moon in Taurus). Still on the money theme, there is possibility today that a shared financial venture or arrangement will run into stormy weather. This could be due as much to a personality clash as to actual monetary disagreement. Try to keep emotions out of discussion; opt for cool logic.

Saturday, September 28 (Moon in Taurus to Gemini 3:26 A.M.). Postmidnight inspiration may concern a deeply practical way of handling a family financial matter for best results all around. Later, pleasure plans predominate, with a somewhat expensive (but delightful) evening-on-the-town part of the scenario.

Sunday, September 29 (Moon in Gemini). Today your alert mind can zero in on just the right route to follow toward a much-desired destination. This may be an actual trip out of town, or it could signal your creation of a game plan for business-career-financial success within a specified period of time.

Monday, September 30 (Moon in Gemini to Cancer 6:59 A.M.). This will not be the best day on which to confer with or confront a higher-up as some influence beyond your control will have muddied the waters of congeniality before you can arrive on the scene. In other words, wait for a more auspicious day.

October 1991

Tuesday, October 1 (Moon in Cancer). Today there may be a slight gap between what you expect and what you get, particularly in a business negotiation. Someone may have exaggerated the prospects, or perhaps there is a lack of communication between you and your opposite number. Avoid overaggressiveness in the P.M.

Wednesday, October 2 (Moon in Cancer to Leo 9:59 A.M.). Signals may get crossed concerning the date, time, or place of a social or romantic meeting; be sure to check details. Though morning hours may feature some form of delay or disappointment, this is not a major issue. Proceed as planned for late-day activities.

Thursday, October 3 (Moon in Leo). Decidedly mixed trends today support a number of your personal interests— and provide you with a great assist in communications and creativity. However, be prepared for a volatile personality (at work or at home) to enter into your plans and activities when least expected.

Friday, October 4 (Moon in Leo to Virgo 12:46 P.M.). Give your undivided attention to a work assignment you receive today. This could be the opening strains of a new and lively job performance (with multiple dollar signs as the frosting on the cake). Romance may be of the quiet, subtle brand this evening.

Saturday, October 5 (Moon in Virgo). A scheduled workout may be postponed or a friend might be unable to join you in a shopping spree or cultural activity. Alternate plans turn out enjoyably, although communications could be a bit clouded in the P.M., when you and another person may be on totally different beams.

Sunday, October 6 (Moon in Virgo to Libra 4:01 P.M.). You will probably take the lead in today's plans and activities and others will be only too glad to follow your ideas. Whether you're in an outdoorsy, sports-oriented mood or drawn toward an elegant evening on the town, you are sure to attract admirers.

Monday, October 7 (Moon in Libra—NEW MOON at 4:40 P.M.). An early-A.M. upset in the day's agenda may stem from the actions of an unpredictable colleague or a sudden business development that catches everyone off guard. This is followed by a misunderstanding of major proportions in the afternoon! Seek a quiet, creative P.M.

Tuesday, October 8 (Moon in Libra to Scorpio 9:01 P.M.). Your dynamic decisiveness in the late morning might avert an unwise business move, or it could be a smashing new money idea you come up with that gains you attention. But speaking of money, don't risk or overspend yours in the P.M., on a covert venture.

Wednesday, October 9 (Moon in Scorpio). This should be a fairly simple and successful financial day, so proceed with confidence and follow generally conservative, sound business practices for best results. Inspiration could emerge from a study session this evening, as you adapt an old format to new dimensions.

Thursday, October 10 (Moon in Scorpio). Money dominates the scene again today, especially in the A.M. when you'll tend to stick with a sure thing rather than to rush off diversifying in multiple directions. Your personal finances are also shaping up, perhaps because you are following some of the advice you give to others.

Friday, October 11 (Moon in Scorpio to Sagittarius 4:59 A.M.). You usually welcome worthwhile advice on any project with which you're involved, but today's offering may not be that worthwhile! Or, perhaps the adviser doesn't understand all the angles. In any case, think twice (or more) before following suggestions.

Saturday, October 12 (Moon in Sagittarius). Routine errands may turn out to have a silver lining, as someone you meet could be just the type of person with whom you have immediate—and fun-loving—rapport. Unexpected benefits may emerge from a phone call or visit, while a near-future trip is also in the works.

Sunday, October 13 (Moon in Sagittarius to Capricorn 4:11 P.M.). This will be a good day for an out-of-town trip, a family gathering, or acquiring information about a legal or academic project. If you do not travel, you may decide to entertain a few close friends in your home, comparing notes on a shared interest.

Monday, October 14 (Moon in Capricorn). Today's events center on home, family, engagements, anniversaries, or the unpredictable behavior of someone you all know. Recent antagonisms melt away (at least for the moment!) and you can also accomplish some practical goals as well, such as resolving a business problem.

Tuesday, October 15 (Moon in Capricorn). Yesterday's smooth rapport was probably too good to last; the sound of clashing wills may again be heard throughout the home.

On a different note, a lovely romantic bonanza is also on the agenda for today, so enjoy time spent with your loved one and cheer up.

Wednesday, October 16 (Moon in Capricorn to Aquarius 5:05 A.M.). A cultural activity could have more than just aesthetic benefits; it may be a fertile ground for achieving one of your goals—a stepping-stone perhaps, to helpful contacts and information. Today might also require that you monitor messages and funds.

Thursday, October 17 (Moon in Aquarius). Postmidnight hours may bring a strong temptation to speculate or take other financial risks, which would be very unwise. In fact, other than just the simplest of everyday monetary activities, you should leave all money-related maneuvering strictly to other people.

Friday, October 18 (Moon in Aquarius to Pisces 4:54 P.M.). The day begins on an upbeat romantic note, as a call or message from your amour puts you in a happy mood for the day. Other developments that can add to your contentment include co-worker rapport and a promising money-making opportunity related to your job.

Saturday, October 19 (Moon in Pisces). Mixed trends combine a few romantic delights with an unfortunate urge to risk security or even health by pursuing an agenda that's short on sleep, rest, and commonsense nutritional values. On the plus side, your creativity is intensified and a family member is helpful.

Sunday, October 20 (Moon in Pisces). Things seem to be back on track today and you might be getting an early start for an outdoorsy day trip, or a hike or bicycle tour. In case you elect to stay at home and laze about, a business-related communication early in the day can be profitable as well as informative.

Monday, October 21 (Moon in Pisces to Aries 1:34 A.M.). Partnership is emphasized today, though you will need to keep your eyes open this evening as a wave of impulsiveness could find both you and your companion willing to sacrifice mutual benefits simply to prove a relatively unimportant point.

Tuesday, October 22 (Moon in Aries). You and your spouse or partner may begin the day on a note of misunderstanding and proceed from there to a full-blown argument. Try to keep away from sensitive subjects, to begin with, and if you inadvertently stumble on one, remember that you are a tactful, diplomatic Libran!

Wednesday, October 23 (Moon in Aries—FULL MOON at 6:09 A.M.—to Taurus 6:56 A.M.). Your first enthusiasm for a money deal may fade when you learn of all the strings that are attached to it. You might also encounter resistance from your mate or partner if you try to promote an iffy financial proposition. P.M. supports personal interests, creative thinking.

Thursday, October 24 (Moon in Taurus). This is a generally fortunate day for routine job-career-money interests, except that there's a special warning to bypass even the most innocent-looking investment offers. There is still a residue of antagonism in a partnership linked to diverse views on joint funds.

Friday, October 25 (Moon in Taurus to Gemini 10:10 A.M.). Postmidnight hours with a loved one may turn out to be mostly talk and very little action. Nevertheless, the subject of the conversation should please you. By noon you should receive a message that gives you a green light on weekend plans, possibly a trip.

Saturday, October 26 (Moon in Gemini). Try to avoid taking on more activities or challenges than you can handle during postmidnight hours (and avoid transportation risks, too). A social or romantic interlude may not live up to expectations, but you can make your own conviviality with a few close friends.

Sunday, October 27 (Moon in Gemini to Cancer 12:38 P.M.). Your industrious mood today could prompt you to live up the upcoming week's activities in helpful detail, with a special emphasis on money potential and the search for due recognition. You'll be able to handle domestic affairs with ease and keep everyone happy.

Monday, October 28 (Moon in Cancer). If you can avoid being taken off guard—or irritated—by a colleague's unexpected opposition to your carefully planned ideas or procedures, you should be able to make a success out of the day's agenda. Financial prospects look promising, but support may be lacking at home.

Tuesday, October 29 (Moon in Cancer to Leo 3:21 P.M.). Encouraging information reaching you during postmidnight hours can be put to good use in a business transaction. Less encouraging are reports about a speculative venture. Evening produces lighthearted social or romantic contacts, fun invitations.

Wednesday, October 30 (Moon in Leo). Keep in mind the favorable potential in one of your business-financial projects, even though it may appear to fade after an encouraging start. (Next week may be a better time to promote this matter.) Tiptoe your way carefully through today's rather spotty schedule for best results.

Thursday, October 31 (Moon in Leo to Virgo 6:48 P.M.). Those exciting social, family, or romantic plans you are formulating are almost sure to be more costly than you anticipate. It's a question of priorities, really; is your need to keep down expenses just as demanding as your need to be a fulfilled Libran?

November 1991

Friday, November 1 (Moon in Virgo). This could be one of those satisfying days when all the items you list on your "must do" agenda are smoothly accomplished, and enjoyable plans turn out to be just as pleasant as you'd hoped. Confidential support from a key person can help to make a business matter successful.

Saturday, November 2 (Moon in Virgo to Libra 11:13 P.M.). This should be another smooth-running day, with a special emphasis on service (working on a humanitarian project, visiting the sick, etc.). Recognition (the nicest kind, with money attached) could be on its way to you for prior job efforts.

Sunday, November 3 (Moon in Libra). Postmidnight hours favor a serious love relationship; unattached Librans could be ready for wedding bells. Unexpected support from your domestic circle can mean a home-improvement project could get an earlier start than you anticipated. A P.M. guest may be a mixed blessing.

Monday, November 4 (Moon in Libra). Your judgment may not be at its sharpest during postmidnight hours, so sidestep any serious decision-making. Later, communications open up pleasantly and profitably, as you receive word of a personal or financial development. News concerning a child or a creative project uplifts.

Tuesday, November 5 (Moon in Libra to Scorpio 5:10 A.M.). A barrier to your swift completion of a monetary arrangement might turn out to be for the best; perhaps there are additional facts due to be revealed. Nevertheless, continue to make your plans and line up support for a business transaction soon to be implemented.

Wednesday, November 6 (Moon in Scorpio—NEW MOON at 6:12 A.M.). This is an altogether favorable day for money matters, whether personal finances, joint funds, or routine business dealings. Postponed items or decisions could now be acted upon to good advantage. P.M. links household improvements with income upsurge.

Thursday, November 7 (Moon in Scorpio to Sagittarius 1:22 P.M.). Still another smooth-sailing money day, when your own inspiration burns brightly and very pragmatically—and others seem to fall neatly into your overall game plans. A chatty friend makes late-evening hours a veritable feast of news and gossip.

Friday, November 8 (Moon in Sagittarius). You may need to restrain an urge toward fiscal recklessness this morning, which would be a smart thing to do inasmuch as this can be a super day for business-financial matters, career advancement, and earned recognition. Try to deal exclusively in certainties.

Saturday, November 9 (Moon in Sagittarius). The single theme that seems to dominate this day is one of your favorites: love, love, love. Whether glamorously romantic, rooted in family relationships, the special warmth and concern for friends, or the ample supply you reserve for pets and plants, it's a love fest!

Sunday, November 10 (Moon in Sagittarius to Capricorn 12:17 A.M.). Your early-A.M. anxieties or worries could be unfounded; in fact a communication or incident later in the day could set your mind at ease. A family gathering in the late P.M. could iron out more than one pesky problem, with unexpected support.

Monday, November 11 (Moon in Capricorn). Prospects are excellent today for a property transaction, finding a future-oriented solution for a past-oriented family problem, and making plans for a fabulous party at your house (maybe for Thanksgiving?). You might also achieve rewarding success in academic or artistic efforts.

Tuesday, November 12 (Moon in Capricorn to Aquarius 1:07 P.M.). Watch your step in travel or transportation today, and make a note not to believe all statements or promises made to you. Creative thinking blended with a bit of romantic inspiration add up to a very productive evening in one way or another.

Wednesday, November 13 (Moon in Aquarius). You may find that a friend's advice is every bit as helpful as a whole series of appointments with a counselor. You might also realize that news you've been gleaning from various sources will come in very handy as you continue to build up a case for or against a special project.

Thursday, November 14 (Moon in Aquarius). The path of true love is reported to never run really smooth, and that can be your consolation today as anything that can go wrong in a relationship probably will. It does seem that money is in some way at the base of most of the arguments. The solution is available.

Friday, November 15 (Moon in Aquarius to Pisces 1:34 A.M.). It's back to smooth sailing today, with a special emphasis on dynamic financial developments. Your work schedule ought to proceed as planned, and a domestic or property interest is accentuated by a late-evening phone call or visit to your home.

Saturday, November 16 (Moon in Pisces). The work project in which you immerse yourself today could be a tough one, but you are strongly motivated and are likely to get through it by late afternoon. Mixing a little business with pleasure can be rewarding on both counts this evening. You'll learn by listening.

Sunday, November 17 (Moon in Pisces to Aries 11:09 A.M.). A key associate is in the limelight today. This could be your spouse, partner, or collaborator in creative work. In any case, you'll both do much better as a team than as solo performers, whether the objective is fame, fortune, or simply self-expression.

Monday, November 18 (Moon in Aries). Until this evening, today may seem to be one challenge after another— most of them based on a clash of wills between family members or friends bound together by common interests. Guard your words and actions in order to minimize hurt feelings and maximize harmony.

Tuesday, November 19 (Moon in Aries to Taurus 4:50 P.M.). Don't allow a treasured romance or ongoing relationship to be endangered by impetuous reactions this afternoon. Count to ten (many times, if necessary) in order to maintain a calm and logical attitude. In the evening, try to sidestep financial arguments.

Wednesday, November 20 (Moon in Taurus). The storm clouds having passed over, today should be a profitable one for business dealings and a rewarding one for personal alliances. A prior friend, teacher, attorney, or romantic companion may reenter the picture this evening. Study and creative work is also favored.

Thursday, November 21 (Moon in Taurus—FULL MOON at 5:57 P.M.—to Gemini 7:23 P.M.). Some individuals in your environment could be high-strung or overwrought today; don't let this type of reaction to tensions rub off on you. The subject of money is what might touch off the tremors, so don't bring it up.

Friday, November 22 (Moon in Gemini). Don't pay too much attention to gossip or rumors at work, since there's a strain of exaggeration present in today's communications outlook. The other side of the coin shows a romantic trend in the P.M., when you and your loved one may share a congenial evening with friends.

Saturday, November 23 (Moon in Gemini to Cancer 8:26 P.M.). If you've planned an early start to the day's out-of-town trek or a group entertainment project, don't be surprised if there is some mix-up in directions, time of departure, or who's in charge of what. All should turn out well by day's end, however.

Sunday, November 24 (Moon in Cancer). Mixed trends today favor festive gatherings, meeting key people in connection with your favorite project, and perhaps a business opportunity as well. On the debit side is a familiar listing: potential for dissention or misunderstandings on the home front, or property worries.

Monday, November 25 (Moon in Cancer to Leo 9:38 P.M.). A postmidnight dispute with your true love can dim your optimism, but only temporarily. Later in the day, excellent financial trends ought to do something for one of your special goals. And, in the late P.M., a mini-reconciliation is due for your mini-spat.

Tuesday, November 26 (Moon in Leo). There may be an obstacle to be overcome before plans for a convivial near-future holiday gathering can be finalized. You could be just the right one to charm various holdouts and "sell" them on the advantages of the affair. Your own personal social calendar is filling up, too.

Wednesday, November 27 (Moon in Leo). Today's only problem might be finding the funds to support a few of your more grandiose ideas for getting the right people together for a good cause. (Part of that good cause may be your own interest in a special someone you are hoping to know better!) Avoid money risks.

Thursday, November 28 (Moon in Leo to Virgo 12:13 A.M.). The first thing to do today is to put a reminder note to yourself on all lists and schedules that an upcoming slowdown could reflect on some of your plans. (This, plus normal holiday delays, etc.). Remain serene and unruffled and face the weeks ahead with equanimity.

Friday, November 29 (Moon in Virgo). A confidential item could get the go-ahead signal today, although you might have to be extra persuasive to convince a key person to go along with the matter. Information received this evening should be carefully checked for missing pieces before taking any action on it.

Saturday, November 30 (Moon in Virgo to Libra 4:48 A.M.). You wind up the month on a wave of enthusiasm, as social-romantic plans proceed rewardingly and even the usual problem areas seem to be upbeat. Community interests, family gatherings, travel itineraries, and your love life all seem to be flourishing.

December 1991

Sunday, December 1 (Moon in Libra). Today you may find that someone who is ordinarily tuned in to your moods and reactions seems to have developed an insensitivity in such matters. This may have nothing to do with you, actually, so wait and see if the picture doesn't change—and brighten—by late evening.

Monday, December 2 (Moon in Libra to Scorpio 11:34 A.M.). Yours could be the deciding voice in an elaborate social or group plan, and you are sure to add plenty of glamour to the itinerary. A business transaction may dawdle along only to end disappointingly by the end of the workday. But there may be a revival.

Tuesday, December 3 (Moon in Scorpio). Postmidnight hours feature exciting romance potential and/or an intriguing investment proposition. Later in the day, business-financial activities are relatively brisk and you are likely to wind up somewhat more solvent than when you started. Opt for a relaxing evening.

Wednesday, December 4 (Moon in Scorpio to Sagittarius 8:53 P.M.). If you seek an agreement concerning a monetary transaction today, be sure to cover all the details and all possible small-print items. Leaving no margin for error can be the smartest approach in this case. Add your personal touch to a P.M. gathering.

Thursday, December 5 (Moon in Sagittarius—NEW MOON 10:57 P.M.). A lighthearted approach will smooth the rough edges of some communications today. Your creative forces are accelerating, so be sure to make a note of various ideas, flashes of intuition, and inspired thinking. But avoid excesses in the evening.

Friday, December 6 (Moon in Sagittarius). Although expenses may mount and transportation may be slow, you could still enjoy a trip this weekend. Just make sure you have the right time, place, and phone numbers as you start off. A new romance or friendship could be on the horizon, which could enrich your social life.

Saturday, December 7 (Moon in Sagittarius to Capricorn 7:42 A.M.). You could feel nurtured by domestic and household activities today. You may also be preparing for a dinner party or houseguest. So long as you are not on too speedy a tempo, all should go according to plan. A P.M. phone call is exhilarating.

Sunday, December 8 (Moon in Capricorn). This is another upbeat day, perfect for lively exchanges of ideas and for meeting stimulating newcomers to your social circle. Domestic tranquillity reigns, and even an on-again, off-again friendship (that's recently been "off") seems to settle into a comfortable niche.

Monday, December 9 (Moon in Capricorn to Aquarius 8:28 P.M.). Sorry to say, your financial judgment could be totally off target today, so try to avoid being in the position where you have to make important monetary judgments. Otherwise, the outlook is calm enough, until late P.M., when a call is unreliable.

Tuesday, December 10 (Moon in Aquarius). Words of affection from a loved one make your day—after an early-A.M. incident (or maybe a dream) that temporarily quelled your spirits. A social or cultural event could be on your evening calendar, complete with plenty of holiday-type conviviality and romancing.

Wednesday, December 11 (Moon in Aquarius). The results of your creative thinking on a business matter are now in and a higher-up is quick to give you full credit. (Whether or not this is backed up by financial recognition remains to be seen!) On the subject of money, try to avoid being overcharged in the P.M.

Thursday, December 12 (Moon in Aquarius to Pisces 9:20 A.M.). Call on a co-worker if you suspect you may not meet a deadline; on the other hand, don't just goof off because you are getting very much into the holiday spirit! Exercise might be a good tonic for you now, stimulating mental energies as well.

Friday, December 13 (Moon in Pisces). Mixed trends could result in your mind and imagination becoming over-stimulated as you try to do too much in too short a time. Actually, this can enhance your creativity, but at the expense of your overall health. So try to stay on the middle ground and get enough rest.

Saturday, December 14 (Moon in Pisces to Aries 8:07 P.M.). A profitable financial development might be almost immediately offset by an unexpected expense. You tend to view such things philosophically and to feel that the money was provided in order to be spent (Libra logic!). P.M. accents togetherness.

Sunday, December 15 (Moon in Aries). Prospects for adventure and new experiences shared with a partner look rosy today—at least until early P.M. when your companion may make an unexpected departure. As this is not necessarily a romantic partnership, you will not be unduly disturbed by the incident.

Monday, December 16 (Moon in Aries). You could be onto a very promising business transaction today, but you could double your power by including a partner in the proceedings. Also, the steadying influence of someone with expertise could help to offset your current tendency toward slightly flawed judgment.

Tuesday, December 17 (Moon in Aries to Taurus 3:11 A.M.). You may feel hesitant or confused when faced with a financial decision today, perhaps because you do not fully understand the inherent risks in the transaction. At the same time, you are enthusiastic about an imaginative and original money-making project.

Wednesday, December 18 (Moon in Taurus). Decidedly mixed trends and a reverse of the recent "slowdown" effect make this a lively but somewhat hectic day—particularly in the realms of job, finances, career interests. There are gains to be made today, but try to sift the possible from the highly improbable.

Thursday, December 19 (Moon in Taurus to Gemini 6:22 A.M.). A trip (business or personal) could be a key event today—or perhaps you will be involved in a legal matter, such as entering into a contract negotiation. In any case, you'll need to keep your wits about you and balance wishful thinking with reality.

Friday, December 20 (Moon in Gemini). Being the early bird that catches the worm may not be such a good idea this morning, as various things could go wrong or key people may not show up. Later, taking the day's events in a more leisurely manner can be more rewarding. Many of you will be leaving today for the holidays.

Saturday, December 21 (Moon in Gemini—FULL MOON Lunar Eclipse at 5:24 A.M.—to Cancer 6:55 A.M.). With such a stellar uproar going on, this can still be a remarkably peaceful day. You may be putting finishing touches on a career project, preparing for a social bash, or leaving for a winter vacation.

Sunday, December 22 (Moon in Cancer). If you are out of the house in the wee small hours, avoid transportation and other risks. Later, adroitly sidestep a domestic misunderstanding, then enjoy a pleasant and leisurely day that could feature a social gathering or perhaps a dinner party in your own domicile.

Monday, December 23 (Moon in Cancer to Leo 6:39 A.M.). The emphasis today is on a love relationship, which may be on a rocky road right now. This is not the time to push, but rather to pause and reflect; could it be you are expecting too much from this alliance? If the answer is truly no, then stop worrying!

Tuesday, December 24 (Moon in Leo). Except for an early-P.M. round of bickering with a loved one, this can be an upbeat day for matters of the heart. It could also have a nice financial tinge, as you may hear good news about your income or receive a worthwhile money gift. Try to spend the evening with friends.

Wednesday, December 25 (Moon in Leo to Virgo 7:24 A.M.). This can be a pleasant, warmly relaxing day, which will be best spent with loved family members and/or a few close friends. You may be in a creative and philosophic mood and, if time and the occasion permit, could produce some worthwhile creative work.

Thursday, December 26 (Moon in Virgo). It looks as though you'll be plunging right back into super activity, whether it takes the form of shopping (returning?), enjoying a winter sport, catching up on neglected tasks, or wading through voluminous correspondence. Try to avoid traffic tie-ups in the evening.

Friday, December 27 (Moon in Virgo to Libra 10:38 A.M.). Postmidnight hours can be delicately romantic, but strong enough to send your heart soaring. Later, you become a whirlwind of activity as you promote favorite projects and catch up on various matters. Try to avoid a conflict with a domestic partner in the P.M.

Saturday, December 28 (Moon in Libra). The one really bright light in today's agenda is your mental clarity, which gives you the ability to sift through a welter of moods and reactions (other people's) and tangled business-financial agreements. If someone promises you the Moon (*and* the stars) in the P.M., don't believe it!

Sunday, December 29 (Moon in Libra to Scorpio 5:04 P.M.). Your charisma is in full force today and can enable you to promote pet projects, as well as yourself and your talents. See key people if you are seeking a favor or support. P.M. hours are tinged with business-financial potential, so be on the alert.

Monday, December 30 (Moon in Scorpio). You may awaken with an intangible worry concerning love or money, but later events can dispel your fears. Domestic harmony is also on tap, and much can be credited to your own attitude and reactions. Entertaining friends in your home this evening can be a pleasant experience.

Tuesday, December 31 (Moon in Scorpio). The cost of entertainment is sure to have an influence on your New Year's Eve plans and whether you have decided to go out on the town or stay home with friends. Actually, whichever you choose, this is due to be a pleasant year's end celebration, with a special loved one.